ALL IN
GOOD TIME

ALL IN
GOOD TIME

BRIAN TOBIN

WITH JOHN LAWRENCE REYNOLDS

PENGUIN
CANADA

PENGUIN CANADA

Published by the Penguin Group

Penguin Books, a division of Pearson Canada, 10 Alcorn Avenue, Toronto, Ontario,
Canada M4V 3B2
Penguin Books Ltd, 80 Strand, London WC2R 0RL, England
Penguin Putnam Inc., 375 Hudson Street, New York, New York 10014, U.S.A.
Penguin Books Australia Ltd, 250 Camberwell Road, Camberwell, Victoria 3124, Australia
Penguin Books India (P) Ltd, 11, Community Centre, Panchsheel Park,
New Delhi – 110 017, India
Penguin Books (NZ) Ltd, cnr Rosedale and Airborne Roads, Albany, Auckland 1310,
New Zealand
Penguin Books (South Africa) (Pty) Ltd, 24 Sturdee Avenue, Rosebank 2196, South Africa

Penguin Books Ltd, Registered Offices: 80 Strand, London WC2R 0RL, England

First published 2002

1 3 5 7 9 10 8 6 4 2

Printed and bound in Canada on acid free paper ∞

NATIONAL LIBRARY OF CANADA CATALOGUING IN PUBLICATION DATA

Tobin, Brian, 1954–
All in good time / Brian Tobin.

ISBN 0-14-301377-7

1. Tobin, Brian, 1954– 2. Canada—Politics and government—1993–
3. Newfoundland and Labrador—Politics and government—1989–
4. Cabinet ministers—Canada—Biography.
5. Prime ministers—Newfoundland and Labrador—Biography. I. Title.

FC636.T62A3 2002   971.064'8'092   C2002-904906-7
F1034.3.T62A3 2002

Visit Penguin Books' website at **www.penguin.ca**

To Jodean

CONTENTS

Acknowledgements   ix

GUNFIRE ON THE GRAND BANKS   1
GROWING UP IN THE BIG LAND   7
THE ROAD TO OTTAWA   22
THE TRUDEAU YEARS   36
BIRTH OF THE RAT PACK   50
THE RETURN OF JEAN CHRÉTIEN   63
THE BATTLE TO SAVE A DWINDLING RESOURCE   77
CONTINGENCIES FOR ARMED CONFLICT   103
SHOTS ACROSS THEIR BOW   119
A CROWDED RALLY, A STARLIT SKY   139
NEW ROLE, NEW TEAM, NEW CHALLENGES   155
MEMORIES OF JOEY, AND MEETING HER MAJESTY   172
A REVOLUTION IN PROVINCIAL EDUCATION   182
THE MOST PROGRESSIVE PROVINCE IN CANADA   197
TALL TALES FROM VOISEY'S BAY   206
HEALTH CARE IN CANADA—PERSONALITIES AND PROPOSALS   218
RETURN TO OTTAWA   228
A YEAR ON PARLIAMENT HILL   240
A NEW AND PRIVATE PERSPECTIVE   258

Index   265

ACKNOWLEDGEMENTS

I MUST CONFESS I am a reluctant author. In fact my initial response to Diane Turbide, editorial director of Penguin Canada, was, "No, I am not interested in writing a book." Diane said, "Fine, but we are looking at doing a book anyway. You can work on it yourself or we can find a journalist who might be interested in doing a book about you."

She knew exactly how to strike terror into the heart of a reluctant politician. My courage collapsed, my emphatic "no" became a "maybe" and the rest is history.

Diane, John Lawrence Reynolds, my exceptional and patient collaborator on this book, and the rest of the superb Penguin team, including Joel Gladstone and Debby de Groot, have been kind, considerate and always encouraging to this novice scribe. Any shortcomings, and no doubt there are many, are mine and mine alone.

I also want to thank those whose participation in, and memories of, the events described herein helped to keep the record straight. In particular, I want to thank: Connie Abbott, John Alho, Gary Anstey, Josée Bedard, Judy Bolt, Heidi Bonnell, Margo Brown, John Butler, Gerry Byrne, Pat Chamut, Chris Clark, Benoit Corbeil, Karen Dmytryk, Cathy Dornan, Francie Ducros, Raquel Fragoso-Peters, Chuck Furey, George Furey, Gerry Glavine, David Gourlay, Tony Grace, Penela Guy, Peter

Harder, Kitt Howley, Linda Ivanoff, Bianca James, Eddy Joyce, Mike Klander, Dean MacDonald, Janice Marshall, Jack McCarthy, Paul McCarthy, Dave McInnis, Greg Mercer, Rodney Mercer, Eva Mills, Barbara Morrisey, Meredith Naylor, Bonnie Noseworthy, Aileen O'Rafferty, Seamus O'Regan, Ross Pilgrim, Bruce Rawson, Art Reid, Gay Rice, Ed Roberts, Bill Rowat, Malcom Rowe, Jeff Ryan, Max Short, Rosalie Short, Rosemary Smith, Paul Sparkes, Claudette Squires, Terry Tobin, Frederique Tsai, Guy Valin and Visjna Zaborski-Breton.

They are amongst the many staff and dedicated public servants with whom I have had the pleasure to serve during more than 24 years in public life. Space does not permit me to name them all. The truth is, however, that public office-holders are only as good as the men and women around them, who work so hard in the interest of their fellow citizens.

One of Penguin's edicts was, "No, Brian. You cannot thank everyone you ever worked with or you ever worked beside in seven election campaigns!" I wish I could thank you each individually. I owe you all so much.

An elected official is perhaps the most visible manifestation of a community's collective will and aspirations. Public life has its moments of great exhilaration and satisfaction. It also has moments of great difficulty and disappointment. Jodean and I signed on for both. We owe a big "thank you" to our extended family for being there through it all. My parents, Vincent and Florence, Jodean's parents, Joseph and Ginger, and all of our brothers and sisters have supported us through every chapter of this 24-year partnership in political life.

I call it a partnership, but the truth is Jodean has carried the largest share of the burden. She has been the anchor in every stormy sea. She has fought for a place for our family in the whirl of public life. She has always maintained the shelter, the home that has nurtured our three beautiful children, Heather, Adam and Jack.

It is to Jodean whom I dedicate with love and profound thanks this reflection on a public life.

ALL IN
GOOD TIME

GUNFIRE ON THE GRAND BANKS

I F SOMEONE SHOULD ASK ME what precipitated the events of March 9, 1995—the day that a Canadian ship fired at the naval vessel of another country for the first time in nearly 50 years—I'll quote a range of legal and ethical motives. "We needed to protect the last remaining fish stock on the Grand Banks," would be my immediate reply. "Nobody was taking Canada's concerns about fish conservation seriously." I could also toss in, I suppose, the need to establish a reasonable precedent for countries to act where and when negotiations to protect the environment failed. I might add that virtually every other country around the world was at least tacitly agreeing with the need to rein in the Spanish fishing fleet. All are true, and all have been widely reported, discussed, evaluated and criticized in the years since.

The incident with the Spanish trawler *Estai*, in which permission was granted to fire four bursts of 50-calibre machine guns across the trawler's bow, stunned the world. The event changed the way nations view the protection of global fishing stocks and shattered the sense of impotence that many of them were feeling over the rapacious nature of certain countries. The fact that Canada, of all nations, had taken such precipitous action underscored the seriousness of the problem. Who could be behind such an atypical act?

Most people, of course, would point to Prime Minister Chrétien and me, and we were indeed the most visible characters in the venture. We were supported by a degree of cabinet unanimity and enthusiasm that I had never seen before, and have rarely seen since. This was not a rash decision, made in the heat of passion and frustration. We had explored and ultimately exhausted every other alternative in an effort to manage our coastal fish stocks effectively. When we took action, we did it with measured steps and careful consideration for the safety of everyone concerned.

That's the accepted and rational explanation for the events of March 9, 1995, and it is totally true.

But it doesn't mention Max Short.

When I was appointed federal minister of fisheries and oceans a year earlier, I came in like the proverbial new broom, determined to sweep clean and make a difference. One of the differences was to strengthen communications between the ministry in Ottawa and the deep-water fishing industry on both coasts. I could have run the ministry from Ottawa, with periodic forays into Halifax, St. John's and Nanaimo. But the heart and soul of fishing in Canada is located elsewhere, much of it in the outports of Newfoundland, a region as unfamiliar to most Canadians as Patagonia.

No one personified the nature of Newfoundland outport people better than Max Short, and soon after settling in Ottawa I asked him to play the role of my unofficial link with the east coast fishermen. Max is from St. Anthony, on the northern peninsula of Newfoundland, 300 miles northwest of St. John's as the crow flies. This is one of the most spectacular and inaccessible regions of Canada; the brooding flat-topped Long Range Mountains run for a hundred miles along the peninsula's length, looming over fishing villages that cling to the coastal plain on the northern limits of the Gulf of St. Lawrence. It is a unique place, and like all unique places it has fostered unique people—people like Max Short.

Standing barely five feet three inches tall, Max had grown up in Lock's Cove, a tiny fishing village on Hare Bay. In Max's day, a boy either became a fisherman or he moved away, and Max stayed to fish for 16 years with his father and brothers, even though he never liked it much. Eventually, Max jumped ship to become a union organizer, performing most of his work on shore. In my encounters with Max, I found him to be fair and highly principled. Best of all, he was a good source for grassroots views and opinions, and I could always count on Max to give me the straight goods, devoid of bureaucratic babble and political what-ifs.

Max had a classic outport style when it came to speaking. During various heated debates, many conducted via conference calls between Ottawa and Newfoundland, I might grow emotional about some hard decision I had to make. Whenever I did, Max's raspy voice would come through the speaker from the regional office in St. John's and into a room crowded with staff members in Ottawa. "Now calm down, just calm down there, Minister," Max would advise. "It's just another inch off your cock."

The first time he said this, in the presence of some rather senior officials who were unfamiliar with colourful Newfoundland phrases, I managed to reply, "Max, that may not be a big deal to you but believe me—it's a big deal to me!"

On the afternoon of March 9, 1995, Max happened to be on the 15th floor of the ministry building on Kent Street in Ottawa. Along with Deputy Minister Bill Rowat and staff members, I had been huddled in a special Operations Centre with Gordon Smith, undersecretary for foreign affairs, and Jim Bartleman, the prime minister's foreign policy adviser and assistant secretary to the federal cabinet. For several hours, we had been tracking Canadian fishing-patrol vessels pursuing the Spanish trawler *Estai* as she fled east off the nose of the Grand Banks. If the term "fishing trawler" raises in your mind the image of a quaint sailing vessel, with a weathered helmsman at the wheel and a pipe-smoking crew singing sea shanties, erase it. The *Estai* was more than 200 feet long, a steel-hulled vacuum cleaner capable of removing hundreds of tonnes of fish from the ocean floor, and then processing, freezing and storing them.

Nor was this a maritime game of hide-and-seek. When the patrol vessels *Cape Roger* and *Leonard J. Cowley*, and the Coast Guard ship *Sir Wilfred Grenfell*, approached the *Estai*, and an RCMP assault team tried to board her, they were repelled and their boarding ladders were tossed into the sea. Then, cutting her nets, the *Estai* steamed away at full speed. The three Canadian vessels attempted to hem in the *Estai*, but they were constantly harassed by other Spanish boats in the area. Our patrol vessels were armed, a Restigouche-class destroyer was on its way to join them, and Spain, which already had one naval patrol vessel in the area, was ready to dispatch its warship *Vigia*, armed with a 76-mm gun and two machine guns. The arrival of the *Vigia* would represent a serious escalation of the encounter. The risk of a collision and injury or loss of life was high. Yet without proof that Spain's fishing policies would doom the last remaining commercially viable groundfish on the Grand Banks, nothing would be resolved—just as nothing had been resolved about illegal fishing in the region for the past decade.

For four hours the *Estai* had been running east, and the scene was becoming frantic: we were firing water cannons at the *Estai*, the Spanish boats were trying to ram the Canadian vessels, the sea was growing rough, visibility was down to 650 feet and I feared that one misstep could lead to disaster.

I was authorized to give the order to fire across the *Estai*'s bow as a warning and to threaten the next step—firing into the vessel itself—if the *Estai* failed to heave to. A decision had to be made, and soon. The more time that passed, the less likely we would be to decide things in Canada's favour. But giving the order to fire in the direction of another country's vessel, on the high seas well beyond our 200-mile limit, was a serious matter.

I took a break to walk the hall outside the Ops Room for a few moments and collect my thoughts. During that stroll I encountered Max, and an idea surfaced in my brain. "Come with me," I said, and practically dragged Max into the Ops Room, where I introduced him to everyone. "Max," I said, "that damn *Estai* has been running for hours now and she won't stop. What do you suppose those Spanish fishermen aboard her are saying right now?"

Max rubbed his chin. I saw the wit and wisdom of several generations of Newfoundland fishermen in his eyes. "Ah, they're feeling proud, Minister," he said finally. "Proud of themselves, and proud of their fleet. They're making fools of us."

"What are the Canadian fishermen going to feel if we don't stop the *Estai*?" I asked.

Max became sombre. "Minister," he said, "it will haul the guts and soul right out of them if we don't stop that boat."

I asked him what he thought we should do in this situation.

Without hesitation, Max barked, "We should chase her all the way to goddamn Ireland if we've got to!" All the pain, all the power and all the disillusionment of eight generations of Newfoundland outport fishermen were wrapped in his reply. He managed to express what I and everyone else in the room had been feeling since the *Estai* began to run.

I thanked Max, and he left. Then I turned to the others and said, "Gentlemen, I'm ready to sign the order to have our vessel fire across the *Estai*'s bow and make her stop. Who will sign it with me?"

Bill Rowat, deputy minister of fisheries and oceans, didn't hesitate a moment. "I'll sign it," he said, and I handed him the pen.

We needed the signature, as well, of the undersecretary of foreign affairs, and Gordon Smith didn't hesitate any longer than Bill Rowat had. "I'll sign it," he said, and when he finished adding his signature, I shoved the paper across to Jim Bartleman, then the prime minister's foreign policy adviser and now the lieutenant-governor of Ontario. We didn't need

Jim's signature, and it might have been wiser not to have it, if only to provide the prime minister with deniability should he need it. Besides, Bartleman had been among the most dovish of advisers when the question of taking direct action against the Spanish fishermen arose. But after hearing Max Short's words, Bartleman seized the pen and signed the document.

It was done. We called the captain of the *Cape Roger* and granted him authority to fire the warning shots, according to our rules of engagement. A few minutes later, when four bursts from the heavy machine guns aboard the *Cape Roger* sailed over her bow, the *Estai* cut her engines and heaved to.

There was no celebratory backslapping or high-fiving when we received the word back in Ottawa. I seem to recall a few tired smiles and some nodding of heads. Seizure of another vessel on the high seas, after all, is serious stuff, and a most un-Canadian act. It ran counter to all that we stood for, and all that we were respected for around the world.

I find it strange that while we have a difficult time defining just what a Canadian is, or explaining a Canadian sense of style and identity, we can easily tell an un-Canadian action when we see one. There is a lesson in that realization, one I had been learning all my life, starting as a kid in the small Newfoundland and Labrador town of Stephenville, and carrying me through senior federal cabinet positions and a provincial premiership.

We expect other countries to demonstrate the same tolerance and values that most of us accept without question. When they do not, we are disappointed. And when we act as they might in similar situations, they are surprised and often critical.

Canada, it seems, is always expected to turn the other cheek.

GROWING UP IN THE BIG LAND

STEPHENVILLE, NEWFOUNDLAND, is in many ways a microcosm of Canada, a self-contained model of this country that includes many of the social, cultural, linguistic, economic and international challenges Canada has faced since Confederation. Not surprisingly, my exposure to these challenges in Stephenville, and my later experiences in Happy Valley-Goose Bay, influenced my view of Canadian life.

If you're not familiar with my birthplace—and let's face it, few Canadians are—let me sketch it for you.

Stephenville lies in the southwest corner of Newfoundland, almost 500 miles west of St. John's. The settlement on the north shore of St. George's Bay was once known both as Acadian Village and Indian Head, the latter name deriving from the resemblance of a Native face on an adjoining mountainside. The first settlers were mostly Roman Catholics, both French- and English-speaking, attracted by the rich fishing grounds and good farmland. English settlers arrived in the mid-19th century from the Margaree region of Cape Breton, and among them was a man named Felix Gallant. When he and his wife returned to Cape Breton to have their son baptized, they persuaded others to follow them back to Newfoundland. Their first-born's name was Stephen, as was the name of the first-born of the LeBlancs, another local family, and the town's name was derived from either (or both) of them.

Over the next hundred years, the area grew steadily but not spectacularly, its prosperity subject to weather, fish stocks and prices, and the usual perils of isolated communities. It took the Second World War and the 1941 Anglo-American Lend-Lease Agreement between Britain and the United States to change the face of Stephenville. Under this agreement, created so that the United States could assist Britain without disrupting its official neutrality at the time, Stephenville was selected as the site of a new US Air Force base. The area's location and excellent flying conditions made it an ideal "jumping off" point for aircraft bound for Britain, and Harmon Air Force Base eventually became the largest American military airport outside the continental United States, employing 1,500 local residents.

At that time, of course, Newfoundland was British territory. When Newfoundland entered Confederation in 1949, all the elements that make Canada a unique and challenging society were at hand: the presence of both French and English, a strong British tradition and a powerful American economic and cultural influence.

There was a "two solitudes" aura to the place, just as we find in certain regions of the country today. French-speaking families resided on the Port au Port Peninsula, the only corner of Newfoundland where the French language and culture survive. They maintained their own music and traditions, and they made the peninsula something of an exotic land to us. The residents of Port au Port came into town for shopping and business, but we anglophones seldom ventured onto the peninsula. Many French residents became anglicized, and some changed the pronunciation of their last names to reflect this pressure.

There was no overt tension between the two groups—none that I was aware of as a young boy—but I always felt a sense of imbalance and unfairness. Much has changed since then. A large number of Newfoundlanders embrace the French language and culture, and residents of Port au Port receive the kind of respect from anglophones unimagined during my childhood. But my memories of the distance between the two groups back when I was a child, hearing the French families being referred to in unflattering terms, still bother me. This may be the reason I took such immense pride when, as a rookie MP, I worked within the federal government to help establish the first French-language school in Newfoundland, located, naturally, on the Port au Port Peninsula.

MY FATHER, VINCE TOBIN, was employed at the US air base as a fireman, but with nine active children, he often held a second job as well. Florence, my mother, also worked during most of my upbringing, usually in retail sales. She has always been full of compassion, involved in various volunteer groups. She was president of the Ladies' Legion Auxiliary, commissioner of the Girl Guides, a busy church volunteer and more. This makes her sound like an extrovert, but she is not. A rather reserved woman, she prefers to stay busy getting things done over simply talking about it.

Mom was physically small but full of energy and incredibly well organized. I remember rising early in the morning to watch as she began her day of frantic activity. I'd slip out of a bunk bed in our small three-bedroom house and stand over a hot-air vent in the kitchen to ward off the morning chill, while Mom set out freshly pressed school uniforms, prepared and packed school lunches, gathered up school bags and maybe even shined a few pairs of shoes before waking my brothers and sisters for breakfast. While she worked, she sang softly to herself. I can still hear her singing "A Mother's Love Is a Blessing."

Perhaps the best example of her compassion and independence of mind occurred during the emotional Newfoundland and Labrador nurses' strike in 1999, when strikers were shouting less-than-flattering words to describe me, the premier, as they picketed in rather nasty spring weather. To the picketers' delight, and my amusement, my mother showed up to pass around hot coffee to help the strikers stay warm. For many years she had been the president of the Ladies' Hospital Auxiliary, and the nurses were front-line workers whom she had supported. She had warned me that it wasn't a good idea to get into a fight with nurses. There's not a politician in the land who would disagree with that assessment, and many of us (including her son) have the scars to prove it.

My father, in contrast, was a private person who achieved much in his work as a fireman. He began as a rookie in the fire hall and worked his way up the ranks. He became a classroom instructor, teaching the techniques of battling the dangerous blazes encountered on an airfield, and retired as deputy fire chief. He was a big, burly man with large hands. "Fisherman's hands," he called them. All that power in those hands and in his body was reconciled with a gentle, almost shy manner. As much as he enjoyed his work, I think he might have been happiest in the bush, hunting and fishing and just being close to the land.

Like most firefighters, police officers and rescue workers, my father never discussed the reality of fighting fires or the risk of injuries and loss of life. Not until I watched the tragic events at the World Trade Center unfold did I fully appreciate what my father and people like him do for a living. They are the ones who are rushing in to face disaster when the rest of us are rushing out to avoid it.

My father was the eldest child in his family, as my mother was in hers, and he awoke every day with a mental checklist of chores to be accomplished. With Dad as sergeant major, we boys were lined up to cut grass, shovel snow, wash the car, feed the dog, deliver newspapers or hustle off to some part-time job that we counted on for spending money in our teenage years.

My dad played hockey as a boy and as a young man, and my brothers and I followed in his path. *Hockey Night in Canada* and the fate of the Toronto Maple Leafs demanded the attention of everyone in our house. I enjoyed watching the games with him, but I enjoyed watching him watch the game even more.

Between the efforts of our parents and the sharing among siblings that all large families learn to assume, we were always well fed, well clothed and well cared for, although we were never wealthy by any stretch of the imagination. Large families face their share of challenges and rewards, and as the fifth child of nine, I was always smack in the middle of things, literally and figuratively. When the school bus disgorged us at the end of the day, it looked more like the arrival of a baseball team than a working-class family, but we all developed into strong individuals. Team Tobin consisted of Terry, Sherri, Janet, Gloria, Brian, Alice, Ross, Craig and Paul, all two years apart in age.

I am grateful to my parents for the way they nurtured our happiness and encouraged us to fulfill our dreams wherever possible. The values they passed on to me and my brothers and sisters were essentially the same values they had been taught by their parents: you work hard, you lead an honest life, you take care of your family and you try to better yourself. Your family is the core of your identity. You stand together and support each other. You celebrate your successes, and you share your disappointments and sorrows. Loyalty, fidelity, honesty, all those traditional values that sound old school today, were the foundation of their lives, and they impressed them upon us.

Life in Stephenville changed in 1966, when the US government announced that it was closing the Harmon air base, the main source of income for Stephenville residents. My father's livelihood, and the livelihood of my friends' fathers, vanished.

We were more fortunate than some. My father was offered a similar position at the US air base in Happy Valley-Goose Bay, Labrador. But the deep tremors that this event generated in our family, and a similar upheaval we suffered five years later when the Americans closed their operation at Goose Bay, created a special empathy in me for working-class families who find themselves set adrift as a result of decisions made in distant locations.

No one can, nor should, expect to avoid the effects of change, whether for economic, technological, political or social reasons. But it is equally wrong, and morally weak, to expect those who are affected by these changes to "roll with the punches" and deal with the situation entirely on their own. This does not reflect the special values we recognize as Canadian.

As a result of those experiences, I identify with people who feel the sudden impact of change beyond their control. I watched my father set off alone for Goose Bay, where he lived for several months while the rest of us took up the slack in his absence. I saw my mother assume sole control of the house and coordinate all the steps needed to relocate us in the middle of a school year. I measured my own reactions to the change being imposed on us: fear at venturing to an unknown place, and excitement at exploring a new location, a new home, a new school. When you are 12 years old, these emotions are substantial, and many of them remain with me as clear and powerful as though I felt them last month and not more than 35 years ago.

The first adventure was the airplane ride in an aging DC-3 propeller-driven aircraft, hopping north over the Long Range Mountains and across the Strait of Belle Isle into Labrador. The engines sputtered and roared, the windows rattled, the wings creaked, and above this noise I could hear my older sisters, Sherry, Janet and Gloria, crying over the boyfriends they were leaving behind in Stephenville.

Landing at Goose Bay was almost like arriving in another country. Having left a region divided between French- and English-language communities, I arrived in a place where, although we were civilians, we lived on an American-managed base and attended a school run by the Royal Canadian Air Force. Our schoolmates included children of personnel employed by the RCAF as well as families of Department of Transport officials, civilian employees of the United States Air Force, and Inuit and Innu children whose families lived in the area. (A brief aside here to explain the terms *Innu* and *Inuit* for those unfamiliar with them. *Inuit*, "People of the Sea Ice," is now a global term for people formerly known as Eskimos; they reside primarily in coastal regions. *Innu* are First Nations people who reside primarily inland within Quebec and Labrador.)

Because we resided on the American air base, we had to carry security cards bearing our photograph at all times. Men with southern accents, automatic weapons and severe expressions could challenge us to prove our identity at any time, and they did. And just to make us feel even more alien—that's a decidedly American term—on my first day at school I arrived wearing the grey slacks, white shirt, tie and jacket that I had worn at St. Stephen's Catholic School in Stephenville, only to discover everyone dressed in T-shirts and jeans.

We had been warned that we would have to make an adjustment, but it was more like a major transformation.

Yet I soon learned to love Labrador. To me, it remains one of the most beautiful places on earth. The land has an almost feminine quality about it, thanks to the gently rolling hills surrounding Goose Bay. The air is fresh and usually soft, and the sky appears more blue and expansive than anywhere else I have been. When the sky is as clear and blue as it can possibly become, people in Labrador call it "a large, large day," and until you experience it for yourself, there is no larger day than the one spent in the pristine environment of the big land.

Just as Stephenville planted an awareness of biculturalism and bilingualism in me, Goose Bay opened up wider vistas when it came to dealing with different cultures and values. I often say that Goose Bay was like a classic "global village," in the sense that people from so many different social structures managed to live together in relative harmony. A little discordance crept in during weekend hockey games, when every faction was cheering as lustily for its own team as any group of rabid NHL fans ever did, but that's another story.

Soon after I arrived at Goose Bay, I sensed a growing appreciation for the land—the wildness, the untamed beauty of it—that I had never experienced back in Stephenville. As a teenager, I would trek into the bush, usually with the family dog, Caesar, trailing behind me, and walk for hours. Sometimes I took a hunting rifle, but I rarely hunted. It was the solitude that appealed to me, and the excitement of following a path or stream to encounter a new vista, or to surprise a caribou or partridge. Often I returned home from these treks realizing that I had reached some decision or sorted out a difficult problem along the way.

Even today, my idea of a relaxing vacation is to spend several days with family or friends at a remote camp in Labrador or elsewhere in Canada. One of the great benefits of political life is that I have seen so much of this beautiful country while doing my job, and my family and I continue to visit places such as the Kootenays and Queen Charlotte Islands in British Columbia, Algonquin Park in Ontario, Mahone Bay in Nova Scotia, the Eastern Townships of Quebec and the foothills of Alberta. These and other Canadian sites are food for the soul. Amid their beauty, problems become simpler and solutions grow more accessible, and spending a night beneath a sky clustered with stars is a spiritual experience in the broadest sense.

I have learned that we all need solitude from time to time, to be alone with ourselves and our thoughts. When I was working as executive assistant to Don Jamieson, leader of the provincial Liberal Party in Newfoundland, he informed me that nothing could be scheduled for him each Wednesday between 10 a.m. and noon, without exception. "Why can't anything be set up on that day, during those two hours?" I asked.

"Because I need them," Jamieson replied.

"For what?"

"To think." He did nothing else during that time—no telephone calls, no dictation, not even any unnecessary reading. Just thinking. Amid all the pressures of his job, and all the people tugging at his sleeve to get his attention, Don Jamieson stole those two hours from every week to give himself time to think in silence.

It was a good lesson, and one I still apply. A long walk in the woods works best for me. A stroll along Ottawa's Rideau Canal is soothing, too. Whenever I return to Labrador, often with my wife Jodean and our children, I find time to take walks in the bush, just as I did as a teenager. My family and I have spent many days and nights under a big Labrador sky. We even celebrated one New Year's Eve with Jodean's family 60 miles from Goose Bay, in the middle of nowhere, setting a bonfire on a frozen lake at midnight.

I can't scoot off to Labrador whenever I need an injection of solitude, so I search for it in other ways. Losing myself in a good book, attending a thought-provoking play, visiting a gallery or listening to favourite music are forms of solitude to me. It's like that old cliché that advises you to stop and smell the roses. It's not the aroma that refreshes you, but the pause from all the distractions whirling around you.

FOR MY THIRTEENTH BIRTHDAY, my parents gave me a set of classic books, all arranged on their little shelf, and I can think of few events that changed my life more. I was busy with other activities: playing hockey and soccer, Boy Scouts, that kind of thing. But the experience of losing myself in those books—tales of Robin Hood, Gulliver's Travels, King Arthur, and the rest—is something I have never forgotten. I discovered the places you can go in your mind and the power of imagination set in motion by the written word. The simple joy of reading was a revelation.

My parents' gift, one they could ill afford with a family of nine, changed me in ways that I am still discovering. After I absorbed all the stories in those books, I began seeking others to read, and the more I read, the more impressed I became with the power of language. I didn't stop at books, either. Thanks to the strong US influence at Goose Bay, copies of *Time, Newsweek, Life* and other periodicals were everywhere. I would grab a magazine, whatever its publication date, and read about politics, international affairs, business dealings, science, Hollywood gossip—it didn't matter. It was all information, it was all fodder for my curiosity, it was all literature of one quality or another.

Sharing a house with 11 people—and it was not a large house, believe me—I discovered I could always have my own space as long as I could locate a quiet corner and something to read. The gift of those books provided me with the ability to look beyond my own circumstances and beyond my own back-yard to imagine a world bigger and more expansive than the one in which I was living. This was important, because back in those days, you couldn't drive to Goose Bay; you either flew or sailed in and out of it. I believe that people who live on an island have a different viewpoint of things, compared with those who live on the mainland. I have heard this as a way of describing the special nature of the Brits, the Irish, Australians, Newfoundlanders and residents of PEI, among others. Goose Bay was something of an island back in the 1960s. Its isolation and the unique perspective of the outside world that books and magazines afforded generated their own influence.

I began applying these lessons in the essays I wrote at school. The use of verbs, the construction of sentences, all the mechanics of good communication, began to flow more easily for me. Encouraged by two of my teachers, Mona Goudie and Peter Heighton, my friend Cyrus Bird and I became the only members of the Robert Leckie High School debating club. Cyrus and I did pretty well for a couple of guys who had to be talked into taking on the task. We held our own in St. John's in the provincial debating championships, and when an all-Newfoundland-and-Labrador team was selected to go to Port Hope, Ontario, to participate in the National High School Debating Championship, I was chosen for the team. I realize now that I was swinging between two poles: the solitude of being absorbed in a book and the noisy give-and-take of debates. To this day, I love both equally.

Some may question my emphasis on this small collection of books and the path they opened for me. But I believe that doing one good thing at one critical time for one individual can make a profound difference. It did for me.

IN MY THIRD YEAR AT HIGH SCHOOL, the teachers chose a "work to rule" strategy in response to a labour dispute. This meant the elimination of many extracurricular activities, and naturally—this was the 1960s, remember—it led to a student protest. Soon we were two or three hundred kids skipping classes and marching to the town hall, chanting slogans on the way. We managed to attract the attention of local media types, and when they arrived with cameras and notepads, looking for someone to explain our actions, I was pushed forward to act as spokesperson. I had established a reputation not just for talking, but also for being blunt. Today we might call it a sound bite; back then, it was just a matter of "telling it like it is." I recall explaining things as best I could and calling upon the government to resolve the issue so that we could move forward with our education.

The local newspaper and radio station reported my comments word for word. The high school principal was not as tickled as I was, and he called me into his office for a firm talk. Almost the entire student body had left the school without authorization, he pointed out. A small number of standouts, including my future wife, Jodean, already showing her independent spirit, remained behind. This was a serious matter. He made it sound like the end of civilization and the onset of anarchy. It was evident to him, at least, that I was the ringleader in this escapade, and he suggested I have a serious talk with my father about whether I was doing anything productive at school.

Of course, being dressed down by the principal elevated my rank in the opinion of the rest of the students. Now I wasn't just the kid who explained things to the press. I was, in the words of the principal himself, a "ringleader."

The following week, I was at home recuperating from a back injury suffered in a hockey game. It happened to be the week that the school held its student council election. Somewhere between the jigs and the reels, my name was put forward as president. Friends told me later that it had been submitted in the name of fun. One way to hand the principal his comeuppance, the reasoning went, would be to nominate Tobin, the student he had harangued just a few days earlier, to lead the student council. Whatever the strategy, it worked, and I returned to school to learn that I had been elected president. I don't know what the principal's response was; mine was confusion. Almost overnight, I had been transformed from the kid with his nose buried in *Reader's Digest* and *Popular Mechanics* into something of a student politician.

I had never seen myself in that position. Was I flattered? I suppose I was. Did I enjoy the role? To my surprise, I found that I did. I never expected to participate in politics and never expected to live and work anywhere but Labrador. But the possibility was at least on the radar screen now.

POLITICAL AWARENESS, as it related to a high school student council, was something of a game, but more serious events were happening in the world.

The war in Vietnam was raging, and the US facility at Goose Bay was part of the military apparatus serving that conflict. Goose Bay became a jumping-off place for some US Army personnel on their way to Vietnam and an interim stopover for soldiers returning from the front. My friends and I encountered them in shops and at the bowling alley, and we talked with many of them. We may have met a few gung-ho types, but I don't recall them. Most were kids a few years older than me, deeply frightened of what they were about to encounter in Vietnam. Some had just returned and were terrified of being sent back. I saw anger and bewilderment expressed at the protests against the war and the politicians who had sent these boys—for that's what many of them were—halfway around the world to risk their lives for an ill-defined goal. I saw young people on the cusp of their prime losing control over their own destinies on behalf of a cause that many neither understood nor cared about.

My friends and I had been raised in the tranquility of Newfoundland and Labrador, where the US government's convoluted rationale for continuing the war in Vietnam was not a prime subject of discussion. I understood some of the background of the war, filtered through reports in the US weekly newsmagazines, but it was academic and distant until I discussed it with young GIs over Cokes at the base's bowling alley. They talked about the amount of time remaining until their army time ended, of friends who hadn't come back from the fields of Vietnam and of others who had returned severely wounded, both physically and mentally. No matter what the root causes were for that sorry conflict, the horrors that these young men faced, or were about to face, seemed totally at odds with their values. While I understood the concept of making sacrifices for your country or any worthwhile objective, things were out of balance for these young men. The sacrifice they were being asked to make was total; the motives were at best foggy; and the fault lay with the political decisions behind it all and the politicians who made them.

I felt for these young Americans who, in most other aspects, were much like me and my friends. We spent many evenings hanging out in the barracks with GIs whose US government paycheque and base exchange privileges enabled them to fill idle hours drinking cheap beer and listening to music from powerful stereos. We discussed the same music, the same movies, the same sports teams, and we found endless areas of agreement. The key difference between my American friends and me was that they were being sent off to fight, perhaps to die, and I was being permitted to remain in the beauty and safety of Labrador.

My awareness of our similarities makes it difficult for me to take cheap shots at American citizens to this day. I also recall the basic kindness and decency of the many Americans who befriended my family and me over the years. Our countries have their differences, and they often lead to the diplomatic equivalent of shouting across the back fence. But I refuse to decry Americans generally, because I vividly remember those frightened young guys from Iowa and Tennessee and Georgia on their way to a war they didn't understand or even support, telling me that I was lucky to be living where I was, that I was lucky to be a Canadian. We should never allow the failure of negotiations between Canada and the United States to become the failure of a deep and genuine friendship between good neighbours.

I still feel that it's a privilege to be a Canadian. Canadians will serve when called upon, as we have proven from Vimy Ridge to Afghanistan. But this country avoids leaping into just any global conflict, and it does not seek to impose itself on others. We are peaceful and tolerant, and if those words sound like clichés, well, as a very wise man told me once, a cliché is a cliché because it is true.

There is much to admire about the United States. It is, as the Americans keep reminding themselves and the rest of the world, a phenomenal exercise in democracy, and I say that without a trace of irony. Sharing a continent, a language (for the most part) and a democratic tradition, our two nations experience differences that often become fuzzy and indistinct, yet carry major significance. The author Ayn Rand made a career out of promoting the power of individualism, one of the major values in the United States. Living your dreams and sticking to your principles is a fine philosophy, but in Canada the concept is reconciled with the wider welfare of the community. This is not hairsplitting; it represents the root of differences between our two countries. It explains deep divisions in matters such as health care, regional economic disparity, international relations and more. I share the view that the good of the community is just as important as individual liberty, and I suspect the vast majority of Canadians do as well.

THE ROAD TO OTTAWA

WHEN I WAS 16 YEARS OLD, I returned to Stephenville from Labrador for a summer holiday and to renew old friendships. One evening, I attended a dance at the local high school and was struck by the beauty and presence of a petite girl I met there. Attempting to describe her now, more than 30 years later, is difficult without using words better suited for romance novels. She had shiny shoulder-length hair, a spray of freckles across her nose, sparkling eyes that were wise and knowing, a beautiful open smile and a slim figure. Her name was Jodean Smith and, as you can tell, I was absolutely captivated by her. Jodean's father, Joseph, a native of the Annapolis Valley in Nova Scotia, was the chief CBC technician in Labrador. Her mother, Ginger, the daughter of a Presbyterian missionary, had spent much of her childhood in Korea and India, and Ginger's father had been killed by Japanese troops in Burma during the Second World War. They were interesting people, and Jodean had inherited their wide-ranging views.

Jodean and I began talking early that evening in Stephenville, and we have never stopped. I found myself listening carefully to a beautiful young woman whose maturity was far beyond her 14 years. The great debater had more than met his match. During that time, I got the bad news and the good news. The bad news was that she was dating someone else. The good news: she promised to return my phone call when we returned to Labrador.

Our conversation resumed in Labrador, occupying hundreds of hours of telephone calls. We each broke off the relationships we had with others, and the rest of our high school years unfolded like a classic feel-good story: I was student council president, and Jodean was selected to be class valedictorian. In August 2002, we celebrated 25 years of married life together. She remains my best friend, my strongest supporter, my closest adviser and my most severe critic. Jodean is honest, wise and courageous. She also speaks her mind; do not ask Jodean for her opinion if you would rather not hear the truth.

Jodean remains the anchor that has kept our family focused in the midst of all the turmoil and tumult of political life. She is a calming presence to me, and I feel the same aura when she walks into a room today as I did when I first met her when I was 16 years of age back in Stephenville.

AFTER HIGH SCHOOL I set off for Memorial University to obtain a bachelor of arts degree. I took political science as one of my classes, but only because I thought it might help if I became a journalist, which was the only career that appealed to me. To cover my student expenses and provide practical experience, I talked my way into jobs as a reporter and announcer/operator, first for CBC and later for NTV, the local CTV affiliate, using broadcast experience acquired during a summer job back in Goose Bay.

I have always felt comfortable behind the microphone or in front of the camera, and that's a trait that either comes naturally or not at all. Like most young people, I was foolish enough to believe that I could handle anything offered to me and confident enough to suggest trying it. This, together with the free rein common in broadcasting back then, gave me opportunities I would never encounter today. I became host of a Sunday afternoon TV talk show called *Counterpoint*, and when this proved too sedentary I began asking for assignments out of the studio—something more exciting and challenging.

Geoff Stirling, the owner and president of NTV, was willing to provide all the excitement I could handle. Geoff, who has always been a revolutionary in his field, operated one of the first 24-hour television services in North America. He frequently debated Joey Smallwood on live television in the studio, sometimes into the early morning hours.

I met Geoff for the first time while working the evening news shift. I had noticed an unfamiliar man hanging around the lobby, and when I asked his reason for being there, he refused to tell me. I called Harry, the security guard, pointed out the strange man and asked that he be escorted from the building. "Are you nuts, my son?" Harry said. "That's Mr. Stirling." Both Harry and Geoff burst into laughter, and I suspect I was not the first rookie to be introduced to Geoff Stirling in such an unorthodox manner.

At one point, Geoff decided to debate MP John Crosbie, and advertised it as The Great Debate of the Decade. I was assigned as moderator, which became impractical when we learned that John had elected to remain in Ottawa. When the show opened, Geoff and I were facing an empty chair bearing John Crosbie's name. I remarked that I hoped Crosbie would arrive soon, and then Geoff launched into his opening statement, tearing the skin off Crosbie. As he was shifting into high gear, I interrupted to announce the debate was terminating and in its place we would be showing a feature movie. The control room operator had the film cued to go, and before Geoff could react it was up and running.

Geoff was not amused. While I waited to be escorted off the premises by Harry the security man, my co-workers began speculating how long it would take for the axe to fall. It never did, although Geoff ordered me on a few assignments that had me wondering about my place in his broadcasting empire. The most notable sent cameraman Ted Lacey and me several hundred miles offshore aboard the Coast Guard vessel *John Cabot.*

Our instructions were to meet the *St. Brendan*, a re-created currach sailed across the Atlantic from Ireland by adventurer and historian Timothy Severin. Currachs, tiny vessels made of ox-hide sewn over a canoe-like frame of wooden splints, were believed to have carried Irish monks to the shores of Newfoundland back in the 6th century. Severin proved it was at least possible, and Ted and I were the first to greet and interview Severin and his crew as they struggled through high seas to make landfall in Newfoundland.

The sea was rough and, of all the journalists on board, the only two feeling healthy enough—or foolish enough—to board a rubber Zodiac raft and make for the *St. Brendan* were Ted and me. We got our footage and conducted on-board interviews with Severin and his crew, who seemed none the worse for wear. The sight of the massive *John Cabot* disappearing behind waves higher than houses on our return to her was terrifying, and we were persuaded to share our footage with other journalists too seasick to get out of their bunks.

More than one person has suggested to me that ploughing through huge swells in an open raft wasn't sufficiently perilous and exciting for me, which is why I entered Newfoundland politics.

I ENCOUNTERED BILL ROWE, leader of the Opposition Liberal Party, on a number of occasions while performing my journalism chores. Bill is now the host of a province-wide talk show so popular that he has a virtual monopoly on the morning listening audience. One day in 1978, I heard that the position of executive assistant to Rowe was open, and I decided to apply for it. Winning the job would mean dropping plans to finish my degree at university, but the offer was too good to pass up; I could always return to school, but how often would an opportunity like this arise?

The day Bill Rowe interviewed me for his job, he pointed to a map of Newfoundland's ridings on his wall. The PC ridings were painted blue, the Liberal ridings were painted red and the one

NDP riding was green. "See that map?" he said to me. "What's wrong with it?"

"It's not all red," I said. "There's too much blue."

Bill Rowe smiled, and I knew I had the job.

My sympathies had always been with the Liberal Party. I rejected the notion that the community should be a battleground between the left and the right, making citizens casualties of the political wars. I also disliked the idea of politics as a winner-take-all sport. I believe that candidates who obtain more votes are awarded the right to play a lead role in making decisions and executing policy, but they do not win the right to reject and ignore other opinions, other concerns, other values.

People who believe in free enterprise and free expression, and who are focused on the well-being of the community at large, should all be sitting at the same table. That's not a sellout or extreme compromise. It is pragmatism, a method of doing the greatest good for the greatest number of people. The idea is preferable, in my view, to scrapping over ideology, or jockeying for some position that means everything to you and absolutely nothing to people outside the forum. Ideology is fine, but it usually doesn't help an out-of-work fisherman, a single mother in poverty, an abused child, a lonely senior citizen, a disillusioned teenager, a small businessperson or a middle-class family that sees its dreams and aspirations vanish under a fog of intransigent dogma. At the negotiating table or in the House of Commons, let's shut up about ideology and find a way to get things done— that's my credo, and it always has been.

These ideas didn't appear full-blown in my head while traipsing through the bush outside Goose Bay, although they had their roots there. They owe much of their origin to Pierre Trudeau, whom I admired from the first time I saw and heard him speak. He represented the division between the old days when cynical men in three-piece suits gathered in backrooms to decide policy, and the new age when politicians began expressing themselves directly. He challenged the established view of the world and, just as important, he often welcomed those who challenged him in turn. As Canadians, we have to remind ourselves from time to time of the massive impact made by Trudeau's arrival on the political scene. Whether you agreed or disagreed with him, it can't be denied that he inspired an entire generation to become more actively involved in politics—intellectually, practically and emotionally.

Working with Bill Rowe, and later Don Jamieson, was a lesson in life as well as politics. It wasn't just political wisdom that these men passed on to me. It was the ability to observe the intricacies of politics and public service. Too often, we grow fascinated by the dramatics of one and overlook the demands of the other.

Soon after starting my new job, I was introduced to the Liberal caucus, populated by several legitimate captains. I remember Captain Jack Windsor, Captain Earl Windsor, Patty Canning and others. These men were in their later years and had set aside their seafaring days to pursue public service. I can't imagine people more polar opposite from Pierre Trudeau in their approach to politics, but they had things to teach me. My first impression was that it was time for them to move on. I was 23 years old, filled with energy and ambition, and these men were in my way. I couldn't have been more wrong, as I discovered when I began taking morning coffee with them. Listening to their views and experiences, I learned something new each day.

These men participated effectively in the political process because they remained in touch with people in their communities. Each reflected his community's values and concerns, and they all shared the aspirations of the people who had chosen them to represent these values. The men were quiet and conservative; they certainly weren't extroverts. But they had a genuine feel for their communities and how to serve them, and this was a profound lesson for me. The way you look or sound is mere froth in the river of public life. True substance runs deeper and may not be seen at first glance. Being young and aggressive is no substitute for wisdom, experience and passionate commitment.

One day, while working as EA to Bill Rowe, I was informed that someone from the Iron Ore Company of Canada had arrived to pay a courtesy call on the provincial government. He had met with Frank Moores, the premier, and was now asking if the leader of the Opposition, Bill Rowe, was available. Rowe was out of the office for the day, and so I offered to host the visitor, who, of course, was Brian Mulroney.

Like everyone else who has talked one on one with Mulroney, including some of his most vociferous critics, I found him charming, intelligent and knowledgeable about a wide range of subjects. As president of IOCC, Mulroney stopped by to bring key members of the provincial government up to date on the company's activities. If he was disappointed to be briefing an executive assistant instead of the leader of the Opposition, he didn't show it. After we talked, I promised to pass my notes on to Bill Rowe, and Mulroney appeared satisfied.

"How long have you been an executive assistant?" Mulroney asked as he was preparing to leave.

I told him it had been just a few months.

"Let me give you some advice," Mulroney said, in that low gravelly voice we are all familiar with. "If you're going to use your position as a learning experience, fine. Learn about policy-making and political strategy. But don't stay too long as an executive assistant or you'll become so imprinted in people's minds that they won't take you seriously in any other role. Stay a couple of years, then either get some private sector experience or run for office yourself."

During some of the more raucous days in Ottawa, when Brian Mulroney and I faced each other across the floor of Parliament— sometimes generating more heat than light in our debates—I wondered if he ever regretted giving me that bit of guidance. I must say that I never regretted taking it.

MULRONEY'S ADVICE RANG IN MY EARS a year and a half later when Joe Clark and the Progressive Conservatives, in one of the great blunders in Canadian political history, lost a non-confidence vote on John Crosbie's first federal budget. The Tories had gained a minority government barely six months earlier, in May 1979. Pierre Trudeau, labelled "Yesterday's Man" in some political circles, was bearing up stoically while the media relentlessly covered the breakup of his marriage. Unwilling to see himself in Opposition with his family life to attend to, Trudeau had announced that he would be resigning. Let someone else take on Clark and the PCs. Trudeau was tired, and perhaps a little disillusioned.

Clark and the Conservatives stumbled as a result of hubris, bad counsel, betrayal or simply an inability to count when, on December 13, 1979, they came up short in the non-confidence vote, and Canada was facing its second federal election in less than a year. The Tories avoided panicking over the situation, believing that they could easily win a second election with the Liberals effectively leaderless. Their defeat might prove a godsend, providing them an opportunity to win a clear majority and be free from fears of another non-confidence challenge for at least four years.

All of this changed the following week when Trudeau was persuaded to remain in the leader's chair after all. Winning the election and returning as PM would be a chance to cap his legacy with a victory over the independence referendum that René Lévesque was planning for 1980. He might even realize his dream of repatriating the Constitution and introducing a Canadian Charter of Rights and Freedoms. In any event, the election of February 18, 1980, would be critical to both the country and the Liberal Party. We had to gear up and, as executive assistant to the leader of the Opposition in Newfoundland, I was recruited to help out.

"We need a candidate in your old neck of the woods in western Newfoundland," Don Jamieson told me one day. "We've got ten thousand dollars to get a war chest started." He handed me a list of names. "Go to Corner Brook, talk to these people and get one of them to stand as a candidate."

Corner Brook was in the riding of Humber-Port au Port-St. Barbe, and on arrival I found a distinct lack of enthusiasm among local Liberals. It wasn't difficult to understand. Criss-crossing the land seeking votes in the depth of a Newfoundland winter was going to be challenge enough. Campaigning as a Liberal anywhere promised no certain reward. Many people recalled John Diefenbaker's coup of the mid-1950s, when he won first an upset victory over a sitting Liberal government to form a minority government in 1957, and then a big majority the following year. Joe Clark's position appeared eerily similar. Clark was no Diefenbaker, but he was the incumbent and he held a strong hand. A PC victory seemed imminent.

That was the national situation. Things were even more challenging in Humber-Port au Port-St. Barbe, where "The Fonz" was expected to rule for some time. The Fonz was Fonse Faour, a bright, engaging lawyer who had won the seat for the NDP, first in a by-election in 1978, then in the May 1979 general election. Faour had achieved the near impossible by becoming the first NDP candidate from Newfoundland to win a seat in Parliament, garnering almost twice as many votes as the Liberal candidate. He was a popular, hard-working lawyer whom everyone, including me, liked and admired. At 28 years of age, he had a bright career ahead of him, and had he run on behalf of either of the main-stream parties, I'm convinced he would still be in Parliament today. As if The Fonz wouldn't be enough competition, the PCs had nominated Ben Alexander, a well-known professional engineer who was expected to run a tough, effective campaign.

So when I began interviewing potential candidates to run under the Liberal banner, I encountered only apologetic smiles and sad shakes of the head. "Not this time," was the usual answer. "Not against these guys."

Somebody had to run, of course. It began to dawn on me that no local candidate would emerge for the Liberal Party in 1980, and there likely would not be a fight for the nomination. Nobody wanted it. How often does someone under 30 years of age get the chance to represent a major party in an uncontested nomination? "I'll do it," I told Don Jamieson when I returned to St. John's and conveyed the reluctance I had encountered. "I couldn't find a candidate, so I'll run myself."

I half expected Jamieson to shake his head and reject the idea. I was, after all, 25 years old and a political neophyte. Instead, he slapped me on the back and said, "You're a loyal soldier."

This was not quite like sending me to battle with the strains of a brass band in my ears and nymphs strewing flowers at my feet. I believe Don saw me as a guy willing to pick up the flag and march off as cannon fodder. He convinced me of this when he said: "Remember, Brian, you'll still have a job here when this is over."

I had no intention of reclaiming my job. Once I had the nomination, I ran to win. Mind you, even *I* didn't give myself much of a chance.

First, the riding hadn't voted Liberal in years, and the residents seemed to be in love with The Fonz. Next, I faced an articulate, well-known opponent who was going to fight tooth and nail to hold onto his seat. The Fonz would be no pushover when it came to debating and campaigning. Finally, I had virtually no organization, and very little time to assemble one. The seat hadn't been Liberal for 12 years, and most Liberals I spoke to were demoralized. It probably didn't help their mood when they learned that the party would be running a young rookie whose roots might be in the area but whose home address was in St. John's, on the other side of the island.

My next problem was to convince Jodean that running was the right thing to do. When I told her of Jamieson's support for my candidacy, tears welled in her eyes. "Don't worry," I said, comforting her. "I may not win, but I won't make a total fool of myself."

"I'm not worried about you losing," Jodean replied. "I'm worried about you winning. We've taken out a mortgage on a home in St John's, I just started a new job and we're planning a family. If you win, all our plans will change."

As usual, Jodean's insight was sharper than mine. She saw beyond the challenge and thrill of the campaign to the responsibilities and obligations that a young family would face in the event of victory. Winning changed much in our lives, but not everything. Our daughter Heather was born exactly nine months after election night.

Back then, campaigns were 56 days long. That's something of a mini-marathon, but it was to my advantage because it gave me time to build an organization. I began by identifying a Liberal in every community of any size in the riding, and calling to ask whether he or she could set up a pot of coffee in their kitchen where I could meet their friends. During my conversations, I attempted to turn at least two or three of them into true believers, hoping they would become enthusiastic enough about my candidacy to spread their support out, like ripples on a pond. I did this for weeks, travelling up and down the length of the riding, making myself visible and keeping track of people who agreed with my reasons for running. Things began going well, but not well enough to ensure a victory by any means.

Then, with just a couple of weeks to go before election day, something happened to turn the election around. It was one of those events that could not have been predicted or anticipated, but it served to crystallize the entire campaign.

The event was an all-candidates meeting at the Knights of Columbus hall in Stephenville, a place where all three of us— Faour, me, and Ben Alexander, the PC candidate—were comfortable, since we were all Roman Catholics. Newfoundlanders take their politics seriously and with great passion, and that evening the hall was packed to the gills with both Catholics and non-Catholics.

The first question put to us concerned abortion: what was our position on it?

Fonse Faour stood up. "My name is Fonse Faour," he declared. "I am the NDP candidate, and I am a Roman Catholic. I am opposed to abortion." A wave of applause swept the room.

Next was Ben Alexander. He announced his name and party, and added: "I am also a Roman Catholic, and I am also opposed to abortion." More applause.

Now it was my turn. I stood up and said, "My name is Brian Tobin. I am also a Catholic, but I'm not running to be an MP for Catholics. I'm running as a Liberal to represent everyone, and I am pro-choice."

The silence was deafening. People looked at each other, cleared their throats or simply examined their fingernails. After a pause that seemed to go on forever, the next question was asked and the general debate began. Faour, Alexander and I took questions for the next 90 minutes. The room was subdued and impossible to read.

When the evening was over, Jack McCarthy, one of my closest supporters, sidled up to me and said, "You just lost the election, you know." He was referring, of course, to my position on abortion.

I wasn't so sure. For one thing, I had been truthful. If you win by ducking the hard questions, what is the prize really worth? Not much. More than that, I knew that I had separated myself from the other candidates. And I also suspected that I had earned some degree of respect from those in the hall for saying what I believed instead of saying what they wanted to hear.

The next day, my position on abortion was trumpeted in the newspapers and on radio and TV. Without my upfront comment, my name would have been buried among the usual reports of the debate, none of them as interesting or stimulating as the debate itself. But my statement became the lead item on all the stories. It was impossible to ignore, and when I returned to knocking on doors, people knew me immediately. This knowledge carried over to my positions on other issues as well, and it forced people to examine me more closely, if only because I stood out so clearly.

I began hearing variations on the same refrain, over and over again. "Oh, yes," the voters would say. "You're the pro-choice fella. Well, I don't agree with you on that subject, but . . ." Soon we were talking about other issues, other concerns. People started inviting me into their homes instead of talking with me in the open doorway, and I knew that was a good sign.

Newfoundlanders are not mean-spirited, but they can tease a bit. Whenever they challenged me pointedly, or suggested I didn't have much of a chance, I would look them in the eye and say, "I'm not in this to run. I'm in it to win. See you on election day." This surprised and seemed to impress a number of people. No one likes a determined fighter better than a Newfoundlander. Even Jack McCarthy was feeling a little better about the way the campaign was going, and I was constantly encouraged to campaign hard. Julie Briffett had resigned as president of the Newfoundland and Labrador Consumer Association to manage my campaign, and she ordered Eva Mills, who managed the campaign office, to throw me out the door if I showed up.

Eva herself didn't mince words with me. "Listen here, buddy," she lectured me, "you get out there and knock on doors and don't stop until your knuckles are bleeding." So I went. Jodean and I and some campaign volunteers began beating our way through February blizzards day after day, trudging through snowdrifts to reach the front door and never knowing how we would be greeted. I suspect that the sight of Jodean, peeking out from under a snow-covered hood and asking people to support her husband, did more to win votes than anything I had to say.

As the days passed, I could feel the tide turning in my favour. I wasn't totally confident, but I knew I was in the running. I hadn't been cannon fodder after all.

Don Jamieson, who had resigned as leader of the Liberal Party in Newfoundland after the 1979 federal election, was a commentator on CTV television that evening. As the polls were closing, Don began reviewing the party's prospects in various ridings. When he came to Humber-Port au Port-St. Barbe he mentioned my name and said, "Brian put up a good fight over there," before conceding the seat to the NDP.

Don was as wise and prescient as any politician I met, but he was wrong about the riding that evening. We won by almost 4,000 votes, and I earned an apology from Don.

I also learned an important lesson, one that each of us, I suspect, has to learn on his or her own. I learned to accept what I truly believe in my heart and never to apologize for it or change it according to the prevailing wind. Would I have won the election by telling the crowd what they wanted to hear about abortion, instead of what I honestly felt? I don't know. It doesn't matter. I only know that I was comfortable within my own skin about my stand then, as I am now.

In politics, you can be carried with the current or you can sail off in another direction. It's always one or the other, and there is no guarantee that either will prove successful. That evening at the Knights of Columbus hall I decided that I would not be carried by the current. I have made similar decisions to sail off in different directions in the years since and, win or lose, I have never regretted them.

THE TRUDEAU YEARS

I MADE A POINT of travelling to Ottawa as soon after the election as possible, for both practical and emotional reasons. From a practical standpoint, I knew that office space on the Hill was dispensed on a first-come, first-served basis; arriving early meant a better choice of location and facilities. My other motive was excitement at the prospect of participating in House of Commons activities. I considered it a privilege and an honour to be an MP, and everyone who serves in that capacity should be humbled, in one way or another, at the responsibility that is being entrusted to him or her.

After meeting with the party whip about office space, I went strolling around the Hill, feeling a little smug at my success so far. I was getting a sore neck from staring up at the Peace Tower when I heard a man's voice call out, "Brian Tobin?"

Now I was even *more* impressed with myself. I hadn't been in Ottawa for a day, and someone had recognized me already. "Yes," I said. "That's me."

"Congratulations on your election," the man said, extending his hand. He was grey haired, with a broad smile and an open, expressive face.

We shook, and I thanked him with as much humility as I could muster. "And what's your name?" I asked.

He smiled. "Allan J. MacEachen," he said.

I had just failed to recognize our House leader and one of the true giants of Canadian politics, especially in Atlantic Canada. I had always admired him for his activist role and his genuine concern for people. Meeting him in that manner was a lesson to me about restraining my pride until I had achieved something more than winning an election.

The most dominant personality on the Hill, of course, was Pierre Elliott Trudeau. In 1980 he retained all his personal passion and magnetism, but he had a new sense of purpose where Canada's future was concerned. The Parti Québécois had called for a separatist referendum that spring, and early measures suggested that a PQ win was not only possible, but likely. As a result Trudeau, I believe, saw the power and privilege he enjoyed as prime minister in a new light. He initiated an amazing number of changes over the next four years, and we continue to feel the effects of these actions today.

I had spent half my life watching Trudeau from afar, and I shared his conviction that the community, the country and the world could be improved in many ways if sufficient determination and leadership were available. Now I would be almost literally shoulder to shoulder with him, and the only thing I feared was that my expectations would be too high, that Trudeau might have feet of clay after all.

I needn't have worried. I watched in awe during my first caucus meeting as he moulded and shaped the discussion. He listened intently to various views, sometimes agreeing, sometimes challenging, sometimes accepting and sometimes discarding them. Then he tossed the consensus viewpoint back at us so that we could see the strengths of it and the direction we would take on the issue. It was vintage Trudeau, balancing party interests and public needs.

For a man who could fill a caucus room, a TV studio or an entire stadium with his presence, Trudeau was almost shy when you met him in a one-to-one situation. Looking back, I suspect that he kept a quiet corner of his soul apart from everyone else, and this was the place he occupied when in conversation with others. He was a remarkable man, and those of us who were fortunate enough to meet and know him will never see his like again.

Pierre Trudeau was not the only member who attracted my attention. Many others provided valuable insights into the democratic process, parliamentary procedure and basic lessons in life. They were not all Liberals, either. I remember Tom Cossitt, the PC member from Leeds-Grenville, who took great delight in attempting to skewer Trudeau with snarky questions and sarcastic comments during Question Period. Cossitt's questions were always among the first that Trudeau took and dealt with, and when Cossitt died suddenly in 1982, I had a sense that Trudeau regretted his passing more than he showed. Cossitt may have blustered and harangued, but I believe Trudeau saw the passion for serving his constituents that was behind Cossitt's posturing, and he respected the man for that.

Les Benjamin, the NDP member from Regina-Lumsden, was another great character. He was a dedicated socialist who prefaced many comments with, "Comes the revolution, brother . . . ," and he didn't mind having a nip or two of good whisky at lunch to fuel him through question period. His roots were firmly planted in the West, and he was as colourful as anyone when it came to explaining things to his constituents . . . and sometimes on behalf of his constituents. One day he rose in the House to plead for agricultural support:

> Mister Speaker, things are so dry and so windy in southwestern Saskatchewan this spring, not only is there no point in seeding, but the gophers are eight feet high and digging.

Les, who picked up the nickname Boxcar Benjamin along the way, served 25 years in the House, and he enjoyed every day of it.

Besides Trudeau, the Liberal side of the floor was dominated by the physical and intellectual presence of Marc Lalonde, one of the few people in Canadian public life capable of challenging Trudeau intellectually. Lalonde wore his power like a mantle. He had helped instigate Trudeau's entry into politics, and his closeness to Trudeau was well known. When you dealt with Lalonde, you had better have your ideas straight and your answers ready. For this and other reasons, he was considered aloof. In reality, while Lalonde could be tough, he was also fair and personally warm to those he dealt with.

Jean Chrétien was clearly someone special. A veteran MP, he had held a number of portfolios and enjoyed the prime minister's confidence. Although some senior ministers seemed unaware of the existence of ordinary members, Jean Chrétien spent time with rookies and backbenchers who were not likely to make the cabinet, and he was always careful to listen more than he spoke. A few cabinet ministers revelled in the trappings and perks of their rank, but Chrétien always looked a little embarrassed by the size of his office and the fuss that his staff made over his power and position.

To rural MPs and those from small-town Canada, Chrétien gave a conspiratorial and knowing smile, and often shared his sense of humour. He understood us and the people we represented. He had identified his constituency, both in and out of Parliament, early in his career, and he nurtured this awareness all the way to the prime minister's office.

I recall a meeting, soon after the 1980 election, that quickly defined both Trudeau and Chrétien. The meeting, led by Trudeau, Lalonde and Chrétien, had been called to discuss the standoff between Ottawa and Newfoundland Premier Brian Peckford over the ownership of oil and gas resources. Peckford was adamant in his opposition to Ottawa's claim, and *Maclean's* magazine had dubbed him "The Bad Boy of Confederation."

Trudeau wanted to fight back by explaining to Newfoundlanders why they should share their income from the reserves with the rest of Canada. He had defended this position during the election campaign at a boisterous student rally on the campus of Memorial University. He may have won over the crowd by standing his ground and taking on hecklers planted by the Tories, but we failed to win any seats in St. John's that year.

Trudeau began the meeting by announcing that Lalonde would mount an information campaign in Newfoundland and Labrador to explain Ottawa's position on ownership of offshore oil and gas. After some discussion, I spoke out, saying that while it was important for Lalonde to speak, it was also important for the province's MPs to be front and centre in the campaign. Chrétien agreed, as did Bill Rompkey and other MPs from Newfoundland and Labrador. Trudeau disagreed with us, saying there should be one spokesperson for the government of Canada to ensure continuity of message.

"Prime Minister," I countered, "Newfoundlanders and Labradorians are like Quebecers. We want to hear from our own representatives on important issues. If we don't, we wonder if they have been gagged."

Trudeau had inserted a pencil in the wire binding of his notepad, and was twirling the pad around it as I spoke, his eyes burning at my apparent impudence. When I finished making my point, the notepad suddenly flew off the end of his pencil and whizzed past my ear. While I retrieved it, Trudeau conceded that we Newfoundland MPs could speak, but only after coordinating our message with Lalonde. The meeting broke up and, walking down the corridor, I remarked to Chrétien that the PM had just missed my head.

"He didn't miss," Chrétien said. "If he'd wanted to hit you, he would have used a chair."

I WAS UNDERSTANDABLY NERVOUS delivering my maiden speech in the House later that year. With people like Trudeau, Lalonde, MacEachen, Chrétien and others listening, I knew that both the content and the delivery would be assessed, and the speech could set the tone for my future career in Parliament.

I started by pointing out that, of all the MPs from Newfoundland and Labrador, at age 25 I was the only one who had been born a Canadian. All the others had arrived in this world prior to Newfoundland joining Confederation. It was a small point, perhaps, but a symbolic one. There was no question in my mind about the wisdom of Newfoundland's decision made at the impetus of Joey Smallwood in 1949, no second-guessing the vote. At my birth, Confederation was an historical fact. My Canadian birth made a difference to my outlook, my value system and my commitment to both my province and my country.

In my comments supporting a funding bill for 1980–81, I quoted from a speech Lester Pearson had delivered in 1949 decrying the cynicism of many Canadians regarding the views and actions of federal representatives versus MPPs. Pearson had been concerned about it back then, and I expressed similar concerns 31 years later. I have always believed there is no conflict between love and passion for one's province and a similar love and passion for one's country. To underline this belief, I next quoted George Drew, leader of the federal PCs when Newfoundland joined Confederation, who had stated that those who would seek to divide province against province were disloyal to Canada. As I sat down, I noted that both Trudeau and Lalonde were applauding. They may have been giving the customary round of applause to a rookie member's first speech, but their show of approval was reassuring.

NEXT TO TRUDEAU, the most dominant player on the Canadian political scene in 1980 was René Lévesque. It may surprise some people to learn that I, and other dedicated federalists, were actually fond of Lévesque. Had we been hockey players instead of politicians, Lévesque would have been the scrappy guy you wished was on your team instead of playing for the other guys. When Lévesque hit the ice he played with passion, and you'd better watch for his elbows in the corners.

Lévesque reflected the passion of Quebec francophones who were struggling to retain their identity among more than 300 million anglophones and Latins sharing the North American continent. As we seem to encounter often in Canadian life, the sharply divergent goals of Trudeau and Lévesque created a unique dichotomy; in the same year that Lévesque scheduled his referendum to seek separation of Quebec from Canada, the ultimate federalist Trudeau led the Liberals in winning 74 out of 75 seats in that province during the general election.

Some have described the 1980 Liberal victory in Quebec as the practical expression of Trudeau's credo "reason over passion," which he learned at the feet of Jesuit educators. Lévesque, who abandoned his studies in law to pursue a career in journalism, had also been educated by Jesuits. Both men shared the Jesuit credo, and the idea that Trudeau was all reason and Lévesque all passion is clearly wrong. No one was more methodical in planning his strategy than Lévesque, and no one who heard Trudeau defend federalism during the 1980 referendum could ever doubt his passion.

I was a Trudeau man but admired both men, even though one wanted to essentially tear the country apart and the other worked to hold it together. It was clear to me that Trudeau was a hero and Lévesque was the villain. The trouble was, I had difficulty disliking the villain. In the run-up to the 1980 referendum I watched Trudeau gather his team—Chrétien, Lalonde, Jean Marchand, a somewhat reluctant Claude Ryan and others—and tackle the separatists head-on. And I was present, to my surprise at the time, when Trudeau gave his electrifying speech in the Paul Sauvé Arena a few weeks before the referendum.

That afternoon I had been strolling across Parliament Hill with John Dustan, an old friend from Newfoundland. We were heading nowhere in particular when a large yellow bus passed us and I heard voices call out, "Hey, Tobin!" I looked up to see Jacques Olivier, Liberal MP from Longueil, and Robert Gourd, who represented Argenteuil-Papineau, leaning out the window and gesturing. "We're off to hear Trudeau speak tonight," they shouted. "You should join us!"

Well, why not? A rather confused and impressed—I'm not sure which—John Dustan and I took seats on the bus and we roared off to Montreal, among a lusty crowd of Québécois MPs. I seem to recall very little English being spoken while a bottle of decent cognac was passed around, and our enthusiasm exploded into total excitement once inside the arena. John and I became caught in the flood, and to our surprise we found ourselves seated right on the stage, directly behind the speaker's podium.

Trudeau spoke that night strictly off the cuff, with no notes at all, and in many ways his address was the Canadian equivalent of Dr. Martin Luther King's famous "I have a dream" speech, which galvanized the US civil rights movement in 1963. He spoke directly from the heart, something that few politicians these days dare to do.

In a speech the previous week, Lévesque had mocked Trudeau's middle name of Elliott, scoffing at its Anglo origins. That was going too far, Trudeau felt. It smacked of racism, or at least tribalism, out of step with Canadian society. With this as the theme, he played the crowd that evening like an orchestra conductor, building to climax after climax, drawing inspiration from the audience's response and feeding it back to them, over and over. Trudeau may have believed in "reason over passion," but that night passion took over, and it was unforgettable. The speech also reminded me why I had been attracted to Trudeau's thinking and style when I was still in high school. Trudeau, unlike everyone else I saw in politics, was his own man—defiantly so. He spoke his mind, sometimes with less-than-positive consequences, but the events of that evening demonstrated his honesty and the power of his oratory.

I did not agree with everything Trudeau said during his career, nor with every policy and strategy he proposed. I was disappointed at the alienation of western Canada during his time in office, for example, and I am forced to agree with those who blame some of our subsequent economic difficulties on policies enacted during his last term in office (although I wish they would also address the immense contribution of Brian Mulroney's government to the deficit during its eight-year term).

Like every Canadian who heard Trudeau's speech in Montreal that May evening in 1980, when he called the separatists "hucksters of sovereignty" and countered Lévesque's snide comment about the British origins of Trudeau's middle name, I was moved by his words and by his passion for this country. I hope we never again need that degree of passion in defence of Canada as a nation. We continue, however, to need the same level of dedication and personal commitment.

Even Trudeau's critics grudgingly accept the fact that he made Canadians proud of their country—proud of our tolerance, proud of our standing within the global community and proud of our image throughout the world. I don't believe anyone since has elevated our own opinion of ourselves to that degree. Excess pride is dangerous, of course, but pride in the right degree brings confidence, and Canada has reaped major benefits from the confidence inspired by Pierre Elliott Trudeau's pride.

AFTER LEADING A SUCCESSFUL FIGHT against the separatists, Trudeau turned his attention to Quebec's concerns. Many of them, he believed, were rooted in the anomalies of our country's Constitution. Here we were, 113 years after Confederation, still unable to define our country without approval from the British Parliament. Trudeau focused attention on the scope of the problem and, incidentally, took it out of the hands of the provincial premiers who often jockeyed for personal political position, by creating a Special Joint Committee of the House of Commons and Senate on the Constitution. Jean Chrétien was asked to assemble the committee, and he appointed me to it.

The 25-member committee was important for a number of reasons beyond its role in the overall constitutional repatriation strategy. It was the first parliamentary committee in Canada to have its proceedings televised, and its hearings involved more participants and a wider range of topics than any committee before or since. For 65 days, the other members and I listened to 914 individuals, representing 294 groups, testify about the need to address their concerns in drafting the proposed new Charter of Rights and Freedoms.

During the hearings, I recall thinking what a fantastic country we were, not only to create a charter that would supersede the powers of the legislature, but also to perform this task only after giving every interested group the opportunity to be acknowledged and heard. Could we create a charter that would address the diverse interests of all who appeared before us? Of course not. We knew this would be impossible, and those making their presentations knew so as well. All we could do was frame the document in a manner that spoke to the major concerns of the largest number of groups. If we could do that, and avoid infringing on the most acute areas of others, we could claim at least limited success.

Those who made their presentations to the committee were received with respect and patience. The committee's activities were neither political window dressing nor empty formalities. Every ethnic group, every community, every region and every individual that took the time to express its interest was acknowledged. They all left the committee room, I believe, satisfied that they had played a role in shaping the charter.

The lessons I absorbed from that process continue to resonate within me. Some were profound in their impact; others were conflicting, perhaps, but vital nevertheless.

On one hand, I had a wonderful sense of participating with Canadians in an historical event as wide ranging in its implications as anything that our government had achieved since Confederation. It drove home to me how Canada had progressed beyond an exclusively "two solitudes" structure. When the committee meetings ended, I realized that my perception of Canada had changed. This country was and is a nation of tremendous complexity and diversity, unlike any in the world. If these qualities bring unique tensions and concerns with them—and without question they do—we should take pride in our ability to recognize and address them with patience and tolerance, if not with perfection.

On the other hand, the multitude of submissions and points of view also focused on a hard fact of political life: at the end of the day, it is up to the elected government to make core decisions. Some may argue that this is a fatal flaw in democracy and that only a pure referendum puts power in the hands of the people. This may be true, but unfocused power can be dangerous and unproductive. As we have seen in two Quebec referenda on separation, the process is subject to suasion through less-than-honourable means. A referendum has a limited, finite horizon; its life begins with the declaration and ends with the voting day. Any event occurring within the period can skew the results far beyond the impact it deserves. Imagine, for example, a horrific murder occurring during a referendum on capital punishment. Without doubt it would dramatically and understandably skew a large number of voters toward a decision they might not have agreed with prior to the event, and one they may not share a few months later.

By definition, a referendum cleaves the situation into two halves with no room for the middle ground where compromise occurs. Positions harden, leading to passion that overrides reason. During the 1980 Quebec referendum, I recall hearing Jean Chrétien say that the process was dividing his own family, brother against brother, sister against sister. In a referendum you are on one side or the other.

Governments can and must explore the middle ground that is non-existent in referendum-based questions. What's more, governments serve to absorb the negative passions often generated by balanced opposing forces. The situation is similar to the parliamentary procedure that seeks to deflect personal views between opposing parties by insisting that all questions be addressed to the Speaker of the House who is, or should be, an individual of neutrality and high standards when it comes to enforcing behaviour.

Is there ever a suitable time and place for a referendum? I believe there is: when the public interest is thwarted by a constitutional inability to fulfill it in good time, or when the decision to be reached is so basic and so clearly delineated that a yes or no response is appropriate. In that situation, those who propose and implement a referendum should be prepared to step aside if it fails to support their position. Referenda are powerful and dangerous weapons, and people who insist on using them must agree to accept the consequences.

In the case of the charter hearings, the committee could never have reached a consensus had our goal been to reconcile all the testimony and evidence presented to us. More than one group told us, in so many words, that if we failed to draft the document according to their needs, it would not be worth the effort.

There would never be a perfect solution, of course. We knew it, and most of those making the presentations knew it. But this hardly negated the effort. At the conclusion of the hearings, it was up to Trudeau to pour some water into our wine. The document we helped produce plays a role in defining who we are and what we stand for as Canadians. It also, for better or for worse, proves the maxim that politics is indeed the art of the possible.

BY THE TIME the 1980 referendum was completed, I was up to speed on performing the duties of an MP and fulfilling the expectations of my constituents and the party.

In serving my constituents, I still had Don Jamieson's words of advice ringing in my ears. "When you go to Ottawa," he told me after I won my seat, "if you concentrate on being a big success there, you'll be a big failure in Newfoundland. And if you're a failure back here, you won't be around very long." The message was clear: never forget the people who elected you. "First impressions are lasting impressions," Don went on. "If you establish yourself as someone who gets up early each day and goes to work, it will last you all your career. If you get a reputation for sleeping late every morning, you'll never get over it."

I took the advice to heart, and it has never failed me. If I received word on Monday that my presence was requested at a town meeting on Wednesday, I was there. This not only established my reputation as someone who "gets up early each day," but also connected me with community leaders, volunteers, citizen groups and others who needed to know that their MP was paying attention. The results were measured at the ballot box in every election. From 42 percent in 1980, my proportion of the vote rose to 50 percent in the Mulroney landslide of 1984, 68 percent in 1988 and 84 percent in 1993.

This kind of steadily growing support is built not by delivering big projects, which is the old pork-barrel method of securing votes. It's built by answering telephone calls and letters from your community and by being accessible when necessary. I accepted this in my role as an advocate for my constituents, and in reconciling their needs with the concerns being exchanged on the floor of the House. To me, this means listening to the voices of your constituents and the voices of other MPs sitting next to you or across the floor of the Commons. From time to time, reconciling these voices can mean conveying bad news to the people who elected you. Here's an example.

A year or so after I was first elected, I received word that Nickerson's, a large fish processor, was applying for a substantial federal loan to complete a new plant it had started to build in my riding. The firm had already put up structural steel worth $2 million and was looking for a handout of several million dollars more to complete the project. Their appeal was compelling. The plant would create as many as 700 jobs, and the steel was already in place—how could we turn it down?

The company had made no prior request for funds before launching construction, and it was against public policy for Ottawa to run in and rescue the project. Besides, there was a concern about over-capacity in the fishing industry in that part of the province. Still, unemployment levels were high; those 700 jobs were needed. What stand could we take?

I conferred with Fisheries Minister Romeo LeBlanc, who agreed that we could not use public funds this way. Instead of giving the word from Ottawa via press release or some other means, LeBlanc and I flew to St. Barbe on the Great Northern Peninsula and told the people directly. Obviously, it was not what they wanted to hear. St. Barbe wanted those jobs as badly as any place in the country. It was painful for me to deliver the bad news, and more painful for them to hear it. But I have never believed in fudging the truth with the public. In the end, it only leads to trouble. Politicians who tell their constituents "maybe" when they really mean "never" are always losers when the truth becomes known. There was disappointment and some anger at the news that the fish plant could not be completed with federal funds, but the people respected me, I believe, for respecting *them* enough to be truthful with them. In its own way, my directness brought me closer to them. The people who were disappointed that day still call me Brian, and they gave me their solid support in every election.

The steel that the processing company had erected, counting on public funds to complete the plant, stood rusting for more than 10 years before it was torn down. The company didn't like it, the public didn't like it and I didn't like it, but there it was— a monument to people who failed to do things right.

BIRTH OF THE RAT PACK

THE YEAR 1984 was a watershed in Canada's history. Early in the year, Pierre Trudeau took his walk in the snow and decided to end his political career. It was also, of course, the end of an era.

The impact of Trudeau's decision on federal Liberals was softened by the knowledge that an heir apparent was waiting. John Turner was not in the House at this time, having resigned in early 1976 to return to law, but everyone from St. John's to Nanaimo knew that his return to Ottawa was only a matter of time. (In those days, Brian Mulroney referred to Turner as "the Liberal dream in motion.") John Turner possessed the same qualities that made Pierre Trudeau a giant in Canadian political history: keen intellect, and a passion for his country, served with a WASP rather than a Gallic flavour.

I admired Turner from the beginning, and when he returned to lead the Liberals in June 1984, I became almost an extra staff member in his office. I grew frustrated that we were unable to lift him above the caricature he had become in the press, which exploited his nervous laugh and certain mannerisms that made him appear uncomfortable in his own skin. Once the press packaged him as someone out of his element, he was unable to change this skewed perception, to find his own feet the way others might have, most notably Jean Chrétien.

JEAN CHRÉTIEN AND JOHN TURNER fought a bitter battle to replace Trudeau for the leadership position in June 1984. When Turner emerged the winner, Chrétien served for a while before giving up his seat for a return to private life, and everyone settled down to see John Turner demonstrate his abilities as prime minister.

We never had the opportunity to see Turner in government the way others had seen him, when he was as sure-footed as any Canadian parliamentarian. He lost an edge during his first debate with Mulroney in the 1984 federal election campaign. He gained some back when he debated Mulroney on the free trade issue, but the damage had been done, and the rest is sad history.

The experience proved to me that a successful prime minister needs two things in equal measure. One is a broad plan to take this country in the right direction. By drawing on the best talent inside and outside government, an effective PM can locate the particular skills and talents to implement the plan in detail, but it remains the PM's duty to sketch the wider view.

The second skill is an ability to inspire key players, both in the caucus and across the country, to shape and share the vision. This involves challenging regional voices that seek to divide us, and speaking over the heads of mass media and splinter groups to address everyday Canadians. Leaders with that capability can help Canadians see themselves as bigger than their own personal problems and aspirations, and can inspire a new experiment in democracy on the northern half of this continent.

That's a tall order. But you and I have seen these skill sets, or parts of them, in one leader or another. We need to find and exploit them in all our leaders, at every level.

JOHN TURNER FACED a supremely confident Brian Mulroney in the 1984 election. I remember watching the Mulroneys being interviewed on TV and adding up all the positive factors: son of an electrician from small-town Quebec who pulls himself up by the bootstraps and marries his life partner who exhibits charm, grace and intelligence. He is fluent in both official languages and establishes himself with corporate bigwigs and labour leaders. Relatively young, energetic and fired with the strength of his convictions, he has first-rate political instincts and abilities. Then, after imposing some much-needed discipline on the Tory party, he gathers impressive new talent around him. Hollywood's central casting office could not have sent over a Tory leader more devastating to our cause.

John Turner's rustiness, the result of being out of the political mainstream for eight years, multiplied our headaches. Turner was as bright and attractive as ever, but political readiness depends on instinct plus something that professional athletes refer to as conditioning. In 1984, John Turner was weak in both.

Nothing brought this home more effectively than his appearance in my riding late in the 1984 campaign. By then, I was resigned to the fact that we would lose a large portion of our majority. Many polls had us battling it out for second place with the NDP, led by a fired-up Ed Broadbent. At times like those, all an MP can do is look after his or her own backyard constituency. That's what I was doing a week or so before the election when I received a call from Keith Davey on a Friday afternoon. Davey, the legendary "rainmaker" for federal Liberals, was having trouble finding places to send Turner for speeches and media exposure prior to voting day.

"The leader will be in your area on Monday," Davey told me. "Can you set up a rally for him?"

The lead time for a prime minister's visit is usually measured in weeks. We had less than 72 hours to arrange Turner's visit to the riding. Thanks to the efforts of people like my executive assistant Chuck Furey, my brother Terry and other members of my campaign team, we pulled it together. The following Monday evening, after I escorted John on a tour through the local paper mill, we arrived at the hall in Stephenville. Both Turner and the national media covering his campaign had low expectations, and so they were doubly impressed when they found a roaring, cheering overflow crowd. We had bused in Liberals from as far away as Corner Brook, and hired local musicians to put everyone in the mood to stomp their feet and shout and whistle, and they all greeted John as though he were a visiting rock star. The applause shook the walls while Turner beamed and the media recorded it all. Finally, John walked to the microphone, raised his hands for silence and began to speak.

I don't know if it was his astonishment at the size and enthusiasm of the crowd, the fatigue of a long and stressful campaign or the lack of Turner's political edge, but the next few seconds were agony. John lost his focus in front of the people and the TV cameras.

"I'm delighted to be here in Stephenville," he began, "with Brian Mu—, Brian Mu—, er."

Brian Mulroney was still occupying John's thoughts. I could almost hear him shift gears.

"Sorry," he said with a grin. "I'm delighted to be here with Brian P—, Brian Peck—"

He had replaced Mulroney with the then-current premier of Newfoundland, Brian Peckford.

The noise in the hall faded away. The only sound was the clicking of eyeballs as people looked at each other silently.

Then John got it right. "I'm pleased to be here with Brian T—, Brian Tobin!" he said.

By this time I was at John's side, and I leaned toward the microphone and said, "The trouble with this country's politics is that there are too many Brians around." I held up two fingers. "*Two* too many!" The crowd roared its approval.

The rest of the evening went better, but it never regained the fervour of our arrival. It was a painful anticlimax to a painful campaign, made doubly agonizing because I liked John so much. I still like him, and I often wonder how things might have been different had he been able to assume Trudeau's mantle. But he had been away from the fray too long. He didn't have it, whatever the "it" of successful politics might be. There are many ways of tracking the end of an individual's political career, I suppose. For me, John Turner's began that night in Stephenville.

BUCKING THE NATIONAL TREND, I managed to improve my vote tally in 1984. That personal achievement, however, proved to be meagre comfort when we were swept out of power by the Mulroney-led Conservatives. I returned to a very different Ottawa from the one I had arrived at as a rookie MP. We had enjoyed both a substantial majority and a confident Liberal leader, but now we counted just 40 seats among us. Moreover, we faced an overwhelming Tory majority and a revitalized NDP determined to replace us as the official Opposition, and we were led by a man who appeared uncomfortable in his position.

It's difficult, nearly 20 years later, to appreciate just how shaky the fortunes of the Liberal Party appeared back then. The 74 Quebec seats we had boasted in the previous Parliament had shrunk to 17. We had two seats west of Ontario. Our share of the popular vote was barely one in four. Many in the media were referring to us as a "Red Rump," meaning that all the meaningful political give-and-take would be between Mulroney's Tories and Broadbent's New Democrats. Editorialists around the country suggested that Canada finally possessed a clear political choice between the Left and the Right. Some predicted that the centrist Liberal party would fade away to little more than a spiritual presence, like the British Liberals.

Ed Broadbent built on this distinction, taking it further with a nationalistic slant. The federal PCs, Broadbent suggested, represented not only the right wing of Canadian politics, but the *Americanized* version. Hadn't Brian Mulroney served as president of a US-owned corporation before entering the political arena? Hadn't Mulroney's last assignment from his Cleveland,

Ohio masters been to shut down Iron Ore of Canada with minimum expense to the American owners? And weren't his fiscal policies a northern version of Ronald Reagan's trickle-down economics? "We are the real Opposition!" Broadbent was fond of saying, even though the NDP held 10 fewer seats than we Liberals. But in the minds of many Canadians, he seemed to have a point. Had we really been "Trudeau's party" more than Liberals? And if so, what did this make us after Trudeau departed?

To complicate things, most of our party's stalwarts were not equipped to function well in Opposition. Except for the nine-month period in 1979 when Joe Clark was PM, the party's senior MPs had been on the government side since 1963. Those who had managed to retain their seats were disillusioned and no match for Mulroney's swaggering majority and Ed Broadbent's blood-sniffing NDP.

Nature abhors a vacuum. So does a political party. When an apparent vacuum of energy, enthusiasm and ambition appeared among the Liberals after the 1984 election, it was filled with a group of young MPs, including myself, who were determined not to allow Mulroney and his members to have the run of Parliament and treat our party like a rump.

And so was born the Rat Pack.

I BELIEVE TIM HARPER of the *Toronto Star* hung the name "Rat Pack" on us, adapting the sobriquet from the crowd who hung around Frank Sinatra and Dean Martin in the 1950s and 1960s. Some observers ignored that connection and leaned more toward the rodent association, but we didn't care. We began making points in Parliament, earning recognition in the media and serving notice that the Liberal Party would continue to address the wider interests of all Canadians. If we had to make noise to do it, we would. If we had to flirt with being obnoxious at times . . . well, anyone who thinks politics is a ladies' and gentlemen's game has never been deeply involved in the process.

Membership in the Rat Pack varied over time but usually consisted of these core MPs: Sheila Copps, John Nunziata, Don Boudria, Jean Lapierre, Jean-Claude Malépart, our *éminence grise* Herb Gray and me. Together, we covered a wide range of experience and points of view even though we were quite different individually.

SHEILA COPPS CAME TO OTTAWA with impeccable political credentials. Her father had been one of Hamilton, Ontario's most popular mayors, and she grew up immersed in talk of political strategy, values and goals. Fluent in French and Italian, with a smattering of other languages, Sheila earned a reputation as a scrapper in the Ontario legislature, where she ran for leadership of the Liberals. She arrived on Parliament Hill in 1984 totally uninhibited by the fact that we had been booted out of power and into Opposition with just 40 seats. Instead of decrying our situation, she went to work rebuilding the party, and she sensed instinctively that control had shifted into the hands of backbenchers. In Sheila's eyes, we were the people who would bring the party back into power.

Let's be frank here: had Sheila brought all of her energies, all of her talents and all of her dedication to bear as a man, and not as a relatively young woman, she would have been lauded as a "new politician to watch," an up-and-coming powerhouse in Ottawa. Instead, she was assessed differently by some MPs who simply could not abide a woman performing in the House with the same effectiveness as people such as Tommy Douglas, John Diefenbaker and others. She entered every debate armed with equal quantities of passion and preparation, and this enraged some members across the floor. One Tory MP from Burlington, Ontario—practically in Sheila's own political backyard—became infamous for using a sexual slander against her that was picked up on videotape and distributed across North America. His stumbling efforts to deny the slur only made him look more foolish and craven.

Too many male MPs were prepared to accept women in the House as long as they behaved "appropriately," which meant, I suppose, as long as they acted "like ladies." They didn't like it when women like Sheila showed they could be as tough, as brass knuckled, as direct and as raucous as men. Sheila broke new ground in her first term, and like all pioneers she paid the price for doing it. You can question her style if you like, but no one has ever questioned her intelligence, her determination and her insistence on being her own person, come hell, high water or John Crosbie.

John Nunziata impressed me immediately as one of the brightest, most articulate members in the House. He was also one of the most fearless men I ever encountered during the period in Ottawa. No one intimidated him, and he took on everyone from the prime minister down, never giving an inch.

John loved jumping into a skirmish, seizing on a remark from across the House that was contradictory or an attack on working Canadians. The thing I remember most about him is that he had run for office hoping to play a role in governing the nation. He wound up in Opposition, where he made a greater impact than he might have if the Liberals had maintained a majority.

Later, John fell out of favour with Jean Chrétien, yet still managed to be elected as an independent in the 1997 election, which was quite an achievement. But in the next election, John went down to defeat running as an independent against Alan Tonks, the Liberal candidate.

Alan invited me to visit his riding of York South–Weston during the campaign, and I arrived to find John and his wife, Caroline, there, with the usual crowd of media gathered around. As the cameras rolled and flashed, John seized my hand and refused to let go as he said, "Brian, I thought we were friends. What are you doing here?"

I explained that I was there to support the Liberal candidate.

John continued to grip my hand, then loudly demanded that I leave "his" riding. I have to admit that I was uncomfortable campaigning against a former colleague whom I had come to admire over the years, but that's the nature of party politics. John's actions were always based on his own set of principles, and when he proved just as fearless in attacking his own leader over them, he paid the price. He knew what the price would be from the beginning, of course, but he stuck to his principles and soldiered on nevertheless—a classic Nunziata decision. On election day I was pleased that Alan Tonks won, and sorry that John would no longer be making his presence felt in Ottawa.

Don Boudria practically grew up on Parliament Hill. A Franco-Ontarian, Don served as a dining room busboy on the Hill when he was a teenager, watching the comings and goings of MPs, staff, civil servants, media—all the elements that fuel and feed off the federal government. Like Jean Chrétien, Don never forgot who sent him to Parliament, and he maintains close ties with blue-collar workers and rank-and-file public service employees.

Perhaps more thoughtful and cautious than other Pack members, Don remained determined to rebuild the Liberal Party, prepared to do battle with Tories like Erik Nielsen and Harvie André at the drop of a memo. He was also brilliant at planning strategy, looking beyond today's give-and-take to plan tomorrow's attack, and he remains a strong advocate for francophone rights. Eventually, Don rose to become minister of public works and receiver general of Canada, and today he serves as government House leader.

Jean Lapierre and Jean-Claude Malépart added their Québécois viewpoints to Rat Pack attacks; if our policies on Quebec did not receive their approval, we went back to the drawing board. Lapierre was bright and articulate, especially when it came to tackling Tory activities on behalf of Quebec. When Jean Chrétien replaced John Turner in 1990, however, Lapierre's nationalism clashed with Chrétien's federalist views, and Lapierre left caucus to join forces with Lucien Bouchard and create the Bloc Québécois. Today, he is one of Quebec's best-known radio and television personalities. Malépart, from a working-class riding in east-end Montreal, was a true people's champion with a booming voice and a big heart. Tragically, he died much too young, of a brain tumour, and people in his riding mourn his passing to this day.

The Rat Pack was enthusiastic and determined but not undisciplined. Our series of questions and follow-ups on Tory actions and policies were plotted before we entered the House, and quiet, dignified Herb Gray was our master tactician. Gray gave guidance to the missiles we lofted across the floor at the Tories. Once we decided on a topic, such as the controversial Sinclair Stevens affair, we discussed ways to counter every angle on it. Sheila might ask the lead-off question, Jean-Claude might take the follow-up, Don Boudria would approach it from an unexpected angle and so on.

Were there times when we went too far (such as the day Sheila and John let their emotions override their logic and tried to leap some chairs in a committee room to reach a departing Sinclair Stevens)? Yes, there were. Would some questions have been better posed in committee or during debate over a specific bill rather than during the melee of Question Period? No question about it. I make all of these reassessments with the advantage of time, age and maturity.

But I cannot and will not apologize for the Rat Pack's overall strategy. Nor would I be overly critical of any party, facing an overwhelming majority across the floor of the House, employing the tactics we used. Politics can be a messy business at times. We all prefer to act like refined ladies and gentlemen, I suppose, no matter what the situation. The truth of the matter is, if you have passion for the values you want to pursue and defend, there are times when refinement becomes as advantageous as the colour of the shoes you happen to be wearing that day. Trudeau's credo, remember, was "reason over passion," not "reason *free* of passion."

I believe that the antics of the Rat Pack helped prevent the Liberals from slipping into near obscurity, as many of the country's editorial writers were predicting at the time. We were able to assert ourselves as a continuing political force and as a necessary counterbalance to the Tories, while the party elders adjusted to the new realities of the Mulroney era. In the space of a few months we had slid from the majority party, led by Trudeau, to an Opposition outnumbered more than five to one, led by a man whose abilities had atrophied after eight years out of the political arena. As time went on, the party elders, including John Turner, forcefully re-engaged in the discussion, and we returned to a semblance of our attitude in the previous House. But the Rat Pack was needed to bridge the gap.

In spite of the fireworks on the floor of the House, work continued in committees, where most of the productivity in Parliament is carried out. Committee work is rarely covered by the media because it is not theatrical in nature. Nor should it be. Good committee work is the result of diligent research, careful preparation and decision making based on compromise, free from posturing and personal attacks. As a result, the committees are often invisible even while being effective.

I wish more attention were paid to committee work, if only to acknowledge the contributions of MPs who will make neither the front page of newspapers nor the front bench of a government in power. Many members complete long, productive careers without occupying a cabinet position. I sat in Parliament for 13 years before joining the cabinet, and much of that time was spent in committee work. During those years, which included the most notorious episodes of the Rat Pack, I was mentioned in dozens of media stories detailing the activities of Question Period, but only once in reference to my committee work. Even then, it was because my filibuster succeeded in derailing a clause in a bill Don Mazankowski was trying to push through. Mazankowski wanted to apply user fees for transportation services. I argued that the fees would be hurtful and unfair to certain groups, and we managed to have it expunged there in the committee room. So 13 years of committee work yielded one mention in a *Globe and Mail* column written by Hugh Winsor, while 13 minutes of give-and-take in Question Period could earn headlines and evening TV news coverage day after day. That kind of sums it up.

Of all the discussions, decisions and activities taking place on Parliament Hill each day, only Question Period appears on the evening news, where Canadians chuckle or grumble at the antics of their elected representatives. It's easy, but inaccurate, to assume that Question Period represents day-long sessions in the House, and that today's MPs act in an intolerable fashion compared with those in the past. Many Canadians are embarrassed by the antics they see during Question Period, but they shouldn't be.

Remember that a prime minister enjoying the benefit of a substantial majority, like Brian Mulroney after the 1984 election, controls a level of political and executive powers found in few, if any, democracies around the world. The president of the United States, for example, faces a system of checks and balances from the House and Senate that is absent in our system. This is not a criticism of Canadian parliamentary structure—I believe it is superior to a president-led republican system in many ways—but it demonstrates a need to hold the prime minister and cabinet to account in a public forum. Thanks to Question Period, the governing party must reply to queries out in the open, and the public has direct access to the response.

Question Period is something of a gauntlet that the cabinet is required to run each day. It can be painful, unfair and even deadly to the ill-prepared or stumbling cabinet minister, but it is very effective at revealing actions or information that the party in power may wish to conceal or twist to its own ends.

The volatility of Question Period is nothing new. Half a century ago, the legendary Jack Pickersgill played the role of a one-man Rat Pack. Armed with an encyclopedic knowledge of House rules and always prepared for any debate, Pickersgill—another Newfoundland Liberal, by the way—once outraged Tory Leader George Drew with his constant interruptions. When Drew tried to admonish Pickersgill for his "bad manners," Pickersgill shot back: "I submit, sir, that it has never been a rule of the House that honourable members have to submit quietly to being bored!"

No one was bored when Jack Pickersgill was speaking, and boredom rarely prevailed when the Rat Pack was in its heyday.

Question Period is also a uniquely Canadian institution. No other parliamentary democracy conducts a similar activity in the same way. It represents an important aspect of the transparency that is essential to the operation of government in a free society. Neither the British nor the US system has anything like our Question Period. In the United Kingdom, Question Period is a one-day-a-week event in which the prime minister responds to written questions, posted in advance. With that much time between sessions, and substantial opportunity to prepare a response, it's easy for the government of the day to deflect and obfuscate any query that it finds challenging, embarrassing or dangerous. No such advantage is provided to a Canadian prime minister or cabinet, and I don't believe there should be.

In the United States, the president and his cabinet are never subjected to direct inquiry by elected representatives on a regular basis. Imagine if Richard Nixon had faced the kind of probing during Watergate that a Canadian PM must deal with each and every day in the Commons. In many ways, the US system depends upon its press to pose tough questions to elected and appointed officials. We have that benefit in Canada as well, but providing elected representatives with the same opportunity, armed with facts instead of speculation, is an invaluable resource we should take pride in and not be embarrassed about.

That's what makes Question Period an important Canadian institution, and the occasional excesses are justified.

THE RETURN OF JEAN CHRÉTIEN

I T'S EASY TO SAY NOW, but I was fortunate to have those 13 years in the Commons, including 8 in Opposition, before earning a cabinet appointment. There were times when I chafed for an opportunity to shape policy directly. Now I realize that I could not have received a better apprenticeship than by watching first Pierre Trudeau, then (very briefly) John Turner, followed by Brian Mulroney and (even more briefly) Kim Campbell, before being tapped by Jean Chrétien to be minister of fisheries and oceans in 1993. The achievements and errors of those prime ministers and their respective cabinets unfolded in front of me over the years, and they all registered as either techniques to emulate or gaffes to avoid.

After Trudeau, Brian Mulroney's influence on me was as powerful as anyone's. Where Trudeau taught me how to use passion to drive a point home, Mulroney revealed how a positive aspect of your personality can become a negative quality once you're in power.

Mulroney, remember, had advised me not to linger as an executive assistant if I were seriously interested in a long-term political career. His counsel, in its own small way, led me to the House of Commons, and I recognized and acknowledged his wisdom. When he and the rest of the Tories trounced the competition in the 1984 election, I admired his acumen even more. He looked and sounded great, ran a terrific campaign and was totally relaxed and comfortable in the spotlight. As a member of the Rat Pack, of course, I often tangled with him but I never personally disliked him, and I had a sense that he had no deep personal animosity for me either. Like a couple of hockey players on opposing teams, we both expected no quarter to be given, but after the game ended we could possibly share a beer or two.

Brian Mulroney can be charming and totally engaging one on one. This aspect of him, unfortunately, never translated itself to television, where the majority of Canadians form their opinions of political leaders. The same smile that looks warm and expansive across a dining table can look forced on television, which tends to exaggerate every gesture. In my opinion, this is why Trudeau maintained such wide public appeal, even when his policies were at odds with certain groups. Trudeau understated his gestures, and this played well in front of the camera; Mulroney's efforts to be amiable came across simply as slick. He is also a superb host—attentive and thoroughly decent in his dealings with people. It would amaze me when I would witness these qualities in the man throughout the day, and then turn on the TV in the evening and discover the same man appearing defensive, bombastic, loud and too cute by half. In Marshall McLuhan's assessment, both television and Trudeau were "cool"; Mulroney was "hot," and thus at odds with TV.

The other fatal flaw in Mulroney's makeup, in my opinion, was his personal loyalty to supporters, especially those who helped him defeat Joe Clark in the 1983 PC leadership review process. Mulroney preaches that "you dance with the one that brung you" in explaining his allegiance to those who assisted his rise to power. This is an admirable quality for most people, but for prime ministers and premiers, and those who aspire to reach those positions, this same brand of loyalty can prove disastrous.

When Marc Lalonde delivered a tribute to Pierre Trudeau during the 1984 Liberal convention that replaced Trudeau with

John Turner, he referred obliquely to this fact when he said, *"Enfin, je retrouve le tutoiement."* Loosely translated, it means, "At last, I can again call my old friend *tu.*" In French, there are two words for *you*: *tu* indicates intimacy; *vous* is formal and distant by comparison. Even though Trudeau and Lalonde could trace their friendship back to their student days, once Trudeau became prime minister the relationship changed. Lalonde knew what few people outside of government recognize: prime ministers and premiers can have no friends around them. Regardless of how close or long-lasting the relationship might have been in the past, once the seat of power is achieved, the friendship is put on hold. Or, as Graham Fraser put it in the *Toronto Star*, "[the] friendship will be locked away like a bottle of wine, to be opened much later."

Gérard Pelletier, whose acquaintance with Trudeau extended back even further than Lalonde's, noted in his memoirs that he rarely saw the prime minister privately while Trudeau was at 24 Sussex Drive and Pelletier was filling a cabinet position. Some people saw this as evidence of Trudeau's cold, aloof nature. I see it as political wisdom of the highest order.

Politics and public service do not function the same way. Everything you do in public life is part of a transparent process, and a "deal" performed as a way of settling political debts is a ticking bomb. Mulroney, applying his misplaced sense of loyalty, brought some friends and supporters into his cabinet who in hindsight were either in the wrong place or there for the wrong reasons. I believe Sinclair Stevens was one of them, and Lucien Bouchard, for quite different reasons, was another. Bouchard was an old friend and adviser of Mulroney's, and I suspect Bouchard had difficulty accepting the fact that he did not have as much sway over his friend as he had before Mulroney became prime minister. Mulroney the friend and Mulroney the prime minister were different people: the friend was open to Bouchard's advice; the prime minister watered it down to help build consensus.

Bouchard, who arrived in Ottawa prepared to bring Quebec into the constitution, could not accept the necessary compromises. This undoubtedly played a role in Bouchard's decision to oppose the Meech Lake Accord and spawn the Bloc Québécois.

At the end of the day, the prime minister has to manage all the assets at his disposal, human and otherwise, according to the best interests of the country. Decisions regarding who can do the best job in one ministerial area, or who should or should not sit in cabinet, must be made in this light. It can be a very difficult function for anyone to perform, even for battle-hardened politicians like Mulroney and Jean Chrétien. It's not easy to inform loyal supporters who hope for a specific ministry that they will not receive that appointment and that they won't even be in cabinet. On the flip side, it can be taxing to appoint someone whom you would prefer not to socialize with to a cabinet position, on the basis that he or she is clearly the best for the job.

I know, because I've dealt with the situation from both sides of the desk, as a cabinet minister under Jean Chrétien and as premier of Newfoundland and Labrador. Friendships in politics must be peripheral to other concerns, including limits on your time and the process of running the government. Everybody except some of your friends understands these demands. Friends who have difficulty dealing with these realities are the ones who, usually with some justification, expected to play an important role in your government.

In spite of errors that, in my opinion, weighted down Mulroney's public image, he achieved goals that demanded substantial courage and acumen. He managed, for example, to reconcile some of the deep scars and divisions that remained in his party after he replaced Joe Clark as PC leader. His defence of bilingualism is a case in point. His proposal and successful introduction of free trade, long before the majority of Canadians were onside, was another courageous act, no matter what your personal feelings may be about the idea.

JEAN CHRÉTIEN, LIKE JOHN TURNER BEFORE HIM, removed himself from Parliament for a few years before returning to lead the Liberals, this time to a victory in 1993 that virtually obliterated the Mulroney-less Tory party. The contrast between the fortunes of the two men is dramatic and telling.

As soon as he left federal politics in 1976, Turner became the acknowledged successor to Pierre Trudeau. Every time the federal Liberals suffered a setback, or a rumour surfaced of Trudeau's retirement from politics, the media ran a feature or two on John. The next day his smiling face, perfect grooming and impeccable tailoring would appear in newspapers and on television. The man had it all: intelligence, good looks, experience and even an Anglo heritage to continue the traditional francophone–anglophone–francophone pattern of leaders for Liberals. The 1984 leadership convention to replace Trudeau was less a contest than a coronation, which made the overwhelming triumph of the Tories later that year even more painful and dramatic.

Jean Chrétien lacked certain advantages that Turner took for granted. Turner always had a sophisticated bearing, as though he had just walked out of a corporate board of directors meeting or a Savile Row tailor shop. You could describe John Turner in a number of ways, but "just one of the guys" wouldn't be appropriate. Yet that's how Jean Chrétien was thought of during his time in federal government. In spite of occupying a number of important cabinet positions over the years, Chrétien was always one of the guys under Trudeau, and his casual, sometimes self-deprecating nature was in sharp contrast to the intellectually tough and sophisticated personalities of the prime minister and people like Marc Lalonde. Nothing illustrates this better than a story (related by Chrétien himself) about flying with Trudeau to a government meeting. Chrétien was seated next to Trudeau, who buried himself in reading from the moment of takeoff, and never spoke a word during the flight. Finally, after an hour of uncomfortable silence that Chrétien spent staring out the window, he commented, "It's raining outside."

"Well, you wouldn't expect it to be raining inside," Trudeau said, and that was the extent of their conversation through the entire journey.

So how could this *petit gar* from Shawinigan, the guy whom many Québécois considered an Uncle Tom as far as French-Canadian values were concerned, succeed where the charismatic Turner had not? After all, both had been ministers in Trudeau's cabinet, and both had stepped directly back into the Liberal leadership role after a few years out of government.

The answer, I suspect, lies in Chrétien's wide view of Canada and his depth of concern for the entire country. He knows all the regions and all their concerns, all their strengths and all their weaknesses. He also had to work harder to ensure that people in and out of government took him seriously. John Turner was like the boy in high school who scores A's on all his exams, quarterbacks the football team and is tall and handsome to boot. When you have all those qualities on your side, you needn't expend a great deal of effort attracting people to you.

In contrast, Jean Chrétien was like a kid from the wrong side of the tracks who wears hand-me-down clothes and struggles to pass some school subjects. If you want to understand the character of Jean Chrétien, you have to go back to the reality of a young boy sent away to school where he lived in residence, who taught himself how to navigate and negotiate in a crowded environment of competing personalities.

What was the 1960s House of Commons, after all, except an elevated form of boys' club? I am certainly not the first person to describe it that way, with all the connotations it suggests: power struggles, competing groups, conflicting personalities, all of them working in close quarters and forming alliances to achieve a common goal. Many of the skills Jean Chrétien acquired in boarding school are skills he applied with great success in Parliament.

Chrétien has never taken his success for granted. He had to convince people of his abilities, over and over again, until the message got through. John Turner may have inherited his right to sit in the PM's office; Jean Chrétien never stopped working to achieve the same post.

Chrétien is also, by the way, more complex than many people believe. He is incredibly competitive, yet he can be cautious to the extreme. To describe his political philosophy in the shortest possible manner, I would say it is "Avoid making the big mistake." At the same time, he is willing to take risks if the stakes are high enough and his reasoning is solid enough. Nothing demonstrates this better than his introduction, during his second term as prime minister, of the Clarity Bill, which dealt with the rules of engagement between the federal and Quebec governments on future sovereignty referenda. Members of his own party didn't agree with him on the wisdom of that bill, nor did many provincial governments around the country. He was virtually the only person to stand up and say that we needed legislation to set ground rules for future sovereignty referenda because the question of Canada's future was not one to be decided by Quebecers exclusively.

Many people believed the bill would generate resentment in Quebec and encourage sovereignty. In fact, it has taken much of the wind out of the sails of the separatists, and, I suspect, the lack of a backlash amongst francophones in Quebc may have been in part the final impetus for Lucien Bouchard's decision to withdraw from the political arena. It was a bold stroke of statesmanship, and Jean Chrétien deserves every accolade for its success.

He has always had this special ability to see the bigger picture and the best way to deal with larger issues. At the first cabinet meeting I attended, in 1993, the prime minister addressed the question of the country's growing deficit and outlined ways we would put money back into the pockets of taxpayers. His articulation of the situation, and the special talents of Paul Martin to implement the plan, produced a major turnaround for the country. Paul Martin's skills are self-evident to anyone who looks at the record, but my experience in power and in Opposition convinces me that he could not have done the job without the strong and steady support of Jean Chrétien. Paul himself generously pointed this out on the day that Jean Chrétien announced his retirement plans.

One of Jean Chrétien's most potent weapons has been the fact that people often underestimate him. The heavy accent, the rural manner and the folksy personality all disguise a disciplined and intelligent mind at work. Jean Chrétien's success over three terms as prime minister with a comfortable majority in each case was not the result of a fortuitous accident, but the product of dogged determination to fulfill ambitions for himself and his country. After losing the leadership to John Turner in 1984, Jean Chrétien refocused his team for the next race. In the current political environment, Paul Martin shares that same discipline and determination. Martin, like Chrétien, regained his focus after the loss of the leadership in 1990 and began preparing himself for the next time. The next time is now, and Martin's preparation has been so thorough that it is difficult to imagine any serious contender challenging him for the leadership of the Liberal Party in the next 12 months.

Much attention has been paid to Jean Chrétien's refusal to let anyone but himself announce his resignation, and the phrase "clinging to power" was associated with the prime minister's name at every turn. A man who handily won three federal elections in a row, presided over a comfortable majority for almost a decade and faced no leader of comparable ability in the Opposition parties can hardly be portrayed simply as "clinging." He is far more complex than that.

In addition to being one of the shrewdest practitioners of power to occupy 24 Sussex Drive, he is also one of the funniest people I have ever met in politics. No one enjoys a laugh more than Jean Chrétien, and no one in politics is better at putting people at ease just by being himself.

I recall Jean Chrétien visiting the St. George's Bay area of Newfoundland in early 1985, the year after he lost the leadership contest to John Turner, whom I had backed. We travelled the riding together, supporting Liberal candidates during the provincial campaign, and at every meeting we addressed, Jean would respond to those who said he should have been elected leader instead of Turner by saying, "Don't blame me, blame Tobin: he voted for the other guy."

Returning to Stephenville, we encountered a heavy blizzard that threatened to close the highway with massive drifts of snow. One of the drifts across the road we were travelling was so high that traffic going in both directions had to stop until a snowplough could arrive and open the road. So there we sat, a dozen or so cars on our side of the drift and a dozen or so on the other side, trying to be patient and stay warm, when Jean said, "You know what? All these people on this side and on the other side, they're voters! They're stuck here and we're stuck here—let's get out and meet them!"

Before I could speak he bounded out and, with me scrambling after him, walked to the car behind us and began tapping on the driver's window. When the driver rolled down his window, Jean thrust his hand toward the startled man and said, "Hi, I'm Jean Chrétien. How are you?" He worked his way down the line of cars on our side of the drift, introducing himself and talking about whatever topic came up. Then we scrambled over the drift and started doing the same thing to that line of cars. Jean charmed them all until the snowplough arrived and we jogged back to our car to resume the journey. I suspect people who met him that evening still talk about Jean Chrétien walking out of the blizzard, offering his hand and saying in that unique voice of his, "Hi, I'm Jean Chrétien! How are you?"

Another time, Jean Chrétien and I arrived in Corner Brook to speak at a fundraising dinner. Walking toward the entrance of our hotel, we grew aware of noises from around the corner of the building, where we saw some hotel employees were playing a road hockey game. Chrétien approached one of the players, wrestled the man's hockey stick from him and joined the game. By the time everyone else realized it really was Jean Chrétien playing road hockey with them on a hotel parking lot, I think he had scored two goals. He tracked down the man whose hockey stick he had borrowed, pumped his hand and thanked him, and said, "I'm Jean Chrétien. Nice to see you!" Then he was gone.

That visit was also the time we "screeched in" Chrétien at the Glynmill Inn in Corner Brook with the usual ceremony of kissing the cod, taking the oath as an honorary Newfoundlander and drinking a healthy shot of screech. He did it all in good humour, and the crowd watching him loved it—especially when he downed the three-ounce shot of powerful rum. Most people grimace, cough and shudder after drinking it, but Jean Chrétien smacked his lips, grinned and said, "You know, that's good stuff. Could I have another one?" Naturally, the crowd loved it. They loved it even more when he insisted that Eddie Goldenberg undergo the same ceremony. Eddie, as usual, followed the leader. He consumed two shots in a row and then smiled, waved to an appreciative crowd and navigated his way to his room to sleep off the effects.

Some commentators think Jean Chrétien is left of centre politically, but when it comes to fiscal matters he is very conservative. He knows what the vast majority of working families go through every day, looking for ways to save money and stretching the budget from paycheque to paycheque. This innate sense of humanity, I believe, is behind Jean Chrétien's sense of humour, a quality I have always enjoyed, although I must admit I pushed it to the edge on one occasion.

It happened at Jean Chrétien's moment of triumph, during the 1990 Liberal convention that proclaimed him leader. As a

Chrétien supporter, I contributed to his speeches, including helping draft his convention speech. During rehearsals, I noticed he relied entirely on the teleprompter to read the words of his address, ignoring the written copy in front of him. I pointed out that the teleprompter was a mechanical device and mechanical devices have a habit of breaking down at the least opportune moments. To avoid disaster, he should always follow the written text as the only way of staying in sequence should the teleprompter fail. Jean loved having the words unscroll at eye level in front of him, making it appear that he was spinning the polished phrases off the top of his head, and no matter how much I tried persuading him to keep the speech pages in sync with the teleprompter, the printed version remained untouched on the podium.

At the last rehearsal before the big weekend speech, he still insisted on relying entirely on the teleprompter. I was concerned enough to raise the matter with Eddie Goldenberg, David Sussman, George Radwanski and Eric Maldoff, and together we made our point in dramatic fashion. In the middle of his final speech rehearsal, while he was still refusing to turn pages of his written copy, I stopped the teleprompter. The words to his speech vanished from the screen, replaced with *F--- you—you're on your own.*

He was not amused. However, our point was well made. During his acceptance speech on prime-time television that weekend, the teleprompter did fail and he had no idea, when he turned to the printed copy on the podium, where he was in the text. Everyone watched (and some of us stopped breathing) while he flipped through the pages of his speech saying, "One minute, please," before he recovered and resumed his strong delivery.

JEAN CHRÉTIEN RETURNED TO POLITICAL LIFE in the midst of the Meech Lake controversy. The provinces had been given three years to ratify the accord following its drafting in 1987, and by early 1990 it was clear that the agreement was in trouble. On this matter, Jean Chrétien and I were in opposite camps. I had voted in favour of the Meech Lake Accord, which afforded Quebec the opportunity to sign the 1982 constitutional agreement "with dignity and honour," as Quebec politicians put it. Was I totally comfortable with the demands that Quebec wanted fulfilled within the accord? The answer is no. Nor did I like the fact that Brian Mulroney had played a game of high-stakes gambling with the future of the country when he described the process of creating the accord as "rolling the dice."

Nevertheless, having completed negotiations with a federalist premier (Robert Bourassa) to meet Quebec's demands, I appreciated what was being gained: the full entry of Quebec into the Canadian federation, something we had never enjoyed before.

In June 1990, with less than three weeks remaining before the ratification period expired, a special first ministers' conference was convened in Ottawa in an attempt to save the accord. Toward the end of the proceedings, I was asked to come to the prime minister's room in the Ottawa Conference Centre. I arrived to find a distressed Brian Mulroney changing his shirt, showing the stress and strain of the past few days' events. The prime minister told me he feared that Newfoundland and Labrador Premier Clyde Wells was about to bolt the conference and return to St. John's, effectively destroying any hope of ratification of the accord.

I was stunned. The whole country knew that Premier Wells had deep concerns about the accord, but he was not the kind of person to torpedo a conference of this magnitude on a whim. What was behind this?

In an attempt to satisfy one of the concerns Clyde Wells had been expressing over the course of the conference, an amendment to the accord had been proposed. The amendment would introduce a scheduled review of the impact of the "distinct society" clause on the Charter of Rights and Freedoms, as part of an attempt to break the log-jam and permitting Newfoundland and Labrador to sign off on the agreement. Unfortunately Premier Bourassa, who initially agreed with the proposal, changed his mind after consulting with his Quebec delegation, and the amendment was killed.

The news of Bourassa's turnabout was deeply disappointing for Premier Wells. After a week of tough negotiating, Wells thought he had secured at least one amendment, only to be told that he had lost it after all. He felt betrayed by the Quebec delegation and was threatening to cease participating in the conference.

Prime Minister Mulroney explained this, sprinkled with salty expressions of frustration over Bourassa, before asking me to visit Wells and encourage him to remain. We needed the dialogue to continue, Mulroney emphasized, and it would end with the departure of Clyde Wells.

I set off for the Newfoundland and Labrador delegation's meeting room, where I encountered an intense Deborah Coyne, the premier's constitutional adviser. She was not happy to see me, and even less happy when I asked her to leave, permitting Clyde and me a few minutes of privacy. With some reluctance, she finally agreed.

Clyde Wells is a man of enormous integrity, and he was struggling to find a balance between what he believed as an individual and what was best for his province and his country. Everything about him in those few moments we spent together—his body language, his words, his tone of voice—reflected the agony he was suffering. He had arrived in Ottawa determined to do what was best for Canada. He had spent almost an entire week debating points he believed were critical and decisive, until he was assured that one of his major concerns had been addressed. Then the rug had been pulled from under him. Now he was being subjected to intense pressure from all sides, and although he did not threaten to walk out of the conference, he was seriously considering withdrawing from the process. I have never forgotten the evidence of the tremendous emotional pain he bore that day while trying to rationalize the personal betrayal he felt with the responsibility he had to his province and his country.

I could not make his mind up for him, and I didn't try. Instead, I told him that whatever he decided, to sign or not to sign, to ratify or reject, I believed it was important that he not walk out the door. "Stay to the end," I said. "That's all I can ask you to do. Then make whatever decision you have to make later." And I left. I wasn't sure what I had accomplished, but the premier decided to stay to the end of the conference.

Wells explained to me in later years that it was never his intention to leave the conference centre. However, he did seriously consider registering his objection by not participating in the discussions around the conference table.

Clyde Wells did not permit a free vote in the legislature on the Meech Lake Accord before the deadline, and some historians have attempted to place the blame for its failure on his shoulders. This ignores the actions of Manitoba MP and First Nations representative Elijah Harper, who, eagle feather in hand, uttered a single word—"No"—to block the unanimous consent that would have circumvented debate and enabled Manitoba to approve the accord before the deadline. Harper acted first. When he did, Clyde Wells adjourned the legislature because the issue was essentially dead. Assigning the entire blame to Clyde Wells is a matter more of convenience than of fact.

THE BATTLE TO SAVE A DWINDLING RESOURCE

T HE FEDERAL ELECTION of October 1993 changed Canada in many ways. As a Liberal, I was naturally elated that we regained power after almost a decade of Mulroney-led Tory rule. It was, in a manner of speaking, revenge for the landslide of 1984 that had reduced our party to 40 seats and set off speculation that the Liberals were doomed as a federal force in Canadian politics. Now the roles were reversed, but even more so. The federal Progressive Conservatives under Kim Campbell's leadership were reduced to just two seats, the most devastating defeat in the history of Canadian politics and, I daresay, of any political party in a democracy.

This was not, I should add, a source of total unbridled joy in the hearts of some Liberals, including me. A comfortable majority is the goal of every political party. So is the opportunity to elect the best talent your party has to offer, and we boasted an immense amount of talent. But democracy functions in a state of dynamic balance. I believed I was a member of the best party to govern Canada, but I knew that every party governs best when facing a strong Opposition. If nothing else, the presence of an effective Opposition party provides the electorate with assurance that both sides of an issue will be aired. Instead of the Conservatives, the loyal Opposition was now the Bloc Québécois, whose raison d'être was to precipitate Quebec separatism, making the term *loyal* jarringly inappropriate.

To no one's surprise, including my own, I was asked to serve as minister of fisheries and oceans. This has been a traditional post for Newfoundland cabinet ministers and, in fact, I had been a frequent critic for fisheries and oceans in the previous Parliament, challenging John Crosbie across the floor of the House.

I will never forget walking up the lane to the Governor General's residence with other newly appointed cabinet ministers on a crisp sunny day in the fall of 1993, all of us sharing a sense of anticipation and excitement. Part of me, of course, was still the young boy from Stephenville and Goose Bay who read and dreamed of a world beyond Newfoundland and Labrador, and as I approached the front door of Government House a voice in the back of my head whispered, "The kid made it!" Whenever I see the photo of that newly sworn-in cabinet I smile, because I recall what I and everyone else in the picture was feeling: after all those years in the trenches, we were being given the opportunity to serve the way we had dreamed about.

The ceremony itself was low-key and solemn, in contrast to the emotions that were almost boiling within us. The mood was partly to counterbalance the perceived excess and extravagance of Brian Mulroney and his cabinet that had so dismayed Canadians.

Still, there was that matter of the overwhelming majority we had, and the concern it was likely to foster in the minds of many Canadians. Had the electorate made a mistake in handing such a dominant majority to us? Were there enough checks and balances to ensure that we cabinet members would toe the line and behave responsibly?

Our position of overwhelming dominance was a concern to Jean Chrétien, and he made this clear when he had every cabinet member interviewed and vetted by Mitchell Sharp, one of the most venerable individuals to serve in Parliament. In plain yet eloquent language, Sharp spoke to us about the responsibilities, duties and obligations of the offices we were assuming. Whatever our previous experience had been, whatever our personal ambitions might be, the most sacred quality we brought into our offices was the trust of the people who had put us there. It was to be preserved, not spent. Like any asset, once spent it vanished forever. The offices we were filling were larger than ourselves, Mitchell Sharp said. We should always remember that and act accordingly.

Sharp's words were followed by a speech from the prime minister, and I still recall his calm assurance in offering us both support and guidance. More than any other prime minister, Jean Chrétien had served in numerous cabinets in previous Parliaments, and he knew the challenges we newly minted ministers were about to face. He reiterated his focus on restoring public trust in government, and he made it clear that nothing was a higher priority to him. Over and over again, especially in those first few years, Chrétien repeated the need to build and maintain respect for government in the minds of Canadians.

I remember those meetings and the PM's words very clearly, and the memories make recent attacks on his ethics very disturbing to me. Politics is neither a comforting nor a gentle business at times. If you cannot appreciate just how rough the ride can be, you shouldn't get aboard the wagon. But I object to the more outrageous claims of poor ethics on the part of Jean Chrétien and the government he headed. Chrétien is a gutsy fighter: there's no denying that. You don't remain in federal politics more than 40 years without being able to give as well as you take in the media or in the House of Commons. Being a good fighter, however, does not preclude being an ethical man, and I refuse to believe that the high standard of ethics he set in 1994 had eroded eight years later.

EVERY NEW CABINET MINISTER arrives in office determined to change things, a determination that's even stronger when he's replacing a previous administration. After several years in

Opposition, many of them spent tangling with John Crosbie, I arrived at Fisheries and Oceans with an agenda in mind.

The encounters with Crosbie had always been tough, often acrimonious, and sometimes entertaining. How could they be anything less, with Crosbie as an opponent? Beyond our political differences, which run about as deep as the Fundy tides, John was and remains a friend. To anyone who witnessed our debates, this may come as a shock, but it's true. Today, John and I work together with Peter Penashue, president of the Innu Nation and the Innu Healing Foundation, raising funds to build recreational facilities for Innu children in Labrador. Peter is one of this country's most promising and gifted young leaders. He was recently selected as one of Canada's Top 40 Under 40 Leaders.

From the mid-1980s on, it had been clear that the Atlantic fishery was in serious trouble, and the efforts of the PCs to correct its problems were well intentioned but doomed. Crosbie, like his predecessors, had been persuaded that there were limits to the actions Canada could take in protecting the livelihoods of its fishermen and the fish stocks off our shores. In spite of clear evidence of overfishing by other nations, the Mulroney government's policy had been to reject taking overt action on the high seas. We had modern patrol vessels and dedicated crew members aboard them, including teams of constantly frustrated inspectors, but their duties were limited for the most part to patrols and inspections. The policy of the Mulroney government, where foreign fishing was concerned, was based on the notion that discussions and negotiations alone could work. Backroom deals and contractual dogma may work in labour negotiations and corporate mergers, which had been Mulroney's previous milieu, but in the international arena they are rarely successful unless supported by appropriate action.

From time to time the fisheries problem became intolerable, even for the Mulroney government. In early 1993, for example, fishermen from the French islands of St. Pierre and Miquelon were arrested for fishing off the coast of Newfoundland. The trawlers were engaged more in protest than illegal fishing; they were angry at Canada for seriously cutting France's quota for fish taken in our waters, the cuts mirroring an overall reduction in quotas applied by Crosbie's ministry. When countries complained about the quotas, Crosbie responded to them with the telling comment, "I cannot give fish that are not there," referring to the serious decline in fish stocks in the area.

I was stunned by these words. Whenever I had implored Crosbie in the House of Commons to take action, his reaction was more political than practical. "What does the honourable member want me to do?" John postured in response to one of my demands. "Does he want me to close St. Anthony?" Then he continued, naming all the fishing communities in my constituency. "Does he want me to close Port au Choix? Does he want me to close Rose Blanche?" And on and on. I was asking for serious action on every front, and John was suggesting that I wanted to close all the fisheries in my riding instead of dealing with the bigger question of declining fish stocks. It played well in the House and on the evening newscasts, but both John and I knew it was earning him no points back in Newfoundland, where the people didn't want debating strategy. They wanted action.

No one wanted to see any fishing ports closed in Newfoundland. I was pointing out that negotiations, treaties, threats and inspections were having no effect on the excessive catches being taken by foreign vessels in Canadian waters. Even after the government slapped substantial limits on catches permitted to Canadian boats, nothing was being done about foreign vessels.

I was so concerned about the amount of improper fishing by both foreign and domestic fishermen that I spoke to Crosbie privately on several occasions: "John, we have to do something. I'm hearing from some of my constituents who work in the fish plants that they're processing fish barely as big as the palm of their hand. If we keep this up, the stocks will never recover. We have to put our Canadian house in order, and when we have done that, we have to demand nothing less from other nations fishing off our continental shelf." If you looked after the fish, I pointed out, the fish would take care of the fishermen, the fish plants and the outport communities. If you failed to look after the fish, everything else would become academic.

In 1991, scientists retained by Fisheries and Oceans Canada submitted a well-researched report that recommended severe cutbacks on quotas to save the Grand Banks stock. Instead of analyzing the data and looking for ways to implement the recommendations, Crosbie ridiculed the report and attacked the scientists. "Who are these scientists who want to close down our fisheries and put people out of work?" he bellowed in the House. "How dare they!" John's words were reflecting those of fishermen and fish plant workers who wanted to avoid any cuts in quotas. I remember listening in amazement and sorrow at his response, and thinking, "He just doesn't get it." No one could guarantee that the scientists were accurate in their assessment, but I felt that if any error were made, it should be made on the side of caution.

John "got it" the following year when the Tories conceded what was now clear to everyone. The cod stocks were so depleted that a moratorium on fishing was declared, an announcement that came more than 200 years after the cod fishery began, and perhaps in time to avoid the cod's extinction.

I have witnessed no political moment more agonizing than watching John Crosbie announce the closure of the fishery, in a hotel conference room while fishermen pounded at the door, demanding to be let in. That day, the cod fishery was no more. He fought for substantial funding on behalf of tens of thousands of displaced workers, but Crosbie couldn't bring back the fish. No one could.

That was the situation when I arrived as the new minister of fisheries and oceans following the October 1993 federal election.

I had spent many years haranguing the Tories over their lack of action. Now, with the support of colleagues in cabinet, I had the power to do something substantial. If I didn't, I could expect to spend many uncomfortable days in Question Period.

We set the stage in our initial throne speech, in January 1994, with a promise to "take the action required to ensure that foreign overfishing of East Coast stocks comes to an end." What could be more explicit than that? We followed it up in May of that year when Parliament unanimously passed Bill C-29, the Coastal Fisheries Protection Act, providing the authority to enforce rules that would protect straddling stocks from commercial extinction, including taking action beyond our 200-mile limit. "Straddling stocks" included fish that breed and feed within Canadian waters but venture beyond them from time to time. This usually occurred on the so-called Nose and Tail of the Grand Banks—two projections of the feeding area extending more than 200 miles from our shores.

Despite the unprecedented scope of Bill C-29, it passed the House and Senate in record time. Senator Bill Petten of Newfoundland led the charge in the upper chamber, and after I gave Opposition Leader Lucien Bouchard a private briefing about foreign overfishing and asked for his cooperation, he surprised me by promising passage within hours.

The European Union voiced opposition immediately; the United States also filed a protest, although it was considered mild and "for the record." The EU pointed out that our legislation was illegal under international law, since enforcement of fishing regulations beyond the 200-mile limit was the responsibility of the home country of the fleets involved. When fish stocks moved between international boundaries, disputes were to be settled by negotiations, preferably within regional organizations such as the North Atlantic Fishing Organization, or NAFO.

All well and good. But the first option failed to address trawlers flying flags of convenience, a growing occurrence on the

Grand Banks. Could we really expect Panama, for example, to rein in the excesses of a Portuguese trawler with a Portuguese crew taking its catch directly to a Portuguese port, just because the vessel was flying a Panamanian flag? As Max Short would put it, not bloody likely.

And what happens when these options fail? Do we stumble along, knowing that a precious natural resource risks being eradicated, and do nothing but shrug our shoulders? Every international action taken by a country is assessed two ways: legally and morally. Our legal basis was open to question, perhaps, but our moral motives were not. We wanted to save the fish for future generations of every country, and that was the sole objective. What's more, we could draw upon a reservoir of international goodwill built up over decades of fair and honest dealings. In the cool light of rational thought, no one would believe that our actions were based on ulterior motives: we were just addressing a problem that no one else was willing to.

Allan Gotlieb, our former ambassador to Washington, put things well when he said: "We've been very conciliatory and emphasized arbitration on other matters, but when it comes to coastal waters and territorial issues, we need to take unilateral action."

My FIRST DEPUTY MINISTER at Fisheries and Oceans was Bruce Rawson, considered the dean of DMs at the time. Bruce had practised law with the Alberta Attorney General's department and filled several provincial posts before arriving in Ottawa as deputy minister for national health and welfare in the mid-1970s. Since then, he had moved through several senior positions at various ministries and at the Privy Council Office.

There was no questioning Bruce's abilities, dedication and experience. But he shared John Crosbie's belief that Canada could not take unilateral action on the high seas, no matter how strong its case. When I was in Opposition and demanding that more effective steps be taken against the illegal fishing practices of some nations off our coast, Crosbie would often ridicule my position. "Does the honourable member really want us to go out and fire at vessels on the high seas?" he taunted. Hell, yes, if all else fails, was my answer. Crosbie reflected the prevailing attitude of the ministry, an attitude that remained in place when I arrived as minister.

Another key member of the team, and a powerful influence over the ministry's direction, was Francine Ducros. Francine, who went on to serve Prime Minister Chrétien as his director of communications—perhaps the most pressure-ridden job an unelected official can have in Ottawa—was acting as departmental liaison at DFO when I arrived. One of a handful of women in the male-dominated ministry, she more than held her own in heated discussions.

WHEN I BEGAN PUSHING for direct action, the bureaucrats pushed back. Instead of exploring the steps we could take to protect the fish stocks, my own team was giving me arguments against the idea. They could not believe that I intended to do the things I had proposed while in Opposition.

Bruce Rawson kept raising concerns whenever I spoke about taking unilateral action, usually supported by Dr. Victor Rabinovitch. As assistant deputy minister, Victor was the senior public servant responsible for efforts to halt foreign overfishing. Much of Bruce's and Victor's jobs involved keeping their minister out of trouble, and so each time I proposed a new strategy they would respond, "Here is why you can't do that, Minister . . ." I appreciated the motive behind their words, but I was not interested in adhering to the niceties of the job. I wanted support for my efforts to save the Grand Banks fish stocks that remained.

If a DM wants to, and the minister permits it, the DM can isolate the minister from the department, protecting the minister from potential embarrassments. I have always been an inclusive kind of person, welcoming as many viewpoints as possible. It's not in my nature to be aloof from either people or issues, and I grew uncomfortable with this management style.

Bruce often entered my office carrying files for the issues to be dealt with that day. Whenever I asked him the whereabouts of the people responsible for the files, he would reply, "I'll deal with them. You deal with me." It took some time for Bruce to adapt to my style, but eventually he would assemble up to a dozen senior departmental and political staff for morning meetings to assess the issues.

True to the traditions of a good DM, Bruce looked for ways to accommodate the aggressive approach I wanted to use. He suggested that we target flag-of-convenience vessels first, taking on the European Union fishing fleets later. Going after these vessels would send a signal to countries like Spain that Canada was serious about dealing effectively with foreign overfishing.

I passed the word down to our patrol and inspection officials that they were no longer to feel restricted in their actions. If they encountered any vessel that appeared to be taking an illegal catch anywhere on the Banks, including the Nose and Tail beyond our 200-mile limit, they were to seize the vessel and escort it to the nearest Canadian port.

Two things happened almost immediately. Morale among the entire staff soared, and in early April 1994 the *Kristina Logos* was seized about 230 miles off the coast and escorted to St. John's, its captain charged with fishing illegally for cod. Once in port, inspectors discovered more than 100 tonnes of cod and flounder in its hold, all caught in defiance of international agreements.

The case of the *Kristina Logos* was a textbook example of the gyrations commonplace in much of the international fishing industry. Originally registered as a Canadian vessel, the Portuguese owner had transferred its registration to Panama, a popular flag-of-convenience nation, and landed all of the boat's catch in Portugal. Our officials had been tracking the *Kristina Logos* for some weeks, convinced it was engaged in illegal fishing but reluctant to take action on an apparent foreign vessel. A little detective work, however, revealed that the owner might have transferred the vessel to Panamanian registry but he had failed to remove it from the Canadian register. On that technicality, two Fisheries inspection ships and a Coast Guard vessel swooped down on it.

This was the second fishing vessel in a week to be boarded and seized in international waters off the Banks. The first, a Nova Scotia tuna boat named the *Stephen B.*, had been escorted to St. John's and its Canadian captain had been charged.

No one made much comment on the seizure of the *Stephen B.*, but there was a good deal of criticism about taking the *Kristina Logos* into port. Lawyers representing its owners called it an act of piracy. "The real pirates," I pointed out, "are not Canadian fisheries officials or anyone in this ministry, or the *Kristina Logos*'s captain. The true pirates in all of this are the men wearing blue suits, sitting in corporate boardrooms and ordering these captains and crews to break international law in the name of short-term profits."

Bruce Rawson skilfully guided me through these first skirmishes in the fish wars. In the midst of them, I heard rumours that a shuffle of deputy ministers was being scheduled, and I grew concerned about his replacement. I feared that I would be assigned either a fisheries neophyte who didn't know his cod from his elbow, or someone sent over expressly to calm down the new sabre-rattling fisheries minister.

I needn't have worried. The clerk of the Privy Council was Jocelyn Bourgon, a former Fisheries and Oceans staffer, and she suggested Bill Rowat as my new DM. I had met Bill during his earlier term at Fisheries and Oceans and been impressed by his exceptional abilities and attitude. Born and raised on an Ontario chicken farm, he had grown up with a practical approach to getting things done. After all, you don't sit intellectualizing on a chicken farm; you get out and feed the birds, clean the henhouse and tackle the messy jobs. If you don't take care of the birds, the birds can't take care of you, which paralleled my view of preserving fish stocks.

After obtaining his degree in economics, Bill came to Ottawa as a civil servant, and by the time we met he had been posted to Industry and Commerce, Transport Canada and the Privy Council Office, in addition to his earlier experience at Fisheries and Oceans. Bill is intelligent, persuasive and courageous. His familiarity with the Privy Council Office and Foreign Affairs proved vital as we stickhandled around obstacles in our path. He was totally supportive of the goals I set, although they entailed risks to his career (and to mine as well). The members of the team assisting us were simply splendid in their dedication and abilities. They included ambassadors, labour leaders and staff members, all of whom filled critical roles in lobbying support and keeping key players informed.

THE RESPONSE OF THE EUROPEAN COMMUNITY to Bill C-29 had been swift and negative, as expected. Quoting the United Nations charter, the EU claimed that Canada could not subject any part of the high seas to its sovereignty, and that our new law weakened provisions of NAFO. Of course, NAFO had done nothing to solve the problem of fish stock depletion for several years; if it had, there would have been no need for Bill C-29.

The day that the EU announced its opposition to Bill C-29, I had lunch with all the EU ambassadors, including Dr. José Luis Pardos, Spanish ambassador to Canada. For years, countries around the world had complained about Spanish fishermen. The waters surrounding the Iberian peninsula have never been rich fishing grounds, which is why the Basques may have travelled as far as the Grand Banks long before Columbus "discovered" North America. Spain's massive fishing fleet travelled around the globe in search of fish and, in the process, built a reputation for taking more than its share of the catch. Both France and the United Kingdom had tangled with Spanish trawlers—France and Spain had actually exchanged gunfire at one point—and one condition of Spain's entry into the EU had been that it refrain from fishing in the waters of EU member countries for a decade. In fact, the EU conveniently sent the Spanish fleet to fish EU quotas off Canada's continental shelf. Concern over Spain's reputation was so deep that Norwegian voters reportedly rejected membership in the EU if it meant permitting Spain to fish in Norwegian waters even 10 years in the future.

A cultured man and an experienced diplomat, Dr. Pardos was quick to grasp the intent and significance of Bill C-29. I tried to make our case to the ambassador as directly yet gently as I could, to no avail (I learned later my language was described as "impertinent" by the embassy). I mentioned the problem of Spanish and Portuguese trawlers flying flags of convenience, supposedly identifying their home ports as Belize, Cayman Islands, Honduras and Panama. I discussed illegal nets capable of snaring fish below mature size, and showed samples of fish taken from Spanish trawlers. (The embassy later commented snidely that I had displayed "a variety of fish samples from Mr. Tobin's private collection.") Later, I sent Dr. Pardos a list of fishing vessels flying flags of convenience. When I received no reply or comment, the lines were drawn.

In Canada, the immediate response to Bill C-29 varied from enthusiastic support in the Atlantic provinces to cautious support in other regions of the country. Of course, there are always skeptics to be found in any issue. One commentator said that we might have seized one vessel on a technicality, and could perhaps harass boats from Portugal and other small nations, but "just let Tobin try that with the Americans, for example, and see what happens."

Within a few weeks we did just that.

In late July, our fisheries inspectors took two US scallop draggers into port from international waters. The *Warrior* and the *Alpha and Omega II*, sailing out of Massachusetts, were seized on the high seas and escorted into St. John's by two patrol boats and a destroyer. Within a week we added more American boats, charging them with illegally catching flounder within our 200-mile limit.

Seizing the scallop draggers generated a protest from the Americans, since they clearly had been in international waters. But scallops are considered a sedentary creature, and a United Nations convention granted countries jurisdiction over sedentary species when their beds extend beyond the 200-mile limit. The Icelandic scallops that the US boats had been harvesting were an extension of the beds on our continental shelf, and we knew that we were within our rights to protect them. We had never pressed this right in the past, and so the Americans and others simply assumed that they were free to break the rules. Our actions signalled a different story.

Apprehending American vessels in international waters, no matter what a UN convention might say, was certain to produce clenched fists in Washington, DC, and within a day or two I was paid a visit by James Blanchard, the US ambassador. Blanchard was a former Michigan governor who knew Canada far better than most US representatives sent to Ottawa, and he genuinely liked our country. The consensus around Ottawa was that if Washington sent more ambassadors of Blanchard's calibre, our long-term relationship with the Americans would improve tremendously.

No matter how much Blanchard might have liked Canada, he meant business that day. He strode into my office, clutching documents in his hand and wearing a stern expression on his face, and launched into a serious tirade. He informed me that he represented the government and people of the United States of America, and he was here to protest the fact that Canadian vessels, including an armed patrol vessel, had molested and apprehended US vessels that were clearly in international waters.

This act by Canada, Blanchard said, was illegal and intolerable, and he demanded that Canada release both the vessels and their crew immediately.

"Or what, Jim?" I asked when he finished his lecture.

Blanchard blinked, shrugged and said, "Hell, I don't know." Then he suggested that we had to find a way to settle this thing.

The fact is, the United States was in an election year and the two boats were from Senator Ted Kennedy's home state. Kennedy was putting pressure on the Clinton White House to secure the release from Canada of the two vessels. Kennedy also directly called Chaviva Hosek, director of policy and research in the Prime Minister's Office, seeking her support in having the boats released. The pressure was on.

It had never occurred to people in the US State Department, I suppose, that Canada would defy their demands. Jim had no fallback position, and after a little nervous laughter about his predicament, we began a dialogue that included explaining Canada's basis for taking action under the UN convention for sedentary species. Jim agreed to convey our position to Washington, where it was immediately rejected. Along with the rejection came a growing wave of protests over our actions. The theme was clear and consistent: how dare Canada, the Good Neighbour of the United States, interfere with the actions of American fishermen on the high seas? Massachusetts Senator Ted Kennedy, proclaiming that he had always considered Canada a friend, publicly demanded immediate action, insisting that we had no jurisdiction in international waters. Congressman Barney Frank wondered whether the US Navy should send its warships to accompany American fishermen in the future. Others recalled that the War of 1812 had its roots in similar action taken by the British, who had stopped and boarded US vessels to ensure the Americans were not providing aid to France.

Amid all this near hysteria, we reiterated our position: Icelandic scallops on the Grand Banks are sedentary and fixed to the ocean bottom by fine threads. They do not swim. They do not migrate. They are, as a result, covered by the UN convention on sedentary species.

This made little impact on the Americans at first. Their politicians and fishermen mocked us, and things weren't helped when we began taking action against American salmon fishermen off the BC coast. The US fishermen were catching salmon originating in Canadian waters as the fish swam by Alaska. An agreement between the United States and Canada providing a fair allotment for both countries had expired, and the Americans were dragging their feet over negotiating a new accord. With no agreement in place, US trawlers were sailing up from Washington and down from Alaska and pulling in all the fish they could net, seriously affecting the livelihood of the BC salmon fishery.

We were just as determined to protect British Columbia's interests as those on the Atlantic coast, and so in a symbolic gesture we began applying a transit fee to the American boats. This enraged the US fishermen and their politicians to the point where the senator from Alaska threatened to have the US Navy sail in and stop this harassment of American boats—in Canadian waters, by the way. Other US politicians flew into a snit over our actions, ignoring our legal position in favour of barraging Canada with the usual threats and bluster, until a new treaty was drawn up and finalized to protect the stocks of Canadian-hatched salmon.

None of this either surprised or deterred me. In my experience, Americans are always assertive where their perceived rights appear to be threatened. They express their self-interest clearly and respond only to strength and determination, not weakness and conciliation, taking a situation as far as they can as long as there appears to be a benefit for them. Everyone who deals with the United States on international issues knows and acknowledges this fact. This is not to say that the Americans are unfair or intolerant, only that any negotiable conflict with them is a zero-sum game, and if they take 75 percent while you walk away with 25 percent, that's just how things work out.

I made this point several times while the conflict with the Americans continued. I noted, for example, that John Crosbie had tried to halt foreign overfishing on both coasts through negotiations, and acknowledged that he had done a lot of good work on the diplomatic front. But Crosbie had been constrained by a federal bureaucracy seeking to avoid confrontation with the United States and the EU, fuelled by Brian Mulroney's desire to keep his friends in the White House happy. Too often, I suggested, we Canadians tend to apologize for drawing attention to someone who happens to be standing on our foot.

We sat tight and waited for the tirade over the scallops to die down and the legal submissions to be evaluated. On the day before the US Thanksgiving holiday, when no American media outlets would carry it and few American citizens would be aware of it, the State Department acknowledged that, indeed, Icelandic scallops do not swim, and Canada was within its right to seize the draggers and charge their owners and captains. Everyone had shouted when they believed we were in the wrong. Hardly anyone whispered when we were proven right.

In the end Ambassador Blanchard, who understood how important the conservation issue was to Canada, had done a good job of explaining Canada's position, and the scallop crisis worked out for the best: We got US recognition of our jurisdiction, and they got their boats back.

THE SCALLOPS WOULD SURVIVE. Meanwhile, serious and perhaps irreparable damage was being done to stocks of Greenland halibut, or turbot, a particularly unattractive fish that had been almost ignored in the past. Similar in appearance to the common Atlantic halibut, the turbot (*Reinhardtius hippoglossoides*) is smaller and darker in colour, and thrives in the northern Atlantic along the northern continental slope off Labrador and in the Grand Banks.

Like all flatfish, the turbot starts life looking like any other salt-water fish, but as it matures, one eye starts migrating to the other side of the skull. In the turbot, however, the migrating eye fails to make a complete journey to line up with the fixed eye. Instead, it positions itself on the upper edge of the forehead. This, needless to say, does not produce a handsome animal. Many fish—the shark, the muskellunge and the salmon, for example—have a noble appearance. The turbot, unfortunately, is uglier than an old boot. But with the near disappearance of the cod, it represented the last substantial food fish in the entire Grand Banks, and the Spanish fleets were taking them by the hundreds of tonnes.

It's worth noting, by the way, that Spain's voraciousness for turbot was not driven by the need to feed its people. Spain consumes relatively little turbot; most of its catch was sold to Japan. So, we weren't speaking of a direct life-sustaining activity dedicated to putting food from the Grand Banks on tables in Madrid and Barcelona. We were dealing with a strictly commercial venture, as profit driven as the harvesting of wood from Brazil's rain forests or the flow of petroleum out of Saudi Arabian oil fields. This fact made the rapacious nature of Spain's activities even more abhorrent.

Both the Scientific Council of NAFO—the group whose warnings John Crosbie had ridiculed a few years earlier—and Canada's Fisheries Resource Conservation Council (FRCC) were raising red flags about the effect of overfishing on the turbot's future. We could not stand by and watch the turbot follow the cod into economic and environmental oblivion, and so I announced that Canada would ask NAFO to reduce the total allowable catches (TAC) of turbot for all member nations. To show that we were willing to pay a price in this effort, I pointed out that Canada would reduce its quotas by 75 percent for turbot caught off Baffin Island and would abandon plans to develop a turbot fishery off northern Labrador.

This was a major tactic in the strategy to conserve the rapidly declining fish stocks. We needed to prove that Canada was not asking other countries to make concessions that we were unwilling to make ourselves. We drove the point home that summer when we charged the masters of four Canadian fishing vessels caught taking illegal catches of turbot off Labrador.

None of this appeared to dissuade the Spanish and Portuguese. Therefore, in late October 1994 I met with ambassadors from Germany (representing the president of NAFO), Spain and Portugal, along with John Beck, the ambassador of the EU in Canada, to discuss the situation. In an *aide-mémoire* distributed at the meeting, I identified a number of Spanish and Portuguese vessels suspected of serious infractions. "Desiring to obtain cooperation to have the multilateral decisions of NAFO respected," the document said, Canada was "prepared to assist the EU in its efforts to curtail fishing by its vessels in contravention of the conservation rules established by NAFO."

The vessels were to sail to the nearest port, either in Canada or St. Pierre and Miquelon, where enforcement officials authorized by the flag state could conduct full inspections. The *aide-mémoire* also noted that "if a Canadian vessel were found in similar circumstances, it would be immediately ordered into port for dockside inspection and charges laid if warranted." Then we asked for an early response.

The only reply from Spain was an angry note that our proposal was "inadmissible." A few weeks later, John Beck wrote to suggest that Spain and Portugal should be the only ones permitted to inspect their fishing vessels "to ensure that continuity of evidence is maintained." Beck apparently was concerned that our inspectors might plant false evidence aboard the trawlers to make our point. "The Commission believes that the specific action demanded by Canada would not in itself be more effective than the action to be carried out by the [EU]," Beck went on. "Furthermore, the suggestion that these vessels might be controlled in Canadian ports would also unnecessarily increase the already heavy burden on the long-distance fishermen concerned."

His last point ignored the "heavy burden" the fishermen would bear when there were no longer any fish to catch, and that was a certainty unless things changed. And his suggestion that Spain and Portugal alone be entrusted to verify that their vessels were conforming with international law was comparable, given the reputations of both countries in this matter, to asking the fox to check the henhouse.

In my reply, I noted that the vessels in question were continuing to break the law, according to our observations, and that if the EU were uncomfortable with having the ships inspected at Canadian ports, it could be done at St. Pierre and Miquelon.

Neither the meeting, the *aide-mémoire* nor my response to Beck's letter achieved any progress, as I feared they wouldn't. They did establish, however, our intention to seek a solution within the boundaries of NAFO and Canada's traditional role in the organization. Similar efforts to build support for our stand in the past had failed. Presentations, speeches, statistics and the like had not worked before and were unlikely to work for the turbot. If we were to break NAFO's record of inaction over conserving fish stocks, it would require a new, tougher approach.

At the September 1994 NAFO meeting, we proposed a turbot TAC of 27,000 tonnes, a figure substantially lower than the member nations anticipated. By the time all the views and objections from other NAFO countries had been tossed back and forth over this proposal, time had run out and a special meeting to determine allocations to each country was scheduled for January 1995.

Back in Ottawa, we began planning strategy for the January meeting. If we could get a majority of members to side with Canada on our proposed new quotas, all EU countries, including Spain and Portugal, would be bound by the rules. "They vote in blocks," someone pointed out, suggesting the idea was doomed, "and Canada doesn't have much leverage in influencing the votes."

"Have we tried?" I asked. "Have we ever really tried to lobby support and put pressure on countries to vote our way?" Canada, I was reminded, did not play hardball in these kinds of negotiations. We had a reputation for being Nice Guys. Well, I suggested, perhaps it was time we challenged that reputation.

Our first objective was to create a united front for the country's efforts. If we were going to make an abrupt shift from being "Good Old Go-Along Canada" to being a country willing to exert whatever force necessary to see that justice prevails, we needed to avoid second-guessers.

At a cabinet meeting soon after, I asked permission from the prime minister to clear the room of everyone except the ministers themselves. I didn't want a raft of deputy ministers tugging at their boss's coat sleeves and whispering, "Minister, we shouldn't do that because . . ." To the other cabinet members, I presented top secret, irrefutable evidence of illegal actions by EU ships on the Grand Banks, including photographs of secret compartments aboard the vessels, reports of foreign trawlers refusing to accept Canadian inspectors and more.

"We are past the point of debating whether something should be done," I said. "We are now debating what we are going to do about it." I submitted that we had no choice but to take direct action, and I asked for the cabinet's full support.

A number of cabinet ministers were known for their cautious, conservative approach where international affairs were concerned. Among them was Herb Gray, the solicitor general. In measured tones, while all of us hung on his words, Herb recited the concerns of his department should we begin boarding vessels on the high seas. Then he said, "Now let me put on my other hat," and after reviewing all the points I had just made, he promised his strong support for my ministry's actions.

Allan Rock did the same thing. He began with the concerns you would expect a justice minister to have. Then, "putting on his other hat," he agreed that, regrettable as it might be, Canada had no choice but to take action.

David Collenette reflected the cautionary position of Defence before he too switched hats, saying he had had enough and Fisheries and Oceans could count on his ministry.

That's how it went, all around the table—members first wearing the cautious hats of their ministry, reviewing the options and risks, and then switching hats and saying, in effect, "If aggressive action is what it takes, that is what we must do." The prime minister listened in silence, and after everyone had spoken, he reviewed his commitment to deal with the over-fishing problem. Then he directed me to draft a plan for further action and report back to cabinet.

That was one of the most remarkable days I have ever experienced in public life. As each minister proffered his or her support, I grew more and more emotional. Any one of them might have withdrawn from the discussion or chosen to withhold approval, providing an "I told you so!" opportunity if things ended in disaster. Such a stance must have been tempting. There would have been no downside to withholding support for the idea; it would basically be a "no lose" situation for them as individuals. But each looked beyond his or her private welfare and addressed the bigger issue.

In essence, the cabinet said: "We cannot now, with our eyes wide open, continue to do nothing." We were not dealing, after all, with a bunch of rogue fishing boats scooting around like poachers and pirates; the host countries were aware of the actions of their fishing fleets *and appeared to support them.* These countries were violating every decent code of international conduct, and no other country had both the resources and the legal basis to end it. Ignoring their actions would have been more than an error or a simple sin of omission; it would have made us complicit in the destruction of the Grand Banks, one of the world's largest and most important natural resources. How could we do that and maintain our credibility and our pride?

I left the meeting confident that the cabinet was behind us 100 percent. Now we had to make things happen.

WE DRAFTED OUR PROPOSAL TO NAFO, setting the annual TAC of turbot from the Banks at 27,000 tonnes to be divided as follows: 16,500 tonnes to Canada; 3,400 tonnes to the EU; 3,000 tonnes to Russia; 2,600 tonnes to Japan; and the remaining 1,500 tonnes to the other NAFO members. Although the EU agreed to the 27,000-tonne TAC, it proposed that EU nations be permitted to take 16,800 tonnes of the TAC, based on the proportion of turbot caught in the previous year. The balance of 10,200 tonnes would be divided between all other NAFO nations including Canada, which we found clearly unacceptable.

We assigned ministry staff to lobby individual member countries during the weeks preceding the NAFO meeting in Brussels. Their duties were to present Canada's reasons for seeking tough limits on turbot catches by NAFO nations, and to provide incentives for each nation to vote with us on the matter. Sometimes the persuasion was gentle, especially when the nation being lobbied already had serious concerns about Spain's fishing policies. At other times, we felt justified in exerting a little muscle where necessary. Japan, for example, takes a good deal of tuna from Canadian waters, and has done so for more than a century. We made it clear to the Japanese that unless they agreed with our lower quota on turbot, they would find very little cooperation from Canada for Japanese tuna fishing within 200 miles of our coasts.

This wasn't bullying, by any means. It was tough but fair negotiations. We were not asking for something for nothing; we wanted to preserve the fish stocks for all nations, including our own, and we pointed to the strict limits we were setting for our own fishery. Some of the nations we lobbied were clearly shocked by our actions. Why? Because this kind of hard bargaining struck them as so . . . so *un-Canadian!*

We acknowledged this view, and explained that the old ways had not worked in the past, were not working now and would not work in the future. We accepted that the fisheries decline was due as much to past Canadian policies as to those of foreign countries. Then we submitted evidence that we had put our own house in order, and now it was up to other countries to pitch in. We never took the position that we were right and other NAFO countries were wrong, only that we faced a crisis, and we all needed to do something about it. I believe we neither angered nor outraged countries in persuading them to vote our way.

Ministry staff and I flew to Brussels in January 1995, a week before the meetings were to take place, taking with us union representatives, provincial government members and fisheries industry managers. My attendance at the NAFO meeting was, to the best of my knowledge, the first by a Canadian fisheries minister. Therein, perhaps, was one root of our past problems.

We set up a week-long schedule of lunches, dinners and receptions for NAFO representatives. Sunday meant lunch with the Russian representative and dinner with the Japanese delegation; Monday started off at a morning meeting with Norway, followed by lunch with the EU, and a reception and dinner with Cuba; and so it went through the week.

My biggest challenge, I knew, would be dealing with the EU. John Beck's response to my earlier *aide-mémoire* convinced me that the EU would throw barriers in the path of our proposed new quotas. Sure enough, the EU rejected them out of hand, forcing a vote. By virtue of its size alone, the EU had more clout in dealing with other NAFO countries than we had. Most of all, the EU had Emma Bonino as its newly appointed commissioner for fisheries.

Emma Bonino would be a force to be reckoned with, either in a delicate situation such as that NAFO meeting, or driving a truck on a crowded expressway. Giving a new definition to the term "activist," Bonino had served as the chair of Italy's Radical Anarchist Party and had been involved in most of her country's parliamentary, referendum and civil-disobedience campaigns on one side or the other: founder of the Italian pro-abortion movement, founding member of Food and Disarmament International and a key participant in the protest that blocked Italy's development of nuclear power. With degrees in foreign languages and literature from Milan's Bocconi University, and a determination to make her mark at the NAFO conference, she was an intimidating presence. Moreover, she wanted to show how her human rights experience could work in the EU's favour. As Max Short might have put it, she was full of piss and vinegar, and the EU's fishing communities had high expectations for her. If anyone could counter Canada's claims, it would be Emma Bonino.

Actually, her fiery disposition and uncompromising position helped our cause. If she had acknowledged that we had a reasonable point to make, even if she disagreed with us, she might have won some NAFO countries to her side, but her unyielding attitude accepted no middle ground, and this cost her support. She and other EU delegates also suffered from overconfidence. For years, the EU had held sway over most major issues at NAFO and in 1995, unaware of our lobbying in the weeks leading up to the conference, the EU was confident it would win this one as well.

Emma Bonino was so confident, in fact, that she didn't even bother meeting with the delegates on the morning before NAFO voted on our proposal. I spent the time outside the main conference room as, one by one, Canadian officials brought NAFO delegates to meet me and we began counting the votes needed to win. As we say in Newfoundland, it was a case of the raggedy-arsed artillery infiltrating the European Union right on its own territory. Every member pitched in, with Bill Murphy applying his Nova Scotian charm to great effect, and Earl McCurdy (president of the Fish, Food and Allied Workers) and Max Short twisting arms like the union hall experts they were. At one point I placed a call to a Nordic minister of fisheries whose delegate was planning to vote against us. I reached him at a formal dinner in Moscow, and 15 minutes later, his delegate was back in Canada's corner.

It soon became clear that if the Koreans abstained, we had enough votes to win. Bill Rowat, Gerry Byrne (Newfoundland's federal cabinet minister as I write) and I pulled the Korean delegate aside and pleaded with him to stay out of the disagreement between Canada and the EU. It appeared to work, and I left the conference room to head straight for Emma Bonino's office, confident that we would carry the day.

Emma Bonino is a petite woman, as lively and expressive as an Italian can be. So here was the picture: she's smiling and calling me Brian, I'm returning the smiles and calling her Emma, and she is being more than conciliatory. "When this nuisance is over," she says, "we must work together for the mutual benefit of everyone." Naturally, I agree. I can tell by her calm demeanour that she has no doubt about the outcome of the vote.

We both sip our coffee and smile some more. Then one of her aides enters the room, carrying a piece of paper and looking stricken. He passes her the note, she glances at it and turns first white with shock, then red with anger. The EU's proposal has been rejected and Canada's proposal for turbot quotas adopted. Norway, Japan, Russia, Iceland and Cuba all voted in our favour and, as we expected, Korea abstained.

Things changed. Our tête-à-tête came to an abrupt end, without even a fare-thee-well. Emma Bonino, who had some explaining to do to her superiors and, no doubt, some scolding to give to her staff, stood up and swept out of the room.

My staff and I were elated, of course. After much handshaking and backslapping, I invited the delegation for a congratulatory meal, and we celebrated our victory with quantities of beer and mussels at a café on Brussels's Grand Place—a little prematurely, as things turned out.

CONTINGENCIES FOR ARMED CONFLICT

AFTER THE CELEBRATION DIED DOWN, the staff and I knew we had won a battle but had yet to win the war. Under the NAFO charter, the EU had the right to invoke an objection procedure, enabling the EU to set its own unilateral quota for Greenland halibut. The objection procedure literally allows NAFO states to ignore sound scientific advice, to ignore the will of the majority of NAFO members, and to unilaterally take a decision to continue to plunder and overfish fragile stocks. If this occurred, we could be in an even worse position than before winning the vote. Emma Bonino's statement following the meeting indicated she was going to do just that, and so we needed to swing back into action.

Our first step was classically Canadian: we tried working through diplomatic channels. Canadian ambassadors called on each EU country to present our position and ask the member state not to support Bonino's expected objection. We proposed a transitional phase that would gradually reduce the EU's turbot catch by transferring a portion of Canada's allotment to the EU for the coming year. This would cause some grumbling, I knew, from our own fishing industry, but the TAC would be low enough to enable the fish to survive. The quid pro quo for this interim deal was that the EU would agree not to launch the objection procedure.

I made this suggestion in a conciliatory letter to Emma Bonino as soon as I returned to Canada. "I hope this offer will be seen in the spirit in which it is intended," I added. "It will cause me difficulties domestically, as the Canadian fleet is prepared to take all the quota allocated to Canada by NAFO. However, I am prepared to accept these difficulties in order to help you, as the new EU Commissioner for Fisheries, and to ease the transition of the Spanish and Portuguese fleets to their new NAFO quotas. I believe your officials will confirm to you that this is an unprecedented offer of assistance in terms of NAFO history, and the history of Canada–EU fisheries relations."

While I had high hopes for this gesture, I suspected it would not be sufficient to cool things down. My suspicions were correct.

John Beck, the EU's diplomatic representative to Canada, made a speech to the Canada-Europe Parliamentary Association the day I wrote to Emma Bonino. Beck, a Brit who too often took the position that Canada was an errant colony that needed reining in from time to time, suggested the future of Canadian–European relationships was being jeopardized by our insistence that EU countries respect the need for conservation. If Canada did not back off on its plan to reduce the turbot quota as approved in the NAFO vote, Beck suggested, the EU might set its own quota. What's more, both the goodwill and trade between the EU and Canada would suffer.

Once again, the EU underestimated Canada and the response that Beck's comments generated. Those in Ottawa who had been lukewarm toward our stand on the turbot situation were galvanized by Beck's threats. If Beck anticipated weakening our resolve with his speech, he achieved just the opposite.

No one was more infuriated by Beck's comment than Ron MacDonald, the MP from Dartmouth and chairman of the House of Commons Standing Committee on Fisheries and Oceans. In a letter to Beck, sent the week following Beck's speech, Ron set the tone in his first sentence. "I must take this opportunity," he wrote, "on behalf of the tens of thousands of out-of-work Atlantic Canadians dependent on the now-decimated ground fishery, to address your recent remarks concerning NAFO turbot allocations . . ."

Ron pulled no punches and wasted no time in establishing our position:

> Your implicit threat that the EU will once more ignore NAFO quota decisions and set its own quota for turbot is clearly unacceptable from both a resource conservation standpoint as well as respect for international organizations such as NAFO. Any unilateral quota increase would be a threat to conservation, which may lead to overfishing of a stock in a serious state of decline. It is unfortunate that the EU is willing to serve as a broker for Spanish pirates . . . perhaps if a turbot looked more like a baby seal, then European pirates could be more easily dissuaded from decimating the stock.

Such intemperate language to a diplomat from a Canadian! Ron justified his language with four irrefutable points:

1. In 1986 the EU reported catches of more than 30,000t of 3NO* cod despite a NAFO allocation of 14,750t
2. In 1987 the EU reported catches of 1,213t of 3LNO Yellowtail despite a NAFO allocation of 300t
3. In 1988 the EU reported catches of 9,828t 3LNO American plaice despite a NAFO allocation of 510t
4. In 1989 the EU reported catches of 1,900t of 3NO witch despite a NAFO allocation of 0t

---

*These and other initials preceding a fish species identify the fishing area within the Banks where the fish are normally caught. t refers to metric tonnes.

The consequences of the abuse of NAFO objection procedures are shockingly clear: all of the above species are now subject to international moratoria.

There is a saying where I grew up in Cape Breton: once bitten, twice shy. Canada has not just been bitten, we have been subject to a feeding frenzy by a Spanish fleet whose past actions speak louder than their present words. The people who live in the coastal communities along the North Atlantic have felt the real impact of Spain's greed and the EU's complicity. They have no jobs, little future, and have seen their way of life destroyed.

As a Canadian parliamentarian and Chair of the House of Commons Standing Committee on Fisheries and Oceans, I serve notice through you to the EU that this Canadian parliament will not sit idly by while the spirit of international law is violated by the EU on behalf of its member states. You cannot have it both ways—on the one hand claiming to be a bastion of support for international law and resource conservations, and on the other hand using NAFO objection procedure like a spoiled child every time you and your member states do not get their way.

Was Ron over the top with these comments? Perhaps. But the EU got the message that Canada had an attitude toward protecting fish stocks that was poles apart from the acquiescent policies of the Mulroney government.

I made this point to a group of British fisheries officials who, though their government under John Major was harrumphing in disapproval for the benefit of EU members, supported our actions against Spain and Portugal. Europe, I said, must "understand that the colonial days are long gone, and the consequences of conservation and the cost of conservation must be paid by all who ascribe to the notion of civilized behaviour by modern nations."

Jean Chrétien, in my experience, is sensitive about keeping his word, wherever possible. In the middle of one cabinet meeting, when I detected a shift of the PM's support away from standing up to the EU in favour of taking the safe (read: do as little as possible) road being proposed by other ministries, I called Heidi Bonnell, my communications director, and asked her to bring over a special file we had accumulated. In it were news clippings on the question of Grand Banks fish stocks. In each clipping, the PM's statements regarding the need for conservation on the Grand Banks were highlighted, showing over and over again how he had stated Canada would do "whatever is necessary" to stop the overfishing. I passed the file to the PM and asked if he could review the clippings and consider the risks we faced if we failed to act. I suggested it would crush the spirit of every Atlantic Canadian if we went back on our word—or, more precisely, the prime minister's word.

Jean Chrétien read the clippings, gave me a tight smile and agreed.

We had jumped one more hurdle toward fairness for the fisheries.

MEANWHILE, THINGS CONTINUED TO HEAT UP, with notes and letters flying back and forth from all sides. I had issued an internal *aide-mémoire* indicating our response to a possible EU objection. The document reviewed various stages of development over the previous decade. It began with an agreement by all NAFO states that the turbot were in danger; led to the Spanish fishing fleet's move to the Grand Banks after wiping out the hake stock off the coast of Africa (this was a documented event, not a personal opinion); gave scientific warnings of the risk to turbot, dating back to 1989; noted the right of Canada to hold onto its share of the turbot catch on the basis of excessive EU catches; reviewed the legal vote in Canada's favour; and detailed our offer to smooth the transition to the smaller EU TAC over the coming year.

Next, the document presented our options should the EU
launch the threatened objection and unilaterally declare its own
quota. These included

- Increasing the number of boardings and inspections of EU
  vessels.
- Amending the Coastal Fisheries Protection Regulations
  (CFPA), adding Spain to the list of states whose vessels were
  prohibited from fishing for straddling stocks on the Nose
  and Tail of the Banks.
- Introducing legislation that would permit us to interfere
  with certain prescribed vessels if they refused a request to
  stop fishing. This could involve the use of newly developed
  "warp-cutters," nasty-looking instruments pulled by fisheries patrol vessels that could slice through the steel cables
  pulling the net behind a trawler.
- Keeping open the offer for future negotiations.

The various drawbacks of these measures were easy to identify.
Our efforts could generate so much negative response that
countries such as the Baltic States, which had kept a low profile
on the subject, might swing over to the EU side. On a second
issue, Roy MacLaren, our minister of international trade, had
launched a program to start free trade discussions between Canada
and the EU; the EU might respond by cutting off these talks.
Most disturbing of all was the risk that EU countries could send
their naval vessels to the Banks and provide armed protection
for their trawlers in international waters. Given this troubling
scenario, I had the *aide-mémoire* reviewed and approved by both
the Justice and Defence ministries.

The risk of a potential armed encounter meant that we had
to establish rules of engagement and provide them to our fisheries patrol officers and destroyer captains in the vicinity. None
of us wanted to be pondering alternatives in the middle of a
confrontation taking place more than 200 miles off our shore.

We needed to explore every possibility beforehand and determine our response, including the use of force if necessary to halt or disable other ships, and protect our own should they come under fire.

I can't recall a more sobering day than the one spent reviewing these rules, to be drawn up in secret and provided to our naval officers. Up to this point, things had been almost academic. Now we were literally assessing firepower and discussing potential casualty risks. This kind of planning, to civilian Canadians, is something more out of Hollywood action movies than reality. The real language of Canadian rules of engagement are not words you would find in the mouths of a Harrison Ford or an Arnold Schwarzenegger: "In the event that Spanish OPVs (offshore patrol vessels) use deadly force, HMC ship (i.e., the destroyer HMCS *Gatineau*) closes the scene, attempts to hail the OPV and warns it to break off its activity. If the OPV fires on the enforcement vessel, HMC ship is to open fire with the proportional force to defend the enforcement vessel." For a Canadian fisheries minister to seriously consider implementing such actions was almost unthinkable—especially *this* fisheries minister.

But there was no escaping this responsibility, and I remained in contact with DND officials on an almost daily basis, reviewing our rules of engagement and praying they would never be applied.

Meanwhile, Emma Bonino replied to my letter with a mixture of good and bad news. The good news was possible conciliation. "You are certainly aware," she wrote, "that the unexpected NAFO decision on Greenland halibut . . . has raised major concerns within the Community, where it is widely regarded both at government level and in the fisheries sector as economically unjustified and wrong on principles." She used this point to rationalize proposing "an autonomous quota of 18,360 tonnes" for the EU, called "a major effort of moderation" to stay within the agreed-upon global TAC of 27,000 tonnes. This might have helped protect the turbot, but it demanded major concessions from our own fishermen. She went on to propose bilateral discussions between the EU and

Canada, followed by talks involving "all the other contracting parties," which we assumed included all of NAFO.

Bonino ended her letter with an unconvincing plea for calm: "Aggressive rhetoric and sabre-rattling on both sides of the Atlantic can only add to the existing tensions between our respective constituencies, and can ultimately prevent us from working toward a sound and forward-looking composition [sic] of this argument, in the framework of our wider bilateral relations."

In the wake of John Beck's repeated threats, and her own thinly disguised warning—"framework of our wider bilateral relations" we took to include the free trade discussions—this concern rang hollow indeed.

Meanwhile, the Spaniards kept fishing, a point I made to Bonino in my reply:

> As you know, while we are going through this exchange of correspondence, the Spanish fleet in the Northwest Atlantic is catching Greenland halibut at a rate which is extraordinarily high for this time of year compared to this fleet's catches during this same period in previous years. We believe the catch may be as high as 6,000t at this date, well above the levels being reported by the fleets to the Spanish authorities for transmission to your officials. If these levels of catch and misreporting continue, the 27,000t TAC established by NAFO for 1995, and any unilateral quota set by the EU, will be irrelevant.
>
> If your officials are advising you that the NAFO quotas assigned to other countries will not be caught, I can assure you this is a totally unwarranted assumption, and cannot provide any basis for rationalizing an EU decision to disregard the NAFO decision.

I went on to list the EU's record over past years, using data lifted from the EU's own documents.

In 1986, the EU was awarded a NAFO quota of 12,444 tonnes of cod in the 3NO area; the EU objected, set its own quota of 26,400 tonnes and reported taking 30,470 tonnes. In the same year, no NAFO quota for redfish had been assigned; the EU objected and proceeded to pull 23,434 tonnes from one area of the Banks. Also in the same year, after being awarded a quota of 700 tonnes of plaice as a result of negotiations, the EU objected and recorded a catch of 21,162 tonnes. On and on it went, year after year—quotas set for yellowtail flounder, witch flounder, and others were ignored and the safe limit of catches, as determined by scientific evaluation, had been totally disregarded. What, then, was the purpose of any efforts to conserve the fish stock under these circumstances? How could we trust the EU countries, and the Spanish fleet in particular, to respect the quotas?

Summarizing my letter, I wrote:

> These examples illustrate what happened a few years ago, when the EU lodged objections to NAFO decisions and set its own rules. I hope [they] serve to explain why Canada cannot sit idly by in the face of yet another EU objection, and if history is repeated, yet another stock catastrophe in the Northwest Atlantic. I urge you, once again, to agree to a meeting of senior officials to allow us to try to resolve this problem.

I sent the letter with sincere hopes that it would generate a positive response from Brussels, but my instincts told me otherwise.

They were right—that same day, the EU set its own turbot quota of 18,630 tonnes, representing 69 percent of the agreed-upon 27,000 tonnes TAC. Given the EU's past record, I suspected that the Spanish fleet would take the entire 27,000 tonnes for itself.

In fact, we had proof that the fleet had already done so. On February 25, 1995, our DFO inspectors boarded two Spanish trawlers fishing the Nose of the Banks. The log of the *José Antonio Nores* indicated that 30 percent of its catch was turbot, yet our inspectors noted that turbot made up 90 percent of the haul. The same day, an inspection of the log of the *Patricia Nores* showed its captain claimed his main catch was skate and round-nose grenadier. But when inspectors went into the hold, they counted 90 percent turbot. And two days later, aboard the *Pedra Rubia*, its records claimed that only 15 percent of the vessel's total catch was turbot even though 85 percent of the fish being processed and 55 percent of the fish in the hold were turbot. These were just three examples of a dozen or more inspections carried out that week. The problem was beyond challenging; it was criminal and systematic, no matter how you measured it.

WE BEGAN MULTIPLYING OUR EFFORTS. Jacques Roy, Canada's EU ambassador, flew back to Brussels to present our case personally first to Sir Leon Brittan, the EU vice-president responsible for external trade, and then on to Brussels for a meeting with Emma Bonino's chief of staff. In early March, Foreign Affairs Minister André Ouellet urged the EU to change its objection to the turbot allocation, warning that Canada was prepared to act to protect the turbot; Gordon Smith, our DM of foreign affairs, outlined our position to the EU member state ambassadors; and we amended the Coastal Fisheries Protection Act to permit enforcement action against Spanish and Portuguese vessels.

On March 2, Canadian ambassadors to all EU countries— France, Britain, Germany, Belgium, the Netherlands, Italy, Greece, Ireland, Portugal, Spain, Sweden, Finland, Austria and Denmark—were sent an identical letter from Prime Minister Chrétien with instructions to deliver it "at the highest possible level immediately." The letter read:

I am writing to you to bring to your attention a matter which, if not dealt with expeditiously and with the greatest care, has the potential to destroy the last remaining groundfish stock in the Northwest Atlantic.

As the result of fishing practices in the Northwest Atlantic in the late 1980s, all major stocks were fished to virtual extinction with the exception of the Greenland Halibut. NAFO, as a consequence, established a moratorium on most stocks under its supervision, forcing 40,000 Canadian fishermen into unemployment with dramatic consequences for the people of Newfoundland.

In the past several years, European Union fishing boats have taken more than 50,000 metric tons per year of the last remaining stock. As a result of this overfishing, this stock faces a fate similar to that of the other groundfish now under moratorium.

In September 1994, the Northwest Atlantic Fishing Organization (NAFO) established, for the first time, a limit on the total catch of Greenland Halibut in the relevant area of the Northwest Atlantic. The total allowable catch was set at 27,000 tonnes for 1995.

On February 1, NAFO made a decision on the allocation of shares to the NAFO contracting parties. This decision included an allocation of 3,400 tonnes to the European Union. The decision was supported by a majority of the longstanding NAFO members that have had a significant fishing presence in the Northwest Atlantic.

The European Union has, however, decided to make use of a procedure available under the NAFO Convention allowing it to lodge an objection to the February 1 decision, and not be legally bound by it. The European Union has also decided to act unilaterally by setting its own quota of 18,630 tonnes.

Canadian surveillance and inspection experts have established that, by the beginning of March, the European Union fleet had already taken as much as 6,000 tonnes, well over its 3,400-tonne NAFO quota, and is continuing its fishery at unprecedented high levels of effort. Moreover, the fishing is being conducted by 45 fishing vessels from one country in a zone comprising only 20 percent of the fish habitat, further violating the most elementary laws of conservation.

I am therefore most concerned that this resource could well be lost to humanity. I am also conscious of the consequences which this would have on the people of Canada's Maritime provinces.

I should be grateful therefore if you could accord your personal attention to the issue. Your cooperation is sought to bring to a halt the fishing of Greenland Halibut off Canada's Northeast coasts. Canada is, of course, prepared to seek transitional arrangements to phase in the reduction of the catch allocated to the European Union. We cannot, however, allow the resource to be destroyed and would take appropriate measures to prevent that from happening.

We could sense support for the EU softening, in part because the prime minister had invested some of the goodwill he had built up with leaders such as Kohl and Dehaene. That's what political clout is for, after all, and Chrétien used it effectively.

To this point, official British support for our position had been equivocal, although grassroots backing was enthusiastically in favour of Canada. British fishermen had been outraged at the antics of the Spanish and Portuguese fleets for years, and they expressed their delight at our stand in many ways.

John Major's response to the PM's letter, while agreeing with the need to conserve fish stocks, noted that the EU had accounted for more than 75 percent of the turbot catch for the past three years, and that "it is not reasonable to expect the European Community to reduce its activity by 90 percent while other Contracting Parties are able very considerably to reduce theirs." This conveniently ignored the fact that the EU's 75 percent had been excessive, regardless of its historic roots, and that we had offered a transition period. Major closed with the usual concerns against "taking any action or making any announcements which could make the situation harder to resolve." Well, at least we had his attention.

On March 3, David Collenette wrote to the PM supporting my stand on the turbot fishery but expressing unease at the legal ramifications of our action. I understood David's motives in doing this, but I wasn't all that comfortable about possibly clouding the issue at this date. David wrote:

The Office of the Judge Advocate has consistently expressed its grave concerns about the legality under international law of using force, including disabling force, outside Canada's 200 nautical mile Exclusive Fishing Zone. The Judge Advocate General has requested that the Department of Justice and the Department of Foreign Affairs and International Trade confirm that it is Canada's official position that the use of force, including disabling force, authorized under the Coastal Fisheries Protection Act and Regulations, is in accordance with international law.

Absent a positive response from the Department of Justice or the Department of Foreign Affairs and International Trade, the Judge Advocate General will not be able to nor will he certify the legality of the Rules of Engagement. If the Chief of the Defence Staff is ordered to issue Rules of Engagement that cannot be certified as legally correct by the Department of Justice, the Department of Foreign Affairs and International Trade, and the Judge Advocate General, there is a real issue whether any direction given is a lawful command and therefore constitutes a lawful duty.

This is a matter which we must all understand and, I believe, a matter which must be clarified before proceeding further. Officials in my Department are pursuing the matter, and I invite your attention to a critical factor which needs to be taken into account in the management of this issue.

The issue was quickly addressed and dealt with: DND could in fact follow the rules of engagement, under the present circumstances, in accordance with international law. This permitted passage of more amendments to the Coastal Fisheries Protection Act that same day, meaning we could go forward with confidence. The amendments allowed our patrol ships to approach, challenge, board and seize vessels on the Nose and Tail of the Banks, beyond our 200-mile limit and, if necessary, to use armed force to halt and disable the vessels. We were free to act.

I mention this to underscore the fact that subsequent actions were not carried out without thoughtful evaluation and total awareness of the possible consequences. In spite of a few nail-biters in the Privy Council Office, we had DND, Justice, Foreign Affairs and the Judge Advocate General on our side—and, more important, we had Jean Chrétien.

WHILE THE PM'S EFFORTS had generated a new appreciation, and at least tacit approval, for our position, the diplomatic channels became busier than ever on the topic. As each day passed, I realized that I was becoming the topic as much as the turbot were. EU diplomats began pleading with the PM's Office and Foreign Affairs to rein me in, and I began hearing from Foreign Affairs that I should consider pulling in my horns and being "less provocative." It was not a plea that I fully understood. We had won the NAFO vote. We had agreement that the turbot stock was in serious danger of becoming as eradicated as the cod stock.

We had both the legal and the moral authority to take action. How could our resolve be interpreted as a provocation under those circumstances?

I found myself dealing with three influential men who did not entirely share either my concern for the fish or my determination to see this matter through to its completion.

Eddie Goldenberg, the PM's senior policy adviser, saw both sides of the issue and frankly, I suspect, just wanted the whole thing to go away.

Jim Bartleman, the PM's foreign policy adviser and assistant secretary to the cabinet for foreign and defence policy, was among the most dovish of those who cautioned me. Jim, a First Nations Canadian, had achieved a distinguished career, serving in many diplomatic posts in the past (he was later appointed our ambassador to the EU).

Gordon Smith, who had just finished his ambassadorship to the EU and was deputy minister of foreign affairs, was reticent about taking a stand. Both he and Jim are bright, dedicated men who demonstrated all the qualities that have established our country's diplomatic corps as among the best in the world. But in this case, I believe, they were out of step—at the beginning, at least. While they were trying to dissuade me from pursuing the matter, they were also warning Foreign Minister André Ouellet and his people of potential disaster if I stuck to my hard line.

Both Bartleman and Smith were "big picture" men. All their training and experience had been dedicated toward assessing individual events in a broader perspective where relations with other countries were concerned. Gordon Smith demonstrated this best when, during one attempt to convince me that the ministry should back off its position vis-à-vis the EU, he wondered if I really wanted to risk damaging our relationship with the EU over "some smelly little fish" that nobody else seemed to give a damn about.

Of course, it wasn't the "smelly little fish" I was most concerned with. It was the future of tens of thousands of Canadian fishermen, their livelihoods seriously damaged and their future in doubt as a result of the closing of the cod fishery. Saving the turbot was both practical—it gave our people something to catch, after all—and symbolic. We had lost the fight to save the cod; we could not afford to lose this one and still pretend that we supported the idea of conservation and environmental protection.

I have never believed that anything of substance is ever achieved, in either the private or the public sector, unless it is fuelled by a deep emotional commitment. I had witnessed firsthand the impact that a declining fishery had made on the Atlantic provinces, most notably Newfoundland and Labrador. I love my home province and people as profoundly as anyone can love his roots and his heritage, and I often wept inside when I heard of yet another outport closing and another family abandoning generations of life on the sea because countries far beyond the horizon chose to ignore basic conservation practices.

I try to control my emotional response to a challenge but I must admit that, in the midst of the events of early 1995, I permitted my heart to rule my head on occasion. During one difficult phone call with Jim Bartleman, I grew exasperated after listening to his reasons why I couldn't do one thing or another to protect the fish stocks. Finally I blurted, "It's gutless people like you who have sold out fishermen year after year, in the interest of giving no offence to countries of the European Union!" and swept the telephone off my desk.

The phone remained functioning, and I heard Jim say, "I know how you feel. I'm a member of Canada's First Nations community, so I know about being forgotten in the face of powerful interests."

Jim made his point, and after we cleared the air between us he contributed significantly to the successful outcome of what became known as the Turbot War.

SHOTS ACROSS THEIR BOW

I N MARCH 1995 it seemed that much of the northern hemi-sphere was involved in either pursuing or protecting a fish that few people knew about a few months before. If there were to be a Turbot War, it had already begun, with words and threats as ammunition.

Fisheries officers from our patrol vessel *Leonard J. Cowley* boarded the Spanish trawler *Noradina* to discover more than 41 tonnes of turbot in its hold, representing more than 80 percent of the *Noradina*'s catch: yet the captain's log stated that only 37 percent of his haul was turbot. Moreover, the size of the turbot indicated the *Noradina* had netted immature fish, too young to spawn. With no authorization to do anything else, the inspector issued a routine citation to the captain. The relatively small fine wouldn't deter the *Noradina* from future infractions, but the impact of his flagrant disregard for honesty and conservation was invaluable.

We began issuing a steady stream of news releases and policy statements from the ministry to both the Canadian and foreign media, building our case beyond the official channels. Most people, we knew, would side with the idea of preserving fish stocks if the story could be made without excessive rhetoric. The *Noradina* experience, especially our evidence of its crew keeping immature fish and falsifying documents, strengthened our case.

We created T-shirts imprinted with the phrase *Get Off My Nose* on the front, and *Stay Off My Tail* on the back, and sold hundreds to raise funds for the United Way. Bill Rowat and his staff even recruited hockey commentator Don Cherry, who bellowed at the camera during a *Hockey Night in Canada* broadcast, "Way to go, Tobin! Way to go, DFO! Get those people off our Nose and Tail!"

We transformed one of the ministry meeting rooms into an Operations Centre, complete with maps and communications apparatus, where we could maintain direct contact with our fisheries inspectors at sea. And, in the event that anyone doubted the PMO's position on the matter, one of the PM's aides stated that Jean Chrétien was "one hundred percent behind Brian, and that means the government is solid."

The topic arose in Question Period and in media scrums. Would we really seize foreign ships on the high seas? Would we used armed force if necessary? Was this a new direction for Canadian policy? The communications team of Bonnie Mewdell and Heidi Bonnell was superb not only at providing the media with background on our actions, but also at preparing charts and graphics for the TV cameras. Heidi would accompany me in the media scrums and, while I discussed our actions and the urgency to find a solution, she would stand to one side shuffling through cardboard-mounted graphs and holding them at the correct height for TV cameras to capture. She did this so often that her co-workers began referring to her as "Vanna," after Vanna White of *Wheel of Fortune* fame.

The public relations program worked, but some still questioned our resolve and our wisdom in making such a break from previous policies. Bud Hulan, Newfoundland's minister of fisheries, brought it home to them when he said, "I am sick and tired of having to tell families in this province, 'You are not allowed to go out and put food on the table for your children,' while at the same time we are allowing Europeans to overfish [the Banks]."

John Efford and Beaton Tulk, two of Newfoundland's best spokespersons, began organizing rallies all across the province in support of our efforts.

Still, political partisanship held sway in some quarters. John Cummins, fisheries critic for the Reform Party, claimed, "There's no cabinet solidarity . . . He [meaning me] is not dealing with a couple of flagless rust buckets this time and nobody wants him going out there and arresting EU vessels." Cummins was wrong on several counts, of course, as time proved. But his words revealed the depth of skepticism in some quarters both in this country and abroad. It was understandable, given the poor record that Canada had of protecting our fishing interests under previous governments, but it was wrong nevertheless.

Emma Bonino continued singing variations on the same song, except her words were becoming more frantic and less logical with each chorus. "We find it astonishing that Canada is threatening unilateral measures against the European Union," she said in early March, "as any action would be in breach of international law." Her comment stirred more cries of warnings and indignation from EU members. The French minister of foreign affairs noted that we were in flagrant violation of international laws governing the high seas; the Portuguese maritime affairs minister called our warning "a deplorable threat, because Canada does not have sovereignty over the NAFO area"; and John Beck maintained his previous stand by saying he found it "astonishing that we should even be talking about the possibility of Canada, a partner of the European Union, going out to arrest [EU] vessels. It is beyond my comprehension."

I needed to draw attention to the principles behind our action and our resolve to protect the turbot. "The issue is not about who gets what share of the fish pie that's out there," I said on March 6. "What's at stake is whether the fish pie itself is going to be sustained, and whether or not there's going to be any fish for anybody in the future. This wanton destruction of a protein resource that belongs to the world is every bit as irresponsible as the destruction of the rain forest. This is a crime against humanity."

As for the angry shouts and denunciations barraging us from the EU, I said: "This is not the dialogue, the posture, of a modern state respectful of the views of its peers in the community of nations. This is the posture of a bully . . . At what point do we say enough is enough? I think we've reached this point." And so the dialogue continued.

The EU, I suspect, anticipated that we would yield to threats and name calling as we had so often in the past. Soon, they believed, a proposal would emanate from Ottawa, cloaked in the shape of compromise, that would agree to the demands of the EU and confirm our dedication to peace and goodwill among nations, whatever the price. Well, we were as dedicated as ever to peace and goodwill, but we were also damned adamant about opposing piracy and environmental pillage.

One of the most outrageous statements was made by the Spanish minister of foreign affairs, who called David Wright, our ambassador to Spain, into his office for "serious talks," which in diplomatic language means something between a desk-pounding tantrum and a brawl. Spain, we were lectured through Ambassador Wright, was prepared to cut the number of trawlers on the Banks from 38 to 20, although it would not publicly acknowledge this "redeployment" for fear of upsetting the Spanish citizenry. It should be seen as a "unilateral gesture of goodwill."

Our ambassador stated that Spain could have as many vessels in the area as it chose, as long as they weren't fishing. This enraged the Spanish minister, who said, with a straight face, that the Spanish fishing fleet could not have pulled in 7,000 tonnes of turbot since the beginning of the year because the fish stock just wasn't that big.

"That's our point!" Ambassador Wright said. "It proves precisely the need for our conservation efforts."

The Spaniards switched to a threatening mode, lecturing Canada not to "paint itself into a corner" by disregarding the "goodwill gesture" of Spain reducing its fleet.

Nevertheless, the message appeared to get through. On March 7, our patrol vessels noted a major withdrawal of EU trawlers from the Nose and Tail of the Banks; the number of Spanish ships dropped from 45 to 16 literally overnight. There was much jubilation in the ministry and beyond, and we began hearing hints that the EU might agree to discuss the turbot quotas in Brussels. I made a statement about being pleased that we had achieved our goal without requiring Canadian enforcement vessels to take action. "Our determination to resolve this matter is such that we'll preserve the stock by whatever means are required," I said. "I'll either hang in there or be hanged."

It made good press, but even as I spoke the words I knew our celebration was premature. On Wednesday, March 8, six Spanish trawlers remained behind. Their continued presence was intolerable, and I asked the PM for an emergency meeting to discuss our response.

Later that day in the PM's office, I laid out the need to inspect the catch aboard the remaining Spanish trawlers. In attendance at the time were André Ouellet, minister of foreign affairs; André's deputy, Gordon Smith; and Jocelyn Bourgon, the clerk of the Privy Council. Each time I suggested that we provide our inspectors with the authority to board ships on the Nose and Tail of the Banks, including the use or threat of weapons if necessary, Smith or Bourgon pleaded their case to the PM to avoid "provocative" action. After several minutes of this, I grew frustrated. "Why can't we manage this thing?" I said, raising my voice. "We've been fooling with it for 10 years. The turbot is a Canadian resource that happens to swim outside the 200-mile limit. We're being raped and pillaged out there, *and we have to take provocative action, damn it!*" At that, I slammed my fist down on the PM's desk.

Silence followed the thump. When I lifted my head to look at the PM I saw a particular look he used when he wanted to echo Queen Victoria's words: "We are not amused."

Nothing was said. The moment passed. The PM suggested one more attempt at negotiation. He would call EU President Santer and propose a diplomatic solution. If Santer refused, in spite of the PM's expression of our determination to take whatever action necessary, we would have no choice in the matter. Our threat of seizure and arrest would not be an empty one. If it were, how much credibility would Canada have in future matters of this kind?

Santer, to no one's surprise, refused to change his tune. He fully expected us to take the safe, predictable and unproductive route of diplomatic negotiations—the route that had led to a dead end over and over again.

With that, Jean Chrétien gave his authority to act.

THE TRAWLER THAT OUR FISHERIES patrol vessels and aircraft had been watching most closely on the Nose of the Banks was the *Estai*, sailing out of Vigo, Spain. We knew it was hauling in turbot, and its continued presence was something between a test and a provocation. If, after all we had gone through to that point, we failed to challenge the *Estai*, what would prevent other EU vessels from swinging about and returning to the Banks?

I called Gordon Smith and Jim Bartleman, asking both to join Bill Rowat and me in the Operations Centre around noon on Thursday, March 9. Bill and I outlined our position and indicated our intention to order the *Estai* seized and brought into St. John's. Gordon and Jim agreed, and the order was sent to Captain Newman Riggs, master of the *Cape Roger* and other ships in the area. In St. John's, Leo Strowbridge coordinated the chase by our patrol vessels and aerial surveillance being carried out by Provincial Airlines, whose pilots flew as low as 50 feet above the water.

None of us was certain the *Estai* would comply, of course, but even we were surprised when the fisheries officers were repulsed and their boarding ladders tossed into the sea. Then the *Estai* cut its nets and began fleeing east, the *Cape Roger* in pursuit with the *Leonard J. Cowley* and *Sir Wilfred Grenfell*, the latter a Coast Guard vessel, closing in.

"He'll heave to shortly," someone said, meaning the *Estai* captain. "He has to."

But he did not.

For four hours, the pursuit continued in foggy North Atlantic waters. Five other Spanish trawlers joined the *Estai* and began trying to interfere with the Canadian ships, which attempted to repel them with water cannons. Reports circulated that an armed Spanish patrol vessel had been dispatched to the site. That's when I invited Max Short into the Operations Centre and, after hearing his poignant and salty observations, we gave the order for Captain Riggs to warn the *Estai* that he was about to fire across the trawler's bow. If shots were fired and the Spanish vessel failed to stop, the captain would issue a second warning to the *Estai* in Spanish, indicating the next burst of fire would be aimed at the *Estai*'s propellers. The Spanish crew would be warned to leave the rear of the vessel and her propellers would be disabled with 50-mm machine gun fire.

It took four bursts of the *Cape Roger*'s weapon across the *Estai*'s bow by gunner Bernie Riggs to stop the trawler, and the voice of the *Cape Roger*'s skipper, announcing that the *Estai* was heaving to, released a long sigh of relief from everyone in the Operations Centre. Armed RCMP and fisheries officers took command of the Spanish trawler and swung her about, headed for St. John's.

UNEQUIVOCAL ACTION IS THE IDEAL WAY to push fence-sitters in one direction or another, and that was the immediate response to our seizing of the *Estai*. There were no EU boats on the Grand Banks at the time, and the EU suddenly agreed that negotiations were a good idea after all. In fact, the EU grew positively enthusiastic after the usual blustering. A statement out of Brussels, following the *Estai* incident, regretted that Canada had "chosen the course of international aggression," quickly adding that a compromise might be worked out "if Canada shows restraint," and closing with a note that the EU "does not want this situation to escalate."

John Beck, the EU ambassador to Canada, had never been a fence-sitter. He had been among our most severe critics, and upon hearing of the *Estai*'s seizure he could barely restrain himself. "I ask you, who is the pirate now?" he demanded. "Who is the bull?" (An interesting analogy considering the Spanish connection to all this. An appropriate retort might have been, "Who has been waving the red flag?") "If we continue along this path of direct action, of armed action against fishermen, I would not wish to vouch for the consequences," Beck warned.

Emma Bonino first claimed that we had taken action against the *Estai* only to satisfy our "internal needs" and hide our inefficiencies in fisheries management. Then she sputtered, "You cannot expect us to do nothing," and she called an emergency meeting of NAFO.

The head of fisheries for one Spanish region called it "an act of war," and the Spanish government's official response was to say that we had taken the *Estai* to divert attention from our internal problems.

Licino Martins, an official with the Portuguese Sea Ministry, claimed without blushing that "Canada has absolutely no right to prevent our boats from fishing for anything they want beyond the 200-mile limit," and the Spanish foreign minister said that his country was considering moves to limit the "free movement of people" between Spain and Canada, meaning the imposition of visas for Canadian visitors. Bearing in mind the immense numbers of Canadian tourists visiting Spain compared with those coming the other way, this sounded like cutting off your tourism nose to spite your fishing face. (Spain did eventually impose visa rules on Canadians, but it rescinded them later.)

Statements from elsewhere were reassuring. Newfoundland Premier Clyde Wells, who naturally supported our moves against the EU, noted: "They [the EU in general and the Spanish in particular] destroyed the cod stocks and now they want to destroy the turbot, because they don't give a damn what the ultimate consequences are. Their sole interest is in getting as much fish as they can as soon as they can."

Britain began moving to our side, and the country dragged Prime Minister John Major, if not kicking and screaming at least harrumphing and frowning, with it. "Are we going to find the British navy lined up with the Spanish navy [against Canada]?" asked one British MP, who called the hostile treatment of Canada by the EU "deeply offensive." At a lower level, the response to our action was enthusiastic and unequivocal. Fishermen across the United Kingdom cheered our arrest of the *Estai* almost as lustily as those in the Newfoundland outports did. The chairman of the Scottish Whitefish Producers Association promised to back us "one hundred percent," and Canadian flags began appearing in the shops of fish and seafood mongers throughout Devon and Cornwall.

In Canada, the *Estai* incident created strange bedfellows indeed. Lucien Bouchard, the Bloc Québécois leader who often appeared to prefer eating rusty nails over saying something positive about Canada, commented: "Canada had to do what it did. The protection of turbot has become imperative," placing him on the same side as every other Canadian provincial leader. But John Cummins, the Reform Party fisheries critic, still failed to get the message. Proving how out of touch his party was with Canadian public opinion, Cummins called the *Estai* seizure "a PR exercise—it's absolutely disgusting, outrageous!"

For myself, I was relieved that we achieved our objectives without any loss of life. "Canadians don't want to punish the Spanish crew members," I told the *Globe and Mail.* "They will be sent home as soon as possible. Fishermen are fishermen the world over." As for name-calling from some EU sources, I pointed out: "It's not the mark of a pirate to reach out in desperation at the eleventh hour and try to save the last fish stock on the Grand Banks. It's the mark of a patriot."

Tens of thousands of Newfoundlanders gathered on the docks of St. John's to greet the *Estai* with jeers when she was escorted into the harbour. I remained in Ottawa to avoid giving the EU and the Spanish an opportunity to suggest I was gloating over a trophy catch. I also suspected some shocking revelations were forthcoming once we got the *Estai* to port and inspected her hold. And I was right.

First was the discovery that the *Estai*'s captain, like other EU fishing vessels on the Grand Banks, kept two logbooks. One, for the benefit of our inspectors, showed the trawler engaged in legal activity, catching lower quantities of turbot and other endangered fish. The other, maintained for the *Estai*'s owners, recorded the true catch. "The two do not add up," I explained at a March 14 press conference. "You don't usually keep two sets of books because you want duplicates of one or the other. You keep two sets of books because one records the real business that's going on, and the other generates the business you want the world [to think] is going on."

That was the first duplicity. The second was a false bulkhead discovered once the *Estai* was docked in St. John's and its captain in custody. Behind the bulkhead were tonnes of turbot processed, packaged and put out of sight of inspectors. What's more, over 80 percent of the turbot were less than the minimum size agreed upon by international fisheries groups. Some were barely palm sized. We also located a secret hold containing 25 tonnes of American plaice, a protected species. How much more proof did the international community need?

Noting the very small size of fish in the *Estai*'s hold, I instructed our patrol vessels to locate the net that had been cut away with the approach of the *Cape Roger*. Using modern global positioning technology, an FPI vessel quickly retrieved the net and carried it back to St. John's. Even more than the false compartments, secret holds, undersized turbot and illegal plaice, the net proved our point and sealed the *Estai*'s guilt. The basic net size had openings of 115 mm, 15 mm less than the minimum set by NAFO, enabling it to snare smaller fish than legally allowed. That was disturbing enough, but an inner liner to the net was just 80 mm in size. No fish larger than three inches could escape. I wasn't stretching things very far when I described the net as "an ecological monstrosity and a weapon of destruction."

This was enough to nudge the EU still further toward negotiations. Sir Leon Brittan said he was interested in de-escalating things, and Emma Bonino announced she would recommend talks begin if we agreed to release the *Estai* and its captain. We did this, but only after the *Estai*'s owners posted a $500,000 bond; the vessel's captain, who had been jeered by Newfoundlanders when he arrived in St. John's, was delighted to be on his way home. The net, of course, remained behind.

A senior delegation consisting of Bill Rowat, Gordon Smith and Jim Bartleman was dispatched to Brussels. Their duties were not to negotiate, but to set the basis for negotiations to follow. Despite this process, the bellicose Spaniards refused to bend, announcing they were sending more trawlers to the Banks, accompanied by the *Vigia*, an armed Spanish patrol vessel.

Within a week, six Spanish trawlers were in position, and I vowed that our patrol vessels would cut the warps of any ship that was pulling in turbot and refusing to leave the area. That's exactly what happened when the *Pescamar Uno* refused to let our inspectors board her. When the *Sir Wilfred Grenfell* attempted to get into position to cut the Spanish fishing vessel's warps, the Spanish patrol vessel *Vigia* cut across the *Grenfell*'s bow barely

50 feet away, a dangerous move. In spite of this harassment, the *Grenfell's* trailing warp cutter sliced through the steel cables suspending the Spanish trawler's nets, and the net and catch dropped to the ocean bottom.

The presence of the armed *Vigia* on Grand Banks waters was a little disconcerting, although the situation became almost comical when its captain, shortly after the encounter with the *Grenfell*, asked permission to enter St. John's to refuel and permit his seasick crew to recover their sea legs. Crossing the North Atlantic, it seems, was somewhat more treacherous and demanding than patrolling the coast of Spain in the Bay of Biscay. Embarrassment over the *Vigia's* fuel and crew problems, plus our continued strong posture, convinced all the Spanish vessels to withdraw from the Nose and Tail, and the informal talks continued.

"Score one for the good guys," somebody said at the ministry, and I had to agree with them. But only one.

LATER THAT MONTH, Emma Bonino was scheduled to speak in New York at a United Nations Conference on Straddling and Highly Migratory Fish Stocks. I was to speak immediately after her. She and I were still trading charges back and forth across the Atlantic, and I suspected that a potential "she says, he says" exchange in New York would accomplish nothing. Canada needed more than rhetoric. We needed to present irrefutable, concrete evidence that would generate wide news coverage. We had it, I believed, in the illegal net recovered from the *Estai*, and I proposed trucking it from St. John's to New York, complete with fisheries enforcement inspectors and RCMP officers to guard it.

The logistics would be considerable. These nets are monsters, fully 20 stories high when suspended. Aside from the practical problem of transporting it south, I had to overcome concern and skepticism by a number of people, including some of those closest to me in the ministry. Paul Lapointe, our ambassador of fisheries who quarterbacked things for us at the UN, shook his head at the idea. Paul had done an amazing job for us, negotiating a new extension of the Law of the Sea to include enforcement of conservation measures of highly migratory and high seas species. He made the case that oceans everywhere were being depleted by overfishing and that laws were needed to stop these practices beyond the 200-mile zone. He was concerned about the risk of trivializing these serious efforts. I appreciated his position, but the opportunity to state our case so directly was too good to ignore.

Foreign Affairs, as usual, opposed any dramatic action by Canada that might embarrass another nation. Word was leaked to the PM, who called me, wanting to know what I had in mind. While I could bypass Paul Lapointe and ignore Foreign Affairs, I couldn't go forward without Jean Chrétien on my side, and so I asked for a chance to pitch the idea directly to him.

"Are you sure about this?" he said when I finished.

I assured him it would work.

"If it doesn't work," the PM said, "it's on your head!"

At times like those, you have to trust your instincts, and I did. I dispatched the net to New York, arranged to have it displayed on a barge anchored in the East River across from UN headquarters—and kept my fingers crossed.

Emma Bonino, bless her heart, played her role as though I had written her words myself. In her UN speech on behalf of the EU, she ridiculed our description of the net, suggesting we were fabricating the evidence. "Where is this net?" she sneered. "Who has seen this net? I have not seen the net. Nobody has seen the net. Only the Canadians have seen this net!" If the net existed, Canada must have planted the evidence, she suggested. "I would be surprised if they don't find heroin, cocaine—I don't know what next!" She called us pirates, aggressors and a danger to sailors on the high seas everywhere.

I spoke after Bonino, and while I was tempted to address all of her heated charges, I stuck to my written text and made no reference to Bonino's claims. As soon as I left the podium, of course, the press swarmed around me, repeating Bonino's statements and challenging me to produce evidence.

"Do you want to see the net for yourselves?" I asked. Naturally, they did. I invited a much-surprised international press scrum to follow me, and together we walked to chartered buses parked in front of the UN. We drove the journalists and video camera operators to the barge anchored on the riverbank, where Premier Clyde Wells and I held a press conference with the net strung behind us and some stern-looking fisheries enforcement officers and RCMP officers standing by.

Clyde Wells and I displayed samples of undersize fish taken from the *Estai*, explained how the net's illegal liner killed everything in its path and answered the reporters' questions. As we were leaving the barge, Joan Bryden of Southam News shouted, "What are you saying to the world today?"

I responded: "We are down to the last lonely, unloved, unattractive little turbot clinging by its fingernails to the Grand Banks of Newfoundland, saying: 'Someone, reach out and save me in this eleventh hour as I'm about to go down to extinction.'" That's the quote that went around the world, and the turbot was lonely no more.

Was my line a little over the top? Perhaps. But we had set out to protect the dwindling fish stocks on the Grand Banks for future generations, and we were being called pirates, hooligans and liars for doing so. We had to get the message across powerfully, and displaying the net at that time and in that fashion did the job. Canada has nothing to apologize for. Bonino and the EU had challenged us to put up or shut up, and we responded in a manner that left them, not us, speechless.

After inspecting the net with their own eyes, the media, of course, couldn't wait to get Bonino's side of the story, and that's when she lost it. "Why is it nobody believes me?" she shouted. "You always believe the Canadians: nobody believes me!" By

Two-thirds of the Tobin brood, mid-1950s, Stephenville, Newfoundland.
Back row: Janet, Sherri, Gloria; Front: Brian, Terry, Alice

Jodean Smith and Brian, taken in 1977
to announce our engagement.

The original campaign team, Humber-Port au Port-St. Barbe, 1980.

Brian and his father, Vince, in St. David's, Newfoundland, 1982.

With the Right Honorable Pierre Elliott Trudeau, in Ottawa, 1985.
(Jean-Marc Carisse/PMO)

Making Liberal Leader John Turner (centre) an honorary member of the
Rat Pack in 1985. Brian, Don Boudria, Sheila Copps, John Nunziata.
(Ron Poling/Canadian Press)

Christmas, 1988: Jodean, Heather, Jack, Brian, Adam.
The 3 for 3 T-shirts celebrate Brian's third election victory.
(Jean-Marc Carisse/PMO)

The whole Tobin gang. Back row, left to right: Craig, Paul, Brian, Vince, Terry, Ross; Front row, left to right: Sherri, Janet, mother Flo, Alice, Gloria

A Rideau Hall reception after Tobin's swearing-in as Minister of Fisheries in 1993. Jodean, Prime Minister Chrétien, Jack, Adam, Heather.
(Jean-Marc Carisse/PMO)

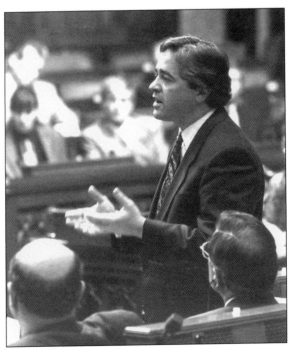

Making a point in the House of Commons, 1994.

The Fisheries patrol vessel *Cape Roger* returning to St. John's harbour after the 1995 high seas dispute over foreign overfishing. *(Gerry Boland/Boland Photography)*

In Cornwall, England, meeting "The Cornishman" in August 1995. Cornwall supported Canada's position on foreign overfishing by flying hundreds of Canadian flags.

In New York, in front of the infamous net cut from the Spanish vessel, the *Estai,* 1995. *(RichardDrew/Canadian Press/AP Photo)*

This cartoon, published in the wake of Tobin's order to fire across the bow of the Spanish boat, the *Estai,* earned him a lasting nickname. *(Theo Moudakis)*

A House of Commons page delivers flowers from a fellow MP to acknowledge the victory in the turbot dispute, 1995.

More than 100,000 Canadians came to Montreal in support of national unity on October 27, 1995. *(Peter Jones/Reuters/Archive Photos)*

On the hustings in Burnt Point, Newfoundland, during the 1996 provincial election. *(Keith Gosse/Canadian Press)*

In Bull Arm, Newfoundland, with the Hibernia Oil Platform in the background, 1997. *(Greg Locke/Stray Light)*

With Her Majesty,
Queen Elizabeth in Bonavista,
Newfoundland, 1997.

With Irish Prime Minister John Bruton in 1997.

Quebec Premier Lucien Bouchard with Premier Tobin in Churchill Falls, Labrador. The two premiers were there to promote the development of the Lower Churchill hydroelectric project, 1998. *(Paul Chiasson/Canadian Press)*

Premier Tobin shares a laugh with Prime Minister Jean Chrétien after accepting the Constitutional Amendment to Newfoundland's Term 17 in 1998. Governor General Romeo LeBlanc looks on.
(Jonathan Hayward/Canadian Press)

Vince and Flo Tobin celebrating their 50th wedding anniversary.

Max Short, Mrs. Short (Max's mother), Brian, Mr. Short (Max's father), and
Ethel Short in St. John's, Newfoundland, 1999.

Fishing with Bill Rowat at the
annual Rick Hansen spinal
cord research fundraiser,
Langara Lodge, B.C. in 1998.

Premier Tobin with Jodean, on election night in February 1999, after
winning a second majority government. *(Bob Crocker/Crocker Photography)*

Premier Tobin with three of the women who became cabinet ministers
in the Tobin government (left to right): Julie Bettney, Brian,
Judy Foote, Howard Foote and Joan Marie Aylward.

Premier's Staff Party 2000—Newly minted Premier Tulk gives Brian his
blessing as he returns to the Ottawa cabinet.

Talking with Prime Minister Chrétien, US President George W. Bush and First Lady Laura Bush, 2001. *(Diana Murphy/PMO)*

At the Committee for Economic Development annual dinner in New York City, May 2001.

With Heidi Bonnell and Jodean.

The Tobin family on the Hamilton River beach
in Happy Valley, Labrador, 1998. *(Michelle R. Baikie)*

this time, the press was either openly hostile toward her or laughing at her, and she stormed out of the session to catch the next plane back to Brussels. One of the newspapers covering the story headlined it as "Bonino Goes Bananas!"

THE NET INCIDENT BEGAN MOVING THINGS in our direction, although it was a longer and rougher journey than we had expected. The EU's support of Spain started to crumble, driven in part by resentment over the practices of the Spanish fleet. From South America to Africa and the North Sea, countries that had complained long and loud about the rapacious habits of Spanish fishermen began applauding Canada's actions. British MPs stood in the House of Commons to pledge support for our efforts. The tabloid *Daily Mail* ran a front-page editorial demanding that Britain stand four-square behind us, and John Major, abandoning the fudging expressed in his letter to Prime Minister Chrétien a month earlier, told the British House of Commons: "I believe Canada is quite right to take a tough stand on enforcement."

Spain, concerned that EU support was crumbling, began fighting a rear-guard action. "What is at risk here is the very credibility of the EU and its member states," Spanish PM Gonzales wrote to the French prime minister. "A split within the Union would be seen as a sign of weakness, and jeopardize the image and efficiency we want for the external relations of the European Union."

"Image and efficiency." Nothing, of course, about illegal fishing practices, concealed catches, duplicate logs and the eradication for all time of a major food source. Frankly, I found such hypocrisy disgusting, which is not diplomatic language, but how far had diplomacy taken us?

THE EU CALLED FOR A ROUND of bilateral negotiations in early April, and I dispatched Bill Rowat to handle things in Brussels. The EU may have thought we were anxious to end things, and of course we were—on our terms. My hasty response to the EU's call had little to do with the prospect of negotiations and more to do with happenings in Ottawa. At the first call for bilateral talks, I began hearing rumblings that Foreign Affairs was pressuring the PM and the Privy Council to assume control of things. Shooting machine guns across the bow of another country's ships was not part of the how-to manual at Foreign Affairs. Its expertise consisted of smiling, nodding, shaking hands and searching for common ground.

This was not the case with our Foreign Affairs people on locations around the world, who supported our fisheries conservation efforts with enthusiasm and energy, earning my deep gratitude. It was the endless second-guessing by some members of Foreign Affairs in Ottawa that irked me and others at DFO. Foreign Affairs, simply put, had lost control of the file. They wanted it back so that they could resume their schmoozing and begin smoothing ruffled relationships.

I understood their concern. I was more than prepared to smile, nod, shake hands and sign agreements. I just wasn't prepared to do this dance to a tune played by Foreign Affairs. The day after the EU proposed the talks, Bill was on a plane with an overnight bag, ready to submit his credentials and exert his authority in hammering out a deal that would save both the turbot and Spain's face, if possible. Bill was soon joined in Brussels by a couple of staff members, whom he welcomed warmly, and by Undersecretary of Foreign Affairs Gordon Smith, whom he merely welcomed.

Smith's arrival launched a tug-of-war to determine just who was speaking for Canada. The EU representatives sensed this fracturing of Canadian leadership and began trying to take advantage of our apparent weakening position. Even after Smith returned to Ottawa after a day or two, we learned that some officials at Foreign Affairs, the PM's Office and the Privy Council Office were sending nudge-nudge, wink-wink messages to the

EU suggesting that Bill and I were posturing and that things weren't as serious as they appeared. At one point, a Privy Council clerk called Bill from Ottawa and demanded to know "what the hell is going on over there," suggesting that we were being inflexible. Reportedly, the EU was informed that the PM's Office and the Privy Council Office were preparing to rein me in, along with Bill Rowat, our ADMs, our staff and the brave men and women on our patrol vessels.

This was outrageous. It encouraged the EU to delay the settlement. Jean Chrétien never asked me to capitulate on Canada's demands for compliance with conservation rules. Had he done so, I would have resigned without question.

Finally, Bill called me from Brussels. "We need some sort of statement from you," Bill said, "that says we're still serious, that we're as determined to protect the fish now as we were when we pulled in the *Estai*."

I told Bill that I didn't think a mere statement by me would accomplish much, but that I would work on something.

Bill woke in Brussels the following morning to hear reports that a Canadian fisheries patrol vessel had almost side-swiped a Spanish trawler in the dead of night on the Nose of the Grand Banks. The Spanish captain reported that a large ship with its lights out had charged his vessel, blowing its horn and causing panic aboard the Spanish boat. Shortly after the incident, a radio exchange between the Spanish fishing captain and the Spanish naval patrol vessel was intercepted, in which the fishing captain complained to the naval captain that the navy was not protecting the trawlers. After calling the Spanish navy "useless," the trawler skipper announced he was going below to change his underwear.

The EU and the Spanish ambassador were in a frenzy, calling Canada's behaviour "reckless." When asked about the incident, I suggested they were surely overreacting and questioned the veracity of the Spanish skipper's account, noting the expert seamanship of our captains and crews. In any case, Bill noted a new sense of crisis on the part of the EU that day. Suddenly the log-jam broke, and helpful proposals started being tossed at him from across the desk. To this day, Bill suspects that I asked one of our patrol vessels to take provocative action. To this day, I refuse to comment.

After more than a week of tough slugging—Bill had planned to be in Brussels no more than a couple of days—we hammered out a deal in principle, and Bill returned home. Almost as soon as he arrived back in Ottawa, the EU began a nitpicking exercise that threatened wholesale renegotiation. We were furious, and announced that we were not prepared to alter the core terms of the deal. To underline our message, we prepared another *aide-mémoire*, this one going into much greater detail on the prospects of armed confrontation between our fisheries patrol vessels and naval destroyers, and armed Spanish patrol vessels (assuming they were better equipped and crewed than the unfortunate *Vigia*). We also drew up an "Operational Plan to Effect an Arrest," listing the fleet of ships available to us on the Banks—seven vessels, among them the destroyer HMCS *Gatineau*. The six patrol vessels carried more than 150 personnel, including almost 40 armed boarders; four of the ships were armed with twin .50-calibre machine guns, and two had warp-cutting capabilities. The operational plan loosened the strings somewhat, providing our fisheries patrol personnel with wider authority. Labelled "secret," its existence was acknowledged among both PMO and PCO personnel. Eventually, I suspect, its details were leaked to the EU negotiators. Supported by our response not to reopen negotiations, things settled down, and by the end of the month we had a deal.

Was the effort worth allegedly breaking one international law to enforce another? Did we gain anything from breaking the widely accepted character of Canada as a peace-loving, non-belligerent nation in defence of an ugly fish?

Yes, yes and yes. Clearly.

We did not bring back stocks that were already lost. But the stocks that were closed—the flat fish stocks, the red fish stocks, the turbot—have since come back in volume to the point where they are once again commercially viable. The biggest loss, of course, was the cod. Ten years after that fishery closed, the spawning rate continues to decline, and the cod may never come back. With their near disappearance, crab have become abundant off the Atlantic Coast, providing economic opportunity to some of the communities displaced by the loss of the cod.

Meanwhile, the effects continued to spread. During the summer of 2002, the first of a number of Newfoundland coastal communities began to resettle when the residents of Harbour Deep voted to pull up stakes and, with assistance from government, relocate to other areas with more promise of opportunity. They were followed by a similar request to move by the citizens of the village of Petites on the south coast. Thousands of coastal Newfoundlanders and Labradorians have abandoned their traditional communities, many moving elsewhere in Canada in search of employment and the promise of a brighter future.

The near eradication of the cod must serve as a warning to the world. With the technology to locate and harvest the resources of our oceans with ruthless efficiency, we can no longer treat the waters beyond a nation's 200-mile zone as lawless frontiers where environmental criminals are free to plunder a species into commercial extinction. In the case of Grand Banks cod, an ecological balance that existed undisturbed for thousands of years was upset within a decade or two.

The same technology used to harm our oceans can be used to heal them. We must monitor fishing activity both inside and outside our 200-mile limit. We must rigorously enforce the rules of conservation and demand that other nations police their fleets when they fish adjacent to Canadian waters. If they fail to do so, Canada should again enforce the rules on our continental shelf beyond the 200-mile limit. If we don't, who will?

Sadly, we appear to be headed back into another overfishing catastrophe. Our fisheries inspectors are once again discovering

illegal nets, fake logs and hidden catches. The Europeans
continue to do this in the face of apparent complacency on our
part. If we do not take appropriate action, we can expect to face
disaster after disaster until all commercial species of fish have
vanished for good.

And consider this: on September 20, 2002, at a NAFO
meeting in Spain, delegates voted a 42,000-tonne turbot quota
for 2003, despite the fact that the NAFO scientific council
recommended a limit of 36,000 tonnes. When NAFO nations
ignore the advice of their own experts and choose to catch more
turbot than the stock can sustain, Canada must act. If this means
unilaterally extending Canada's jurisdiction to include the Nose
and Tail of the Grand Banks in order to manage migratory fish
stocks, then let's get on with it.

A CROWDED RALLY, A STARLIT SKY

O UR EFFORTS TO SAVE THE TURBOT and make our point to the EU and the rest of the world generated a gratifying response. We had stretched the rules to make a point—one that redefined not just how Canada should act to conserve a dwindling resource, but also how each nation should accept responsibility and be prepared, if necessary, to take the flak. We were not insisting on exclusive rights to the fish on the Banks, nor were we focusing entirely on the situation for our own benefit. We were working just as hard for the future of fisheries in other countries as we were for our own, and if it took an uncharacteristically Canadian act of militancy to achieve success, that was unfortunate. But what was the option?

Spain and Portugal never saw it this way, of course. Fishermen in other countries, especially those in Britain, understood it immediately. Jodean and I sampled their appreciation when we vacationed in England during the summer of 1995, visiting Cornwall and Devon. In Cornwall we were guests of the Fisheries Festival, where we had the special experience of seeing all of the coastal towns and villages bedecked with Canadian flags. They were flying from boats, from businesses, from houses in Penzance, St. Ives, Plymouth, Torbay, Falmouth—everywhere along England's southern coast that summer.

It wasn't just fishermen who appreciated Canada's stance, by the way. In one town, the local constabulary presented me with one of its hats and a billy stick. When representatives of an animal rights group showed up to protest Canada's seal hunt, they were warned against attempting to upset the festivities, and it was suggested that they pack up their placards and vacate the town. They did.

We returned home from vacation to the turmoil of the Quebec referendum on separation, or "sovereignty association," led by Jacques Parizeau in Quebec City and Lucien Bouchard in Ottawa.

Parizeau and Bouchard were as dissimilar as any two politicians can be while seeking a common goal. In this case, their goal was the breakup of a country that many people throughout the world admired, then and now.

I have known Lucien Bouchard as a Mulroney MP, as an Opposition leader and as a fellow premier. In case it need be said, I disagree totally with his point of view on Canadian federalism, but I accept that he is a passionate, committed man. I'm just not sure that he is, or ever was, a *séparatiste* in the pure sense of the word.

To my mind, there are two distinct groups of Quebec separatists. The Angry faction are mad as hell and will not rest until Quebec obtains total division from Canada and is recognized by the rest of the world as a separate nation. Their goal has little to do with a proactive vision, or an effort at nation-building, nor is their resentment rooted in contemporary concerns of role and identity within Canada. Instead, it is founded on the outcome of the Battle of the Plains of Abraham, nearly 250 years ago. Many aging Quebec separatists grew up at a time in Quebec when, quite understandably, they rejected the notion that their fathers and families should work a lifetime in industries owned and controlled by the English minority. They looked around and saw too few francophone owners and entrepreneurs in leadership positions in a community and province where francophones were a clear majority. They refuse to this day to acknowledge that the battles of yesterday are over.

Francophones are not only captains of industry in Quebec. They are outstanding Canadian leaders in every field of endeavour, both in our country and around the world. They have formed productive alliances with members of Quebec's minority language business community and together they are shaping a new competitive and dynamic business community. The Angry separatists are still trying to fight battles that have long since been won, and in nursing the wounds of their youth, they have alienated a new generation of Quebecers who are confident and outward looking.

The other faction, I call Visionary separatists. In contrast with the Angry group, the Visionary's self-awareness and vision seek full expression in nationhood that celebrates cultural and linguistic identity. Visionary separatists are more dangerous to Canada, in my opinion, because their efforts can be presented in a reasonable manner. The Angry separatist waving a clenched fist is an anachronism and a walking cliché. But the Visionary separatist in a tailored suit, speaking of negotiations and shrugging off questions of economics and responsibility, appears more plausible and presents a greater risk to Canadian federalism.

IN MID-OCTOBER 1995, I began talking to polling firms across the country asking for comment on the Quebec separatist referendum barely two weeks away. According to pollsters like Angus Reid, who delivered the most disturbing wake-up call, the federalist No side was 7 to 14 points behind the separatists.

I couldn't believe it. I didn't want to believe it, nor could most of Canada outside Quebec. But each of the major polls in the country was saying the same thing: the separatists were going to win and, no matter how much Parizeau, Bouchard and the PQ might sugar-coat it, they would break up Canada. We had senior members of the cabinet saying to each other, "What happens if we lose?" The unthinkable had become a real possibility.

And it could not be ignored. We could not say the referendum didn't matter, that it didn't count, that it would not be "official," because Ottawa had engaged in the process before Lucien Bouchard took command of the sovereignist movement, back when polls indicated the separatists would be rejected. The federal side accepted that the referendum would decide the outcome, notwithstanding the unfair wording of the question, which was a convoluted structure that managed to avoid using the word "separate." The prime minister had become involved in the exercise according to rules dictated by the PQ, and we would be obliged to live with the result.

Things were made more complex by the real possibility that, should the PQ succeed and Canada be required to negotiate with Quebec to determine its new status, the prime minister's authority to speak for Canada would be challenged because he was a Quebec MP. Who would speak for Canada? Who would decide Canada's response in the event of a Yes vote? We were entering uncharted territory here. How many countries in all of history had engaged in negotiations leading to breakup, without the use of military force or political coups?

I attended a dinner meeting with several of my cabinet colleagues over the weekend to talk about these questions and the danger we were facing. On Monday morning, reflecting on everything I had heard, I arrived at my office feeling disheartened. It was October 23, exactly one week before the referendum.

I remember sitting in the boardroom that morning, with the usual group of 14 or so staff members around the table. It was our routine Monday morning review of situations across the country and their possible effect on our areas of responsibility. Ten minutes into the meeting I began looking at all the faces and asking myself, "What is happening here?" Here we are, one week from the possible breakup of Canada, conducting business as usual. It was time to do something.

I suspended the meeting and asked Bill Rowat, my deputy minister, and my executive assistant, Gary Anstey, to join me in my office. I shared with them the latest poll results. "Gentlemen, this whole situation is surreal," I said. "Here we are facing at the very least a possible constitutional crisis in a week's time, and we're behaving as though everything were normal. And it's not."

Somebody asked what we could do in less than a week that would make an impact in our favour. Perhaps, I replied, we could try to influence some scheduled event, some activity where the groundwork has already been done. I asked my director of policy, Francine Ducros, to find something in which we could participate, and she identified a noontime rally of business people scheduled for Montreal's Place du Canada on Friday, four days away.

My first thought was that the entire ministry should be there. We should shut down our office for the day and show up to lend our support. How could we conduct business as usual on Friday knowing that Monday could mark the beginning of the end of Canada as we knew it? It was preposterous.

Once the idea was in place, it began to grow. Why only our ministry? Why not other federal ministries? And why only government members? Everyone stood to lose if the Yes side won.

I always rejected the idea that the question of Quebec separation was a subject only for the people of Quebec to decide. The notion that people in other parts of Canada should be told to "stay home" because the question of separation is an exclusive debate for Quebecers was unacceptable, and it had been a mistake for the federal government to accept the separatists' rules. I refused to acknowledge that a sovereignist government should frame the question, shape the debate and tell the rest of Canada it was none of our business.

Less than a week before the vote, we couldn't insist on changing the rules to make them fair. Nor would threats and warnings about the risks of sovereignty be effective; in fact, they could backfire and generate resentment among swing voters who were waiting until the last minute to make up their minds.

Only one message, it seemed to me, could be effectively conveyed to Quebec by the rest of Canada in the time available. That message would be *we care*. I wanted to give Canadians outside Quebec a chance to express that sentiment, because I knew it was true.

Lucien Bouchard, recognizing some of the weariness that Quebecers and the rest of Canadians were feeling about the separatism question, had been saying to the Québécois: "This debate has gone on too long, and it will not end until we separate." That was bad enough, but he was also saying: "The anglophones don't care. They are tired. They are fed up. And who can blame them? We have put *les Anglais* through hell again and again and again." This was an entirely new strategy for him and the *séparatistes*, this idea of suggesting that separatism would be a welcome event to the rest of Canada, ending the pain Quebec had been inflicting on us. To the soft middle of Bouchard's and Parizeau's constituency—the group that felt uncomfortable with the status quo and equally uncomfortable with the sovereignists—it was working. It was wrong, but it was working.

I became convinced that, if we could demonstrate that Bouchard and Parizeau were wrong, we could sway those who were buying into this new strategy. If they realized that the rest of the country cared deeply and was willing to continue the kind of dialogue that had led to changes in the relationship with Quebec, they would reconsider their support for the separatist cause.

I began by calling Frank McKenna in Fredericton and telling him about the rally. "If we were to organize a federalist rally," I asked him, "could you get the troops up to Montreal?"

Frank quickly sized up the situation and made a decision. "If you're asking me if I can help out by bringing people to Montreal," Frank replied, "you can count on it. I'll be there. Tell me when and where, and I'll bring as many New Brunswickers as I can."

Frank's response gave me a lift. If McKenna believed this was worth the effort, the idea couldn't be that far-fetched.

Next, I asked Lloyd Axworthy, the minister of employment and immigration, about the idea of bringing in people from Manitoba. Lloyd agreed, but raised a serious practical question. "How are we going to get people from Manitoba to Montreal in time?" he asked.

"If we got an aircraft," I asked, "could you fill it up?" Lloyd said he could. I called friends from British Columbia and asked the same question: if I could get a plane from Vancouver to Montreal, could they fill it up with federalist supporters? Ross Fitzpatrick (now a senator) agreed that he could. I repeated the process all across Canada. I called senators, cabinet ministers, MPs, premiers, anyone I knew who shared my concerns and who would agree to take action. My message was the same: we have to do something. There is a rally in Montreal on Friday. Let's gather as many Canadians as we can and have them deliver the two words that could make a difference: *we care.*

Of course, promises weren't going to carry people from BC, Alberta, Nova Scotia and elsewhere to Montreal: planes were. So that afternoon I called Hollis Harris, then president of Air Canada. It was the first time I had ever spoken to Harris (who, incidentally, is a southern US citizen through and through). I emphasized that I was speaking not as a minister of the Crown but as a private citizen. I insisted that he consider the proposal I was about to make in that context, and whatever decision he reached would have no bearing, pro or con, on his dealings with the government.

I outlined the situation to him, reviewing the poll results, mentioning Friday's rally in Montreal, suggesting that a show of concern might swing the decision and confirming that I had obtained assurance that thousands of Canadians would gather in Montreal to demonstrate their support for Canada. Could Air Canada supply the planes to take them, and how much would it cost?

Hollis Harris's response was amazing. "You want planes," he said in his soft Georgia drawl. "I'll get you planes. We'll put them where you need them. Count on it."

I thanked him and immediately called the president of Canadian Airlines. I told him I had just spoken to Hollis Harris, who promised to supply aircraft where and when we wanted them, and then I asked what Canadian Airlines could do for us. The airline promised to get back to me, and within a short time a representative called to announce a special "unity rate" for anyone choosing to fly to Montreal for Friday's rally. The unity rate cut fares by as much as 90 percent and, of course, Air Canada matched the fare immediately. The next day, VIA Rail announced a 60-percent reduction on all round-trip fares to Montreal for the weekend.

I had yet to discuss any of this with the prime minister, and so at the cabinet meeting the next morning I asked permission to speak outside the normal agenda. The PM agreed, but first he gave his overview of the referendum situation. It was sobering. The next day he would be moved nearly to tears when addressing caucus on the subject, and he would later challenge undecided Quebecers, in a TV address, to come up with "one good reason to destroy Canada."

When the prime minister finished, I mentioned the upcoming rally in Montreal. "We can't just sit on our hands," I said. "Premier Bouchard has been successful at convincing Quebecers that the rest of us are indifferent, that we don't care. That's not true, as everyone in this room knows, but it is a very effective line. We must give Canadians a chance to show Quebecers that they *do* care." I proposed that we have as large a delegation as possible in Montreal. The prime minister asked what kind of showing we might have there. I thought perhaps 3,000, 4,000, maybe even as many as 5,000 people, would come to Montreal on short notice.

By that time, I had received responses from government leaders coast to coast, as well as the solemn support of Air Canada and Canadian Airlines. "In the very worst-case scenario,"

I said, "we will have at least 5,000 people from across Canada there on Friday at noon." I mentioned the premiers who had promised their full support—Frank McKenna, Clyde Wells, Ralph Klein and others. One part of the story that has not been told in detail until now was the solid backing of corporate Canada; all the major business leaders that my office approached opened their chequebooks and asked how much we needed. I reviewed all of this activity and enthusiasm, then said: "Prime Minister, we don't have time to talk about this in greater detail. If you give me the green light, I'll leave this room now and get things moving."

The prime minister polled the other ministers, saying in effect, "Should we let Tobin go and do this?" The reaction, not surprisingly, was mixed. The most common response was, "It can't hurt. It's 'Hail Mary' time after all." And the majority of ministers offered help from their own regions of the country. Some ministers from Quebec were concerned that it could backfire, which was a legitimate concern. It was a gambit, after all, and if the rally created a problem, we would have no time to rectify it before the vote. But there was no time to debate the issue in detail either. When all was said and done, the prime minister looked across the table at me and said, "Brian—go!" And I went.

When I returned to my office and announced that we had full approval, it was like unleashing a tidal wave across the country. I was never more proud of my staff than on that day. VIA Rail came on board, and the bus companies began getting involved. I had young junior staffers, who had never been involved in any kind of campaign, receiving commitments of money from one area of the country and directing it to other areas that needed it. Local committees began springing up to handle things in their districts, and the entire process assumed a life of its own.

The next day, Wednesday, I appeared on CTV's morning news show, *Canada AM*, and invited Canadians to come to Montreal by air, by train, by bus, by any means possible. I thanked Air

Canada for its support and announced the Canadian Airlines unity fare. I did CBC-TV and took calls from radio shows all across Canada, and shortly after lunch Canadian Airlines called and asked me to quit talking about the special fare— they were sold out. Over 25,000 seats had been filled in barely four hours.

I attended a scheduled caucus session that afternoon and several MPs gathered around me saying, "You went on national television this morning and told people if they wanted to come to Montreal for the rally on Friday and needed more information, they should call their MPs. Well, they're still calling! Thousands of them!" There was some good-natured kidding about making extra work for them, but the caucus members were already lining up buses, checking train schedules and filling seats with enthusiastic Canadians, who would carry the message that Canada did care after all, and that Lucien Bouchard, Jacques Parizeau and the others were wrong.

What happened in Montreal on Friday, October 27, 1995, was a spontaneous reaction from Canadians who had been waiting for an opportunity to make themselves heard, to stand up and be counted. All they needed was someone to tell them when and where to appear. No individual, no political party and no organization can generate that kind of response. The urge to participate resided in the hearts of everyone who showed up that day, and everything else was just a catalyst that permitted it to happen. The only thing I can take credit for is issuing the invitation. The people of Canada had been feeling the same kind of anxiety about our country's future that I had been feeling. It was there, it was real and it was powerful.

Canadians were uncomfortable about not being part of the debate. They were desperately looking for a time and a place to express themselves, and they did it by showing up in Montreal waving both Canada's flag and Quebec's flag together. The result was the most magical display of popular support I have seen.

Like me, no one who participated will ever forget the emotion of the day.

I awoke the morning of the rally with the realization that, should the day's event fail, it would be devastating to Canada. Jodean and I, our children and some staff members had taken a room high up in Le Château Champlain hotel overlooking Place du Canada. At mid-morning, I could feel my heart sinking: the square was virtually empty. People were setting up tents, platforms and sound systems, but they were people who *had* to be there. The only people who counted would be those who *chose* to be there, and so far they were notable by their absence. Had there been a collective change of mind? Had the reports that morning of thousands of passengers aboard aircraft, trains and buses heading to Montreal been exaggerated? I feared they might have been.

About 11 a.m. the square began to fill, first with a trickle and then with a flood. I remember cheering at every fresh wave of demonstrators who arrived, waving Canadian flags. They stepped out of cars and off buses, they emerged from subway stations, they walked from hotels and tourist homes and private homes, just to be in the square that day, for Canada. Within an hour, the entire square and all the side streets were crowded with people and flags, an intermingled sea of celebration. I remember the enormous relief I felt for Canada and for everyone who loved the country enough to do whatever it took to keep it together.

No country is more celebrated for its patriotism than the United States, and so the words of Jim Blanchard, the US ambassador to Canada at the time, are as good a description of October 27 as we are likely to hear. "Between 100,000 and 150,000 people came from all over the province [of Quebec] and the country to demonstrate their love of Canada," Jim wrote in his book *Behind the Embassy Door*, "in a colourful, enthusiastic and emotionally stirring show of flags and patriotic speeches. They flew in from British Columbia and Newfoundland for the day; they drove all night from Toronto, and came by bus from

New Brunswick; they brought their children and their hearts. It was a dramatic, powerful, watershed moment in the history of the country."

Did the rally change minds and swing votes to the No side? No one truly knows. I feel that it did. I also know that the rally, at the very least, heartened those who were fighting for the federalist side within Quebec and assured them that Canadians outside Quebec were not indifferent to their fate. Remember that a good many Quebecers attended as well, including thousands of francophones opposed to separation. I watched them reach out and embrace those who had travelled thousands of miles to express their concern. "*Merci*—Thank you for coming," they said to people from Alberta, British Columbia, Ontario, New Brunswick, Newfoundland and Labrador and elsewhere. Remember, too, that almost every premier of Canada was there in the crowd, shaking hands and waving Canadian flags, along with union leaders, leaders of the Opposition, artists and business executives. They all came just to say that they cared and that they loved both Canada and Quebec. The Canadian family stood united in Montreal. How can you be indifferent to that kind of expression? The answer is, you could not, especially if you were a Québécois trying to decide to vote one way or the other.

JEAN CHRÉTIEN WAS UNFAIRLY CRITICIZED in some quarters for not taking a more active role in the referendum. The truth is, he was very active on the No side, working behind the scenes. No one who saw and heard him reviewing the situation in caucus could doubt his commitment. It should also be remembered that, until Lucien Bouchard's assumption of leadership of the separatist referendum campaign a month earlier, the Yes side had been in trouble. Bouchard's entry galvanized things and suddenly the pendulum was swinging in support of the separatists. Until then, there was no advantage for Jean Chrétien to attempt to dominate the debate in Quebec. After all, Jean Charest was the federalist leader in Quebec, and he fought with passion and determination.

Bouchard's arrival altered everything. In late 1995, Lucien Bouchard was something of a modern-day Lazarus. The previous year he had fallen ill to the dreadful "flesh-eating disease," which took his leg and almost his life. He now walked on a prosthesis with the aid of a cane, showing great courage and determination. His plight touched the heart of every Canadian, and so it's easy to understand how Quebecers felt about the man.

Had Parizeau not relinquished the campaign's direction to the vastly more capable Bouchard, the crisis might never have arisen and no one would be second-guessing Jean Chrétien's strategy. Had the prime minister injected his views into the campaign early and generated a backlash leading to a marginal victory for the PQ, the same people who wanted him to become more active would have castigated him for not standing aside and letting things unfold as they should. Politicians learn to tolerate this kind of extreme criticism in the media—at least they had better. We simply accept it and move on, knowing that we have done our best as we saw things. What else can anyone do?

I was invited to be with Peter Mansbridge on the CBC "Decision Desk" on referendum night, and along with millions of other Canadians I spent the evening watching a bar graph edge back and forth as the night wore on. When it moved in one direction, it meant the likely withdrawal of Quebec from Canada; when it moved in the other direction, it indicated a growing repudiation of Parizeau's and Bouchard's philosophy. I never thought I could be so totally mesmerized by a computer-generated graphic.

When the results indicated a tiny margin of victory (50.6–49.4) for the federalists and we were breathing a sigh of relief, Parizeau appeared on camera to blame "outsiders and moneyed interests," unmasking the petty views of certain corners of the movement. In fairness to Lucien Bouchard, I have never heard him speak in that manner.

Parizeau and those who most closely supported him were not focused on opening Quebec to the wider world. They were talking like people who anticipated the creation of a more closed society, restricted in membership and outlook, while Canada was moving in the other direction, embracing diversity and drawing strength from it. As much as anything else, that distinction explains the difference between Parizeau and his followers, and the rest of Canada, and it is all the evidence I need that the PQ and the Bloc Québécois will never succeed.

LUCIEN BOUCHARD WAS A PROUD, intelligent man, a shrewd politician and, according to my categorization, a Visionary sovereignist. It is unfortunate that he could not continue to support the federalist cause, where he would have been very effective. Who knows how far he might have gone in the dismal post-Mulroney years of the PC party? On more than one occasion, I told Bouchard over a glass of wine that he would have made a hell of a PM, had his passion been directed toward building Canada instead of tearing it apart.

In that sense, Bouchard was a little like Lévesque. They were both passionate men who, once you got past political differences, were easy to empathize with. Their passion was understandable in men of their generation. The fathers and grandfathers of Bouchard and Lévesque worked for anglophone masters and anglophone owners, when a French accent or French surname was a barrier to success, recognition and fulfilment. It may be difficult for Anglo Canadians to admit, but it's true. People in Quebec saw their society shaped by a minority in their own province. The wounds from that period may have healed, but the scars remain.

Bouchard fought long and hard on behalf of the separatist movement, and I had several conversations with him when we were travelling as provincial premiers. During one trip, shortly before he withdrew from politics, Bouchard admitted to me that he was growing tired and disillusioned. One of the things that concerned him was the wide gap between his age and the age of his children. He was in his 60s and his children were still in public school. He wanted to provide for their education, but he was not a wealthy man. Political life is rewarding in many ways, but only those who are immersed in it for a lengthy period can appreciate the economic price to be paid, compared with people of similar age and abilities working similar hours in private life. Bouchard had come to the conclusion it was time to put family first, and go back to the practice of law. It would also remove him from the endless glare of the political spotlight, providing him and his family with some privacy. And that's what he did.

Aside from divergent visions of Canada and Quebec, the biggest problem I have with Lucien Bouchard related to his personal attacks on Jean Chrétien. There were times when Bouchard tried to demonize Chrétien in the eyes of Quebecers by pushing hot buttons that he knew would excite and anger them. I told Bouchard I thought these attacks were beneath him and very much at odds with the man I had come to know in private conversation. One of the great ironies of the Chrétien-Bouchard relationship is that they got along well during Team Canada trade missions. They were more than polite; they were courteous and considerate of each other, and they joined with the other first ministers in sharing humorous war stories of life as a government leader.

Lucien Bouchard is a man of achievement, aware of his strengths. In contrast, Jacques Parizeau strikes me as a man who is not at peace with himself, and this flaw is fatal to a politician. Everyone with lofty ambitions has to deal with failure or setbacks in his or her life.

Parizeau tried to walk away from the results of October 1995, but he could not let go. He continued to hang around, haunting Bouchard and later Bernard Landry, playing the role of a self-styled conscience for the PQ. Parizeau is the classic Angry separatist speaking in a cultured quasi-British accent. He is a man who missed his date with history and who has not been able to sleep well since the referendum. Lucien Bouchard, I suspect, sleeps very well indeed.

THE NARROWNESS OF THE NO VICTORY and Parizeau's disturbing comments troubled members of my staff who had accompanied me to Montreal. Driving back to Ottawa with them that evening, I listened to everyone reflect on the night's events. Had we really come close to fracturing Canada? Did Parizeau's comments represent the true heart of the PQ?

We had won, after all. My experience in politics said that if someone wins by 20,000 votes or by 20 votes, they have won regardless. Instead of regretting the slimness of the victory, I focused on celebrating the fact that Canada had survived a crisis that few, if any, countries ever face. A victory was still a victory.

I stopped the car somewhere along the road, and invited everyone to get out and look up at the sky. I remember it was a magnificent clear night and we were midway between the two cities of Ottawa and Montreal. The sky was brilliant with stars. "Look up," I said. "It's a beautiful evening, we are returning to Ottawa and it remains the capital of all of Canada. The stars are still shining on the best country in the world."

NEW ROLE, NEW TEAM, NEW CHALLENGES

T HE YEAR 1995 WAS, by any measure, an extraordinary one for me. It began with a victory over the EU at NAFO, led to the confrontation with the *Estai* and other vessels, saw the completion of the ground-breaking UN agreement on high seas fishing and flowed into the celebration of Canada in Montreal.

That would be more than enough for any year, but at the end of December Clyde Wells announced that he would be stepping down as premier of Newfoundland. Wells had accomplished much as Liberal leader in Newfoundland, and I admired the dignity and integrity he maintained through his years in office.

Even though we were both Newfoundland Liberals, Clyde and I were not always close, and we disagreed from time to time on some issues. Our biggest difference had been over Meech Lake, although the distance between us extended back to my initial election campaign in 1980, when Clyde was Mister Liberal in western Newfoundland. He traced his political ancestry back to the Joey Smallwood days, when Wells was minister of labour. He earned respect when he and John Crosbie quit Smallwood's cabinet in 1968 over policy differences with Premier Smallwood. Crosbie switched parties to become a Conservative, while Clyde returned to private life and practised law for many years.

Running for election as a 25-year-old rookie, I approached Clyde seeking his help in my campaign. He was courteous, but offered no assistance. In retrospect, I can understand his reasons, I suppose. Few people gave me a chance of winning, at the outset at least. It's a form of political triage that many of us practise from time to time when deciding how to allot limited resources.

After I surprised everyone and won the election, I began building my own political base. It excluded Clyde. I was determined to show that if I could win election as a rookie without his help, I could do without his assistance in the future as well. And I did.

Things got better in 1989 when the Newfoundland Liberals were looking for a leader to replace Leo Barry. I received a note from the provincial caucus inviting me to return to St. John's and assume the leadership. It had been a unanimous decision by the caucus and it was very compelling. I gave it a good deal of thought before turning it down, telling myself I was too young for the position. At 34, I believed my career rested at the federal level, and as a hard-hitting Opposition member, I believed I was making a difference.

A better choice, I believed, was Clyde Wells, who had not rejected the idea out of hand. I was part of several delegations of Liberals who went to visit Clyde at his home to say, "Clyde, this is your time. Give up your private life and assume the leader's position." I went with Mel Woodward, one of the most successful businessmen in Newfoundland and Labrador and a former member of Smallwood's cabinet, to make the case on behalf of federal Liberals. Chuck Furey, who earlier had been my executive assistant, and later became a senior cabinet minister, and Walter Carter, whose political career extended back many years over both federal and provincial jurisdictions, brought Clyde a message of support from the provincial caucus. (Walter wrote an entertaining account of his political career, called *Never a Dull Moment.*)

It was clear that Clyde was close to making up his mind to return to political life. During that visit he and I finally established a rapport, and we maintained it from that point on, except for Meech Lake. Clyde's constitutional adviser, Deborah Coyne, was especially vehement about my support of Meech Lake, considering me a treacherous Newfoundland Liberal for refusing to endorse the premier's position. She had received reports from members of the federal caucus that I had spoken out in favour of Meech Lake and against Clyde's position, and I felt my relationship with Clyde grow cool again. Things had become complicated whenever I spoke with members of Clyde's caucus and cabinet, some of whom told me they were ready to support Meech Lake in a free vote. When word got back to Wells and Coyne that his caucus and I had been discussing the matter, this caused further difficulties between us, as you can imagine.

After the failure of Meech Lake, Clyde Wells and I, as premier and federal minister respectively, began to build a better relationship. He and I talked perhaps three or four times a week, and we worked together on shared issues. I found him a man of honour who was as good as his word. So, in late 1995, based on dropped hints here and there, I had a good idea that he had been reflecting on his political career and his personal future.

At one point, he said, "Brian, if I were to leave politics, would you run for my office?" When I replied that I would certainly consider it, he asked if I would contest the leadership if necessary, and again I replied that I would, but only if this happened in the very near future. This was in late 1995, and I suspected that the prime minister would shuffle his cabinet in early 1996. If he did this, whether or not I stayed at my post or accepted a new ministry, I could not leave Ottawa within a month or two of the shuffle, which would be unfair to the prime minister and other cabinet members.

At this stage, we were both talking hypothetically but my message was clear: if Clyde were to leave office and wanted to see me in the race to replace him, it could only be done if he left by the end of the year. If he left after Jean Chrétien completed his cabinet shuffle, I would not go to St. John's.

Did that make an impact on Wells's decision? Was it the factor that triggered the announcement between Christmas and New Year's 1995 of his decision to step down? I don't know. We never discussed it. He did not bow out directly on my behalf; his reasons and motivation were entirely his own. I believe that he wanted and expected a vigorous leadership campaign if he left office, and he saw me as one of a number of people who would seek to replace him.

On December 29, while on a skiing vacation with my family at Marble Mountain near Corner Brook, I read the newspaper headlines announcing his resignation. The media pegged me to replace him (the *Toronto Star*'s headline read: "Wells Bows Out, Tobin on the Spot"), but I refused to make any commitment, saying only that Clyde Wells had achieved something rare in politics: "to be able to leave with as much dignity and integrity as he brought [to the office]." When the media kept pressing for a comment, asking what I was going to do, I replied, "I'm going to talk to the mountain." Later when I decided to run, the headlines declared, "The mountain said, 'Yes.'"

What the mountain said is between me and it. I know that Jodean and I discussed the idea for many hours. I also talked to members of my family, including my father, who always looked beyond the political implications when giving me advice. You need that kind of grounding in any career activity, I suppose, but especially in politics, and I valued his unique view of things when it came to helping me reach a difficult decision.

In the end, I agreed to seek the leadership because exciting things were happening in Newfoundland and Labrador, and I wanted to be part of them. The move surprised many people, I discovered. Step out of the national spotlight to return to provincial politics? What kind of career move was that?

The truth is, I have never considered politics to be a risk-free venture. Nor should it be. You make decisions based on personal values and existing circumstances. If every decision a politician makes is founded on ensuring his or her own survival in the short run, what does that politician stand for in the long run? Everything I have ever done in politics carried risk. If you seek a job that entails making major decisions and accepting personal responsibility for them, you better be prepared to take risks. If that idea frightens you, then you're the wrong person for the job.

I WISH I COULD SAY that my return to Newfoundland politics was all smooth sailing. The truth is, for the first six months, I was quite lonely. In January 1996, I moved to a small apartment in St. John's, assuming I would be contesting the leadership. As it turned out, I was acclaimed. Jodean and I had agreed that, rather than disrupt the children's school year, they and Jodean would remain in Ottawa until June.

So there I was, living in a spartan apartment, away from family for the first time since 1980, telling myself I had made the right move. And I had. It just didn't feel that way for a while. When you've spent years balancing the rough and tumble of politics with spending time among your close-knit family, the sudden absence of spouse and children becomes almost painful. This was exacerbated by the fact that I was the party leader and premier. In that role you're not one of the troops, one of the caucus or even one of the ministers. Like it or not, you are isolated to a large degree, and without Jodean and the children, the isolation really hit home.

Having been sworn in on a Friday, I called an election three days later, on Monday. While I was grateful to have my party's endorsement, I knew real authority could only come from the people themselves. I asked the voters to assess our platform and give me a mandate to proceed. In opposing me, the Progressive Conservatives based their strategy on attacking my decision to accept pension payments earned over almost 17 years as a sitting MP.

Anyone who chooses a career in politics with the primary goal of growing wealthy is a fool. If you have the energy, determination and organizational skills needed to be elected as a member of Parliament, chances are you can earn more in the private sector than as a sitting MP.

Considering that politics is also among the world's least secure professions—your job is on the line every four years or less—a reasonable pension at the end of the line strikes me as fair recompense. You and I may disagree about the size of the pension payments, and I would understand and appreciate the basis of our disagreement. But the pensions exist, nevertheless, and I made a decision to accept the payments when I left Ottawa. This decision was influenced, at least in part, by the reality that leaving my position as a cabinet minister to become premier of Newfoundland and Labrador represented a substantial pay cut, and the pension payments essentially covered the difference. I had accumulated little in the way of savings while serving in Ottawa, and Heather, our eldest child, was preparing for a university education.

As they had proven back in 1980, when I did not deny my support for abortion rights, the people of Newfoundland respected the fact that I was upfront regarding the pension from the beginning. I felt I was entitled to it, and I planned to use the income for the good of my family. I refused to play the hypocritical game of saying, in the middle of the campaign, that I would donate the payments to charity or that I would not accept them at all, and then quietly change my mind when the spotlight was off me.

My position was this: if the people of Newfoundland and Labrador felt that the most critical issue in the campaign was whether or not Brian Tobin accepted a pension to which he was fully entitled, then they would vote accordingly. But I intended to take the pension payments.

This disarmed the opposition, who had chosen the pension question as the foundation for their campaign. When I admitted everything they were saying, and did not attempt to weasel out of

the situation, they didn't know how to respond. I was confident
that Newfoundlanders would not make the election a referendum
on my pension. My confidence was boosted by the response
of the voters even before election day, when I heard callers to
open-line radio shows saying, "That man would be a fool not
to take the pension! If I earned the pension, I'd take it, too!"

We won 37 of 48 seats, an increase in both the Liberal
party's share of seats and in the percentage of the popular vote.
Perhaps most telling of all, the pension issue was never raised
again. The fact is, the public always votes on the big issues of
the day, not the fluff that some would try to pass off for
substantial policy debate. The Reform/Alliance party has found
this out as well. They no longer talk about scandalous parliamentary pensions. They take them. They no longer talk about
Stornoway (official residence of the Opposition leader) as a
waste of money. Stephen Harper lives there.

WHEN I ARRIVED IN ST. JOHN'S in January 1996, only one
woman was sitting in the legislature. She was Lynn Verge, a veteran
Conservative and the leader of the Opposition, who went down to
defeat in the upcoming election. This was clearly unacceptable,
and I spread the word that I wanted more women candidates in
ridings where we had a good opportunity of winning. I began
playing an active role in seeing that they were nominated, and
we came up with a slate of impressive female candidates who
became highly effective members of the legislature.

Judy Foote had been director of communications for Clyde
Wells, and I had always found her tough and capable. In the
previous election, Judy had run in her home riding of Grand
Bank and lost. I encouraged her to run again in 1996, and she
won decisively.

Julie Bettney, the mayor of Mount Pearl, had fought the
previous Wells administration over its plan to amalgamate
Mount Pearl with St. John's. Her ability to speak on behalf of

the community in a forceful manner impressed me, and we managed to recruit her as a winning candidate.

Joan Marie Aylward's reputation as president of the Newfoundland and Labrador Nurses' Union was well established, and she won the nomination and seat in St. John's Centre.

Sandra Kelly, mayor of Gander, had been interested in a legislative seat, and she was nominated as well, along with Anna Thistle, who had run in the previous election for the seat for Grand Falls-Buchans. Both won election.

Mary Hodder, long a political force in Burin-Placentia West, became an effective member of the House of Assembly. Yvonne Jones, independent candidate, pulled off the rare trick of getting elected entirely on her own in a riding on the Labrador coast.

The election of these women had a profound impact on the government. Many of the social programs we introduced reflected the insight and concerns of our female members, and the programs were the better for it.

The euphoria of winning the election with a large majority faded when I found myself facing some tough decisions as premier. The province's deficit was bigger than I had thought, and revenues were dropping. Something had to be done, but I had few choices. In fact, I soon discovered I had only one, and that was to cut the public service workforce by 10 percent.

Telling people they no longer have jobs is a terribly difficult thing to do, and it doesn't get any easier whether you make that announcement from the office of the premier, or on the shop floor. The early months of 1996 saw continual protests by public employees on the front lawn of the legislature buildings, and feisty debate inside the House. We eventually achieved our goal of introducing both a balanced budget and improved programs, and the first provincial income tax cuts since Newfoundland joined Confederation in 1949. These achievements took a determined and principled caucus and cabinet, and I was fortunate to work with both during my years in St. John's. I was a reformist premier happily surrounded by women and men of like mind, strong courage and big hearts.

I had also managed to assemble an exceptional staff. Back in 1980, one of my first actions after being elected was to hire Eva Mills as my constituency secretary. Eva was precisely the kind of constituency worker that every politician needs to achieve success. Dedicated and hard working, Eva performed unglamorous work such as staffing the telephones and organizing the polling organizations. When Heidi Bonnell, a school friend of Eva's daughter, expressed an interest in politics and public relations, Eva gave Heidi an opportunity to gain experience in one of my campaigns. When she finished university, Heidi became a junior communications assistant in my office and later director of communications in my premier's office. Today, she is vice-president, communications, with Hill & Knowlton, the largest and most prestigious public relations firm in the world.

Gerry Glavine, my chief of staff, and House Leader Beaton Tulk are two examples of the high quality of people from a wide range of backgrounds that I had on my team. Beaton, a tall, strapping fisherman's son from Ladle Cove on the Labrador Sea, obtained a master's degree in English literature before being elected to office in 1979. He spent 10 years as an effective Opposition spokesperson on education, social services, fisheries, labour relations, forestry, agriculture, treasury board and the environment. Beaton had represented the electoral district of Fogo for several years, but with the restructuring of districts in 1996, Fogo "disappeared," and so Beaton ran and won in the new district of Bonavista North. I appointed him minister of forest resources and agrifoods, as well as government House leader. Later he became minister of development and rural renewal. By August 2000, he was deputy premier and subsequently became premier upon my leaving office.

In contrast to Beaton Tulk's involvement in political matters, Gerry Glavine had spent almost 30 years in education and was a high-school department head when I tapped him to be my chief of staff. He was also a former grand knight of the Knights of Columbus, and so you can imagine the heat that he took while helping me reorganize the education system, which involved removing the Catholic Church's 200-year control over public schools.

Tony Grace had served as a senior research officer in the Government Members' Office before joining my staff as executive assistant. He became my right hand, travelling with me everywhere, organizing the competing demands on my time. He was the first staff person I saw each morning and the last staffer I saw each night.

Another talented and quietly efficient person who joined my staff at this time was Margo Brown, who served as my director of operations in St. John's. Margo had worked with Premier Wells and knew how to make things happen in the premier's office. When I assumed the Fisheries and Oceans portfolio in 1993, I came across a paper written by Malcolm Rowe, a long-time adviser to John Crosbie. The paper was critical of my proposals to deal with overfishing. I didn't agree with his conclusions, but I was so impressed with the clarity of his thinking and his communication skills that I invited him into my office to talk about it. Malcolm, of course, felt a little like Daniel entering the lion's den, but we hit it off so well that I offered him a contract to give me advice on matters of international law. He accepted, and during all the hectic action that followed in 1995, his observations and interpretations were critical to many of the key decisions made in the ministry. Later, he served with me as clerk of the Privy Council in Newfoundland and Labrador and eventually was appointed to the Newfoundland Supreme Court.

Joan Marie Aylward is an especially gifted woman who contributed much to Newfoundland and Labrador over the years, especially during the emotional confrontation with the provincial nurses' union. When she won the St. John's Centre seat in 1996,

I immediately appointed her minister of the Department of Social Services and, a year later, elevated her to head the Health ministry. In this latter position, she led the government's efforts in dealing with members of her former union when we lifted a freeze on public service salaries that had been in place for several years. The freeze had followed an attempt by the previous Wells administration to grant substantial wage and salary increases for public service employees. Negotiations were completed and contracts were signed before the government realized it simply could not afford to pay the amounts it had agreed upon. As a result, legislation was passed rolling back the contracts, and public service wages and salaries were frozen indefinitely.

The freeze needed to be lifted, but to avoid a repeat of the previous administration's experience we offered public service employees an across-the-board increase of 7 percent over three years. It would be implemented only if the public service unions agreed to it, and they all did with the exception of the nurses' union, which refused to come to the table. Their situation, the nurses said, was different, and they insisted on receiving more than the 7 percent being offered everyone else.

Few public service personnel can make a stronger emotional plea for special consideration than nurses. Through protracted negotiations, we tried to explain that all the other unions had agreed to the terms of our proposal on condition that no union receive a wage offer that was better than another's. Were Newfoundland nurses underpaid compared with those of other provinces? Yes, they were. So were other categories of public servants. Could we have paid them the 17-percent wage increase they were seeking? No, because we couldn't afford it, and because I had given my word it would have broken faith with the other union presidents. I believe the unions would have called a general strike and demanded a whole new series of negotiations, and who could blame them?

The nurses remained resolute. They demanded special consideration, they tapped the emotions of the general public and they brought in people like CLC President Bob White and others from elsewhere in Canada to declare their solidarity. Meanwhile, Joan Marie Aylward and I became targets for their anger and frustration. I accepted the flak, but it was especially hard on Joan Marie, who had moved from being president of the nurses' union, fighting for rights and benefits for her members, to being the person to explain that 7 percent was all we could afford, and that was that. Joan Marie's courage and negotiating abilities were challenged and friendships ruptured in the face of a difficult standoff.

The dispute extended through the 1999 election campaign, with nurses using the election that year as a springboard for their demands. Wherever I appeared during the campaign, a delegation of nurses arrived, carrying placards, shouting slogans and handing out pamphlets. Usually I exchanged greetings with them. Some of our discussions were more passionate than others, but I respected their position and their right to protest in support of their demands.

After the 1999 election returned us to office, we began concentrating on the nurses' situation, seeking a way through the problem without a strike. Negotiations went on, often into the wee hours of the morning, and at one point I thought we had a deal but the union negotiators returned with fresh demands. When we explained that these new demands could not be met, the nurses walked out on March 24, 1999. With great reluctance, after nearly 10 days of strike activity, I asked the House of Assembly to pass legislation requiring them to return to work under the best terms we could offer: a 7-percent increase in earnings, spread over three years (identical to the offer to other public service employees); 200 part-time jobs converted to full-time nursing positions; and the hiring of an additional 125 nurses.

The conflict attracted national attention to both sides. The nurses received support from other members of their profession as well as from the public across Canada. I received support from provincial premiers, saying things like, "Hold your ground—health care costs are escalating and we've got to get them under control!" If I held the line, they informed me, it would be easier for them to hold the line as well. Well, I held the line, but it wasn't easy. I learned a good deal from that experience, and while I would not—I *could* not—do anything differently, it helped me shape some thoughts on our national health care situation.

Every poll confirms that Canadians value their health care system above all other government programs. They also value the contribution of the medical professionals who provide this care, especially the nursing staff. Ask the public if nurses should receive twice the pay they're earning now, and many will say they should get *three* times as much. At the same time, the public expects fiscal responsibility on the part of the government. Canadians don't want crippling taxes, and they don't want the kind of massive debt that confronted us after the Mulroney years. Ask the same group of people who propose paying nurses three times their current salary if they agree to have their taxes raised, and the answer will be no. That's a contradictory response, and Canadians are aware of that. It doesn't matter. They expect elected officials to find a solution that satisfies both needs. Sometimes we do. Often we don't.

The dirty job of saying no when you really want to say yes is part of elected public life. Politicians are paid to make hard decisions. If you're not prepared to take the kind of pressure I experienced during the nurses' strike, you're probably not suited for public office. But it is never pleasant. Nor, I point out, was it pleasant for the nurses, who sincerely felt they deserved more.

DURING MY FIRST YEAR IN OFFICE, I needed a deep commitment from my staff, cabinet and caucus to achieve goals we had set for the government. Chief among them were fiscal matters, and solving them would take more than slashing public service jobs.

We began a line-by-line examination of government programs, discarding those that were not worth the resources needed to operate them. Governments are very good at launching programs but they are notoriously bad at ending them. A program that makes sense today may not be able to justify its existence 5 or 10 years down the road, yet some continue because no one has the political will to shut them down.

The public service employees operating those terminated programs became redundant, and we sought ways to make things easier for them. This included offering early retirement to long-term workers, as well as retraining programs enabling them to move within government or into the private sector. We tried to hang on to the next generation of employees who brought special skills in computer operation, information technology and other talents to their work. The buyouts opened positions at the top of the job pyramid, creating opportunities for advancement among ambitious and impatient younger people. This latter goal was important: many of our brightest young men and women in public service were leaving the province, because they couldn't see room for advancement within the public service.

Paul Dicks, our minister of finance, led the way in establishing a three-year plan to balance Newfoundland's budget. We achieved that, and it enabled us to do something that no other Newfoundland and Labrador government had done since joining Canada: we cut payroll taxes, corporate taxes and personal income taxes.

The impact on the province's economy was positive and substantial, but I believe we made a more fundamental and enduring change. By shrinking the size of Newfoundland's public service, we departed from the long-held notion that all wealth, prosperity and opportunity comes from government. It also invited greater participation by entrepreneurs and small businesses, and made Newfoundland a more attractive place for both domestic and foreign investment.

OVERRIDING ALL OUR EFFORTS was my sense of a need to restore confidence to the province. I wanted to create an environment in which the citizens of Newfoundland and Labrador could believe in the future and in the notion that the future resided in our own hands. We had to escape the feeling that Newfoundlanders, to one extent or another, were victims, subject to the whims of decision makers far removed from us. We needed to become convinced that we could act in our own best interests.

In 1996, Newfoundland and Labrador was in its fourth year of the cod moratorium, and open-line radio shows reflected the anger and helplessness of the situation. Inevitably, the tone of the comments was victimization: people felt disadvantaged, ripped off, forgotten and abused by "the system," whatever the broader topic might be that day. The same attitude ran through local television news broadcasts. The newscast seemed to cover only economic bad news, the destruction of communities, forecasts of disaster and so on. If you listened long enough, you would become convinced that this was a province in decline, without hope. No one focused on stories of success, or cared to speculate in a positive way on planning for the future. Over all of Newfoundland and Labrador, it seemed, hung an oppressive cloud of doom and gloom. It wasn't a media-driven thing, either: I also heard it in private conversations.

I decided we had to lift that cloud by focusing on our strengths. We had to marvel at the size of our potential and not allow the size of our problems to overwhelm us. That attitude could not be created out of whole cloth, of course. It needed to be founded in reality, and so I began looking for ways to celebrate our achievements and those of the entrepreneurs, business leaders, political leaders and others who were behind them. It was a way to achieve balance and light a path through the gloomy atmosphere. Here is one example.

The Hibernia petroleum development project was scheduled to begin production from the oil field located 200 miles east of

St. John's and 250 feet beneath the ocean. Negotiations with the petroleum companies over Terra Nova, another petroleum deposit southeast of Hibernia, were dragging on. As a government, we wanted to accelerate the Terra Nova negotiations to reach an agreement faster. And we did. I was soon able to announce that talks had concluded with terms favourable to both sides, and Terra Nova would enable Newfoundland and Labrador to launch a home-based oil and gas industry.

Hibernia and Terra Nova were on their way toward full production, but both projects had been delayed for years by seemingly endless negotiations. What if Newfoundland and Labrador introduced a generic offshore oil and gas policy that could cut through the red tape and reach agreement faster? We sent representatives to discuss the proposal with oil and gas company executives in Alberta, Texas and elsewhere. We drafted a set of regulations incorporating common elements that has since been largely copied by Nova Scotia and British Columbia. Designed to fast-track these otherwise complex agreements, the document avoids "one-off" contracts by establishing a set of rules fair to both parties, providing an incentive for investment dollars to flow into the province.

We also began working with the Newfoundland and Labrador Manufacturers Association to introduce programs that would help that sector grow. Much of our effort was related to encouraging companies working on information technology, supported by a joint federal/provincial fund and managed by a private-sector task force led by retired banker Sam Walters. The effort paid off in a surge of development and agreements with companies as large as Sun Microsystems and as small as one-person start-up firms. Companies like Zedcomm, an award-winning IT firm founded in 1992, proved both the capabilities of Newfoundlanders and the practicality of the project. Recognized as a pioneer in harnessing the potential of the Web, Zedcomm maintains offices in St. John's and Ottawa as well as in Irvine and San Jose, California, designing, developing and implementing custom e-learning solutions and Web-based business applications.

I made a point of talking about our private-industry successes, letting everyone know that Newfoundland and Labrador was an untapped source of talent and initiative. Young men and young women in Newfoundland and Labrador were creating employment and generating wealth. Governments can be partners, they can facilitate, they can encourage, but they cannot create wealth on their own. They need to understand what an entrepreneur may require in the way of tax measures, R&D investment and infrastructure to help ensure success, and then stay out of the way as much as possible.

I spent a good deal of time searching for success stories and spreading the word. If we had a big petroleum development, I asked who were the Newfoundland or Labrador suppliers to these global oil and gas companies. Who were the workers? Who were the people building these enormous sophisticated drilling and recovery devices that operate offshore? They were not always people from our province, of course, but that's the way of the world. You have to bring in specialized services and talent from time to time. But I kept telling people that we had to learn to do those things ourselves, over time, and capture as much value as possible for our own people.

MEMORIES OF JOEY,
AND MEETING HER MAJESTY

No one who enters Newfoundland politics can avoid the legacy of Joey Smallwood, the last Father of Confederation. He is more properly identified as The Honourable Joseph Roberts Smallwood but he was simply "Joey" throughout his political career.

My entry into politics occurred after the departure of Smallwood from the political scene, but his spirit remained a presence in Newfoundland and Labrador, as it does to this day. The last time I saw Joey was in the late 1980s, and as I drove up the lane to his home near the entrance to Conception Bay, I thought, "Take a good long look, my son, for once he is gone you'll not soon see his like again." It was a sunny day, and Joey stood in the doorway of his home waving a welcome. A stroke had left him bereft of speech, and he sought the support of walls, doors and helpful arms. My heart went out to this man who had dominated the political life of Newfoundland and Labrador for so many decades.

Joey's body might be failing him and his oratory lost, but his spirit remained strong and determined. He shook hands with surprising energy and swept his arms in an invitation to take in the beauty of the day and his special place under the sun.

Inside his home were photos of himself with dignitaries and royalty, plaques and certificates of appreciation and recognition, letters from presidents and prime ministers, silver shovels that had turned sod for new projects and samples of offshore oil that held promise for his beloved province. He was especially proud of his first editions of Newfoundland and Labrador literature. Joey's first act following the province's entry into Confederation had been to establish Memorial University, providing thousands with the opportunity for higher learning within their own province. His final act, one that eventually exhausted both his physical stamina and his assets, was to produce the *Encyclopedia of Newfoundland and Labrador.*

I can think of no figure in Canadian history who surpassed him for the scope of his vision, the depth of his passion and the extent of his impact on a province and people he loved dearly. "Develop or perish" became his rallying cry. Inevitably, mistakes were made, as Joey himself acknowledged. But let's never forget that they were mistakes of the heart.

Joey died a week before his 91st birthday, a relatively poor man. He had poured the last remaining measures of his energy and money into his encyclopedia, never living to see it completed. I have a set in my home today, occupying a place of honour.

I cannot leave Joey's memory without recalling an incident that occurred on my way to his funeral in December 1991. Brian Mulroney's government made an old Armed Forces Lockheed Constellation available to those who wanted to attend the services, and I boarded the flight along with Frank Moores, Jack Pickersgill, Jean Chrétien and several others. The Constellation was a four-engine propeller-driven aircraft long past retirement age. It was noisy and shaky and did not inspire much confidence in its passengers. Together we indulged in several bottles of Scotch on board, except Frank Moores, who had given up alcohol.

Between the Scotch and the stories about Joey Smallwood, the flight grew bearable until, with a sound like a shotgun being fired, the rubber seal around one of the pressurized doors blew out. Suddenly, everything and everybody not tied down was sucked toward the partially opened door. This was disturbing enough, but the sight of a crew member marching up the aisle with a bucket of water and a roll of toilet paper had us wondering what was next. He calmly dipped the toilet paper in the water and used it to replace the missing rubber seal. As the toilet paper froze, it resealed the door. The plane repressurized. The whole business was too much for Frank, seated next to the door whose seal had blown.

Moores looked around wide-eyed and said, "That's it—I'm off the wagon! Somebody give me a goddamn Scotch," and Frank's teetotalling days were over, at least temporarily.

It's the kind of story Joey would have loved to hear.

JOEY SMALLWOOD HAD DONE MUCH to attract industry to Newfoundland and Labrador, too often with disastrous results. One industry that I felt had not received as much attention in the past as it deserved was tourism. Tourism is clean, renewable, environmentally friendly and potentially endless. Petroleum developments are impressive, but they have a beginning, a middle and an end. Some day the oil reserves will run out, and that's the end of that economic asset. If you build tourism carefully and sustain it, it will be around for generations. We began investing in the marketing and promotion of tourism to Newfoundland and Labrador. We supported development of the infrastructure, launched agreements with the federal government, assisted small-business operators with venture dollars and constantly nurtured the idea that Newfoundland and Labrador could profit tremendously from tourism.

Governments can't throw money at an industry and hope it succeeds, but they can launch initiatives that spill over into the private sector and return dividends, if the right opportunity presents itself. One of these opportunities was our support of the re-creation of the voyage of the *Matthew*, John Cabot's sailing ship. Cabot and his three sons, with the blessing (but without the financing) of Henry VII, sailed from Bristol, England, on May 2, 1497, and landed at Bonavista on June 24.

Clyde Wells, an avid sailor, had started planning the Cabot celebrations. I saw the event as a chance to draw the world's attention to Newfoundland by commemorating the 500th anniversary of Cabot's journey and his landing at Bonavista. We proposed a ceremony in Bristol on May 2, marking Cabot's departure, and another at Bonavista on June 24, when a replica of the *Matthew* would sail into port. Since Cabot had claimed the New Land for Britain, we asked if the Queen could take part in the event, and Buckingham Palace responded with enthusiasm. What's more, Prince Philip would steer a replica of the *Matthew* out of Bristol harbour, using the same tiller-style steering device that Cabot's ship used. Queen Elizabeth would be on hand when the *Matthew* replica landed at Bonavista, and she would follow this with a tour of the province. In all, Her Majesty would be with us for an entire week.

I was elated at the palace's response, but it occurred to me that even more could be done to mark this important anniversary. Cabot, after all, had been a Genoa barber named Giovanni Caboto. Why not commemorate the Italian connection with the presence of that country's president, His Excellency Oscar Luigi Scalfaro? The Italians agreed and commissioned a beautiful marble relief commemorating Caboto's voyage to be unveiled by Scalfaro at Bonavista, Newfoundland. We should also, I felt, acknowledge the Irish roots in Newfoundland by inviting the *taoiseach* (prime minister) of Ireland, John Bruton. Talk to almost any Newfoundlander and the impact of the Irish culture on the province is immediately apparent. In addition to this cultural connection, Ireland was the last European point of land from which Cabot set out on his voyage.

I wanted to strengthen the traditional bonds between Newfoundland and Ireland for another, very practical reason.

During the 1990s, Ireland achieved a dramatic turnaround in its economy, becoming a powerhouse in computer and information technology. The country, whose economy had drifted and declined for decades, was being hailed as the Celtic Tiger. I believed we could learn from Ireland's experiences and perhaps apply the lessons to our own economy. As a result, I had gotten to know Prime Minister Bruton quite well, and I knew he would be delighted to share in our celebrations. As a matter of fact, he had developed a special rapport with our province. Bruton had visited Newfoundland as a young man and had recently returned for a visit as prime minister of Ireland on his way home from visiting President Clinton in the White House.

Bruton's office responded with enthusiasm, and plans moved forward. In addition to the queen's visit, choirs from 10 countries would gather in St. John's, Corner Brook and Labrador, singing not only in cathedrals, but under the sun as well. The festival would be capped by a gala performance featuring a 400-voice children's choir and a 400-voice adult choir supported by more than 100 musicians. Everything flowed smoothly until rumblings began to be heard, through the Foreign Affairs ministry in Ottawa, that the palace was not happy at the prospect of the Queen sharing the platform with the Irish prime minister and Italian president. Worse still, I was told that unless invitations which had already been accepted by the Italian head of state and the Irish prime minister were withdrawn, the Queen might not come to Newfoundland and Labrador at all.

I have no evidence, but I am certain that the Queen was not made aware of these machinations. Having been in government for many years, I suspect that things have been said in her name that she knew nothing about, and that it was cooked up by minions whose only purpose in life is to make things as complex and intrigue ridden as they can be, regardless of the practical and human aspects.

I refused to uninvite either guest. Soon I received word that the Italians were sending their regrets; while President Scalfaro indeed would pay a state visit to Canada in June, he would unfortunately not be able to attend the ceremony at Bonavista. It was made clear to me that this decision was in response to express wishes from the House of Windsor, and while the Italians naturally complied, they were not happy. Buckingham Palace was not alone in applying this pressure tactic; I was informed that the British government had been recruited to persuade Italy to change its mind. The Italians sent a significant delegation to Bonavista anyway, with the beautiful marble relief as a gift to the province. I appreciated their presence and regretted the absence of His Excellency President Scalfaro.

Soon after this news arrived, I received a telephone call from John Bruton, who explained that he and his office also had been the target of similar requests and pressures from London. "I have received informal messages that it would be preferred that I not come," John explained. "Brian, what should I do? Should I withdraw or should I come?" I asked him what his preference was. "I prefer to come," he said, and I replied, "Then come."

A few days later, I received a visit to my office from a very senior official of Buckingham Palace. In strong terms, this individual advised me to withdraw the invitation to the Irish prime minister. If I failed to, I was told, the Queen might remove herself from the event.

I recall the frustration building within me as I listened to this bureaucrat deliver threats in the haughty upper-class manner that so offends even some dedicated anglophiles. I could not understand how such a momentous occasion, a reason for celebration among four countries, could be threatened because the Queen was being asked to share a stage with the Irish prime minister.

I informed the individual that I would not withdraw the invitation to the Irish prime minister and that, having recently spoken with him, I did not expect him to cancel his plans to attend the event. I stated that if the Queen withdrew, I and the people of Newfoundland and Labrador would be extremely disappointed, and I would call a press conference to explain why the Queen's visit had been cancelled. I would make public these unusual requests to uninvite other guests, and I would comment very negatively on the circumstances. I would state, I explained, that the palace was seeking to take over an event celebrating the culture, heritage and history of Newfoundland and Labrador, turning it toward its own goals and interests. I could not accept, given the historical linkage of Newfoundland with Ireland, that the head of state of my country (i.e., the Queen) could not share the same platform with the prime minister of Ireland. In summary, I would not withdraw the invitation and if the Queen, following the guidance of her advisers, withdrew from the event, I would challenge that decision in the media and reveal details of the representations made to me by the palace.

The response was grim-faced silence.

After the palace's envoy returned to London, I was uncertain what might happen. Would the Queen cancel her visit? Would Britain protest my intransigence?

I waited for an angry response from London. But nothing changed. The celebration took place in Bristol with Prince Philip as planned, and arrangements proceeded for visits from both the Queen and Prime Minister Bruton in Bonavista. Smiles were the order of the day and cooperation was everywhere—except from the weather. June 24 dawned cold and blustery, more like a winter's day in Devon than early summer in Newfoundland. It was nothing less than miserable—there are no other words to describe it. I have never seen a worse summer's day in Newfoundland, and I have never seen anyone carry off duties in those conditions with more grace and aplomb than the Queen. She never complained, and she never shrank from any of the commitments made for her—in fact, she added several events to her agenda. She went out of her way to meet people and shake their hands, paying particular attention to veterans and seniors. All of this was done with the utmost charm under conditions that would have persuaded most people to shorten their time out of doors instead of extending it as she did.

Her positive attitude and the special efforts she made to meet people made me question once again if she had been aware of the manoeuvrings that had taken place regarding the presence of the Irish prime minister and the Italian president. I don't believe she had any knowledge of those discussions.

SOMETHING UNSETTLING OCCURRED during the landing celebrations, however, after I introduced the Queen, who spoke of Cabot's landing at Bonavista. As soon as she completed her talk, her entourage appeared and swept her from the stage just as Irish Prime Minister John Bruton was moving to the microphone to deliver his speech. I had no idea this was going to occur, and I was disheartened at the obvious snub to John. It was almost as though the palace officials, who had not succeeded in preventing the Irish prime minister from being present at the ceremony, registered their protest by having Her Majesty turn her back to him and exit even as he rose to speak. I found it rude and uncalled for, and I attribute it solely to some spiteful officials who were unable to get their way otherwise.

Early on the day of the welcoming ceremony for the *Matthew*, a reception had been held prior to the event itself, and John Bruton was scheduled to meet the Queen there. I found John to be an exceptionally friendly and charming man, and during a conversation with him before the reception began, he turned to me and said, "Brian, what do I say when I meet Her Majesty?"

The question surprised me. "John," I said, "you've met the Queen before."

"No, I haven't," he said.

I assured him that Her Majesty was warm and friendly, and that he would find her quite approachable and engaging.

"You know," John said, "this is the first time in history that an Irish prime minister and a British monarch have shared a public platform. History is being made here today, Brian."

He was aware of the historical importance of the event, but no one else was, because the media never picked up on that aspect of the Queen's visit. This made her abrupt departure before he could speak all the more regrettable to me. It was especially unfortunate because peace talks between Ireland and Britain were underway and people on both sides were searching for ways to reconcile the differences that had existed for so many years and had cost so many lives. Having the Queen and the Irish prime minister speak from the same stage, and acknowledge the historical precedent, would have been a wonderful gesture. A great opportunity was missed.

The press may not have been aware of the historical precedent of the Queen and an Irish prime minister sharing a stage, but the British tabloids made the most of a much less significant incident. This occurred as the Queen and I were ascending the steps of the Confederation Building in St. John's. Those steps are tricky even in good weather, but on a blustery day like that one, the wind can literally blow you over. The wind was so strong that I was concerned she might lose her footing so, in a perfectly natural gesture, I placed my hand behind her back to steady her.

The British media reported this as though it were a scandalous international incident. Headlines, photographs and cries of outrage appeared in some British tabloids the next day over the fact that I had touched the Queen. I was amazed that something so trivial would receive so much attention.

A few days later, while touring Labrador with her, I thanked the Queen for not locking me up in the Tower of London for my apparently inappropriate behaviour.

She laughed it off. "The tabloids love to make mountains out of molehills," she responded with a smile. "Don't worry about that."

Her response was so geniuine that I reached to touch her shoulder in a gesture of gratitude and affection. When I did, she recoiled and said with mock horror: "Premier! You were about to do it again!"

IF YOU SPEND ALMOST ANY TIME in her presence, you cannot help being impressed by the charm and the humanity of Her Majesty. She has an enormous sense of duty and great empathy for everyone she encounters, especially the young, the elderly, the ill and war veterans. I write these words as someone who feels Canada no longer needs to swear allegiance to the British monarchy, yet who is a great fan of Queen Elizabeth II. If that strikes you as contradictory, then you have not met Her Majesty. She is a remarkable woman.

A REVOLUTION IN
PROVINCIAL EDUCATION

WHEN I RETURNED TO ST. JOHN'S in early 1996, I threw myself into a number of issues that required attention, but none proved more contentious than the problem of funding and administering education in the province. It demanded reform, and had for several years. Unfortunately, it involved two groups as opposed to reform as any you might encounter: the Roman Catholic Church and the Pentecostal Assemblies. Just to complicate things, the guy who was determined to change the process—me—was Roman Catholic and his education minister—Roger Grimes—was Pentecostal.

Well, at least nobody could charge us with bias.

NEWFOUNDLAND AND LABRADOR'S educational system was rooted in the beginning of the province's history. Its first schools were established by the Church of England's missionary Society for the Propagation of the Gospel in Foreign Parts (SPG) in the 1720s, with the launch of a school in Bonavista. Other schools followed, in St. John's and outport communities, launched by the SPG and open to any denomination. In the early 1800s, the Newfoundland School Society began operating public schools throughout the province. Like the SPG, the school society was privately funded. This ended in 1836 with the first government funding of education, a program expanded seven years later when it was decreed that education grants would be divided between separate Roman Catholic and Protestant school boards.

Over time, the Protestant grant became distributed through Denominational Education Committees, or DECs, representing several denominations including Church of England, Methodist, Salvation Army and Pentecostal. Eventually, this was consolidated into Protestant and Pentecostal, but the role of the DECs remained. They, not the government, determined allocations of the educational budget and established teacher qualifications, and their decisions were made according to the best interests of each denomination. The provincial legislature generated the dollars needed to fund the schools but had little or no say in the expenditures.

Questions of efficiency in spending taxpayers' dollars by the DECs were not their first priority. Each DEC acted in the interests of its denomination. As a result, as birth rates declined, a single community might have three half-empty schools—one Roman Catholic, one Protestant, one Pentecostal—all maintained with public funds, when one or perhaps two non-denominational schools would suffice. Students from one community might be bused an hour each way to a second community to attend a denominational school, and along the way they might pass a bus transporting students in the other direction to attend a denominational school in the first community. It was a maddening situation, one that placed an extra burden on the provincial budget, restricted teacher salaries, resulted in substandard school facilities and had a negative effect on the quality of education overall.

There was also the question of accountability, fiscal and otherwise. The province was in the business, to a large degree, of generating money for the DECs to distribute according to their whims, and the DECs were in the business of protecting their own turf, which included maintaining and strengthening their presence in communities. So the people collecting the money to finance the education system had no influence on the people spending that money, presumably in the best interests of the students.

Control of the education budgets rested with the religious groups and they—the Catholic Education Council and the Pentecostal Education Committee in particular—understandably resisted relinquishing that power. The system, as antiquated and unwieldy as it was, had been embedded in the terms of union when Newfoundland entered Confederation in 1949, though the terms had been left undefined. Until Clyde Wells made an attempt during his term in office, the courts had never been called upon to determine how far these terms enabled either the government or the DECs to extend their power.

In 1992, a royal commission recommended the reorganization of the primary, elementary and secondary education system in Newfoundland and Labrador in order to permit the government to administer it in an efficient manner. The solution to the funding question was hardly Solomonic: a single interdenominational system encompassing all denominational systems.

Unfortunately, this proved unworkable when the DECs resisted reform. Frustrated, Wells went to the people of Newfoundland directly with a referendum. In search of progress—any progress at all—he did not ask for total management of the system, simply a degree of control. He also assumed a hands-off approach, leaving it to the public to make up its mind and avoided personally campaigning on the issue. In contrast, the religious groups took a hard line with their adherents. Nonetheless, the September 1995 referendum passed, albeit with a bare majority of 54.4 percent. A month later the Newfoundland House of Assembly approved a resolution requesting the Parliament of Canada to amend the constitution in accordance with the wishes of the people. In January 1996, Prime Minister Jean Chrétien wrote Clyde Wells confirming that the government would accede to those wishes.

Still the DECs resisted, and when the Newfoundland Supreme Court granted an injunction preventing the closure of Pentecostal and Roman Catholic schools without consent from the denominations, it created an impasse.

When I assumed office and tried to deal with the education funding question, I found things virtually unworkable. Thanks to the partial reforms proposed by Wells and the court's broad interpretation of the DECs' remaining rights, the government's hands were effectively tied. Meanwhile, more controversy than ever was whirling around the subject. On one side, avid reformers felt that things hadn't gone far enough; on the other side, those opposed to reform were looking to the courts at every turn in an attempt to restore power they thought they had lost. Members of the Catholic and Pentecostal communities were furious with the Liberal government for trying to take away their rights, while those on the other side were upset because the reforms they believed they had voted for were not being delivered.

I was unprepared for this raucous debate when I arrived back in St. John's. I had grown up in Stephenville as the son of a Catholic father and an Anglican mother. On Sundays, I usually attended Catholic services in my parish church, but occasionally I would visit the Anglican church with my grandmother. So I never had a sense that I belonged to the Catholic community and not the Protestant community, or vice versa—that kind of exclusive sectarian identity just never occurred to me. Nor was I unusual in that respect. I think this attitude reflected the values of baby boomers everywhere.

In Goose Bay, I attended a Canadian Forces non-denominational public school with separate religious programs for Catholics and Protestants. This attitude carried over to every aspect of our lives. My wife Jodean is a United Church of Canada member, and of my eight brothers and sisters, only two married inside the Catholic Church. The notion of communities that relied so heavily upon their religious affiliation for identity was alien to me.

Arriving as a Catholic premier, I discovered that many non-Catholics assumed I would attempt to dismantle Clyde Wells's efforts to reform the system. Some believed that I would begin conspiring with the bishops to undo everything the previous government had introduced to challenge the DECs. The Catholic community felt that the Wells government had gone much too far and that I, as a Catholic, would be inspired to correct things. I even remember tension, along religious lines, within my own caucus, based on the fear that tackling this issue too forcefully could undermine the credibility of the government.

Having said that, I must point out that Catholic caucus members such as Paul Dicks of Corner Brook, Chuck Furey, who represented St. Barbe, and Kevin Aylward of Stephenville never flinched when it came to finding a solution that would benefit the children of Newfoundland. We refused to bow to the pressures of minorities representing various denominations who were casting this issue as one of religious rights and freedoms. These groups claimed to speak for the broader community but they were largely speaking only for themselves. Not one word of the legislation even hinted at restricting religious freedom. It was intended to improve the education of Newfoundland's children and reduce the load on taxpayers. Most Newfoundlanders shared the determination of Paul and Chuck and the other caucus members to correct an unfair and unwieldy situation.

To run an efficient education system, we would need to close schools that were surplus to the province's needs and consolidate our resources on teachers, computers and better classrooms, instead of busing students and keeping half-empty buildings open.

During my first year in office, I tried unsuccessfully to find common ground with the other side. In fairness to the churches, if you grant an organization defined legal powers, it will exercise those powers. That is precisely what the churches did, especially after the courts strengthened their claim to them. But the public had been given enough time to see that issues of quality education had become secondary to the question of rights. I suspect the public's point of view was also considered against the backdrop of events of the previous decade, especially the revelation of abuses at the Mount Cashel orphanage, identified with the Christian Brothers teaching order.

Clearly, Newfoundland was in the mood for a separation of church and state when it came to education. Beyond that, a generational change had occurred as well. A substantial number of younger men and women in the Catholic Church no longer saw the need for a Catholic incubator to teach religious values within the school system. The place for that, they believed, was the exclusive domain of the church.

The 1995 referendum called by Premier Wells had been painful and divisive, and we wanted to avoid putting the province through another one. Besides, I don't favour referenda generally. A government is elected to get things done during its mandate period and, except in extreme circumstances, it should not have to go back to the people between elections and obtain permission before making one decision or another. But as much as we attempted to find a solution with the DECs, we couldn't get anywhere on the matter. If we tried to close a school with too few students, we would be challenged in court by the appropriate DEC. Based on earlier findings, the court would decree that our action could not be taken without the consent of the Denominational Education Committee, whose jurisdiction included that school.

We clung to the idea of settling things through dialogue and legal means, but the more we tried, the more we failed, and the more we failed, the more we sensed frustration among those demanding reform. I concluded that we must either abandon reform or remove the churches from the education system entirely. I kept that sentiment to myself for some time, sharing it only with Jodean. Then, at a caucus meeting in the summer of 1997, I heard some members talk about the difficulty they faced in returning to their communities where reform was desperately needed to raise the standards of the schools. A few members approached me and said, "Premier, I know this is not the case, but some of my constituents have told me that they suspect this quagmire we find ourselves in is the result of you seeking to undo the modest reforms that Clyde Wells proposed and that you are taking this position because you're a Catholic." Outside of caucus, I was hearing from Catholics who said they could not believe I had betrayed the church by encouraging this reform idea to continue. They resented my constant challenging of the Catholic Church's legal position. Of all the issues we had tackled to that point, including the contentious one of removing 10 percent of public servants from the government payroll to slash the deficit, this was the one that most people felt troubled about.

I may have been the focus of the discontent, but individual members were feeling the heat as well. Gerald Smith, the member from Port au Port, is a former grand knight of the Knights of Columbus and a courageous and principled man. He stood with me on the issue. Beaton Tulk, whose Bonavista riding was almost exclusively Protestant, was accused of betrayal because the government appeared to be dragging its feet on educational reform. Lloyd Mathews, a cabinet member from St. John's North and a full participant in the Pentecostal community, faced a constant barrage of questions from constituents and friends about the government's intention on education and the threat it posed to the Pentecostal Church. He showed courage in sticking to his convictions, as did Roger Grimes, the minister of education. Roger's brother was the second highest ranking member of the Pentecostal Assemblies of Newfoundland and Labrador, yet there was Roger, standing front and centre with me, leading the charge for reform.

All of the public passion and debate over education reform was being reflected within caucus, which agreed on the need for reform. Things could not continue as they had for so many years. We needed to create a better education system, and we had to start by eliminating unnecessary busing, putting an end to half-empty classrooms and increasing the funds available for teachers and materials. We had to use the education system to build an understanding in our children of Newfoundland and Labrador's history and culture; no Newfoundland history was being taught because of a lack of funds for textbooks and teacher training. To top it off, the education question was occupying substantial amounts of the government's time and attention, leaving precious little for other issues.

Eventually, I concluded that there was only one way to solve the problem. We could not retreat in the face of court cases that kept going against the government, nor could we say, "In the interests of peace, we'll stop trying to change things," dooming our children to substandard education. The only alternative was to place all the control over public education in the hands of the legislature, which was providing the funds.

On July 31, 1997, I announced to caucus, with some regret, the decision I had reached. "The time has come," I said, "to call another referendum. But in this one, there will be no confusion regarding the course to be taken. We are forced to remove the churches from the education system entirely. To achieve this, there must be clarity in the question asked and the action to be taken if the referendum passes."

Everyone had a chance to speak and I listened to each view, pro and con. At some point, a leader has to get out in front and lead. I had made up my mind that a second referendum requesting the voters to grant us full power over the province's education programs was essential, and I asked for the support of caucus. The members, who represented every conceivable point of view, backed my decision. It was a courageous thing for them to do, and its impact will be felt for generations.

I intended to frame the question so that the people would understand that the government was asking not for *some* rights from the church organizations when it came to education, but *all* rights. As a Catholic married to a member of the United Church of Canada, I resented the fact that others were dictating how and where our children were to be educated. I rejected the idea that teachers were being hired and fired on the basis of their religious affiliation and that assessments of their teaching abilities hinged on church membership.

A few members were unsure we could win a referendum on that basis, and if we did win, it would be by a margin so small that it would be divisive. If this happened, we would be in an even worse state than we already were, and our credibility with the voters would be severely damaged. I agreed with their assessment. The effects of a loss of credibility and trust in the government would be felt by every member of caucus. Since the decision to go forward with the referendum was ultimately mine, it was only fair that any potential fallout be directed at me. I promised caucus that I would resign my office and ask caucus to elect an interim premier in my place if the referendum failed. In this manner, the government would not be brought down by the issue, and the caucus members would not suffer as a result of my decision.

That evening I announced on a live radio and TV address that the time had come "to protect the rights of the most important group in education—our children." It was time, I suggested, "to elect our school board members because they will exercise their best judgment on behalf of all of us, not just some of us. The government is prepared to take decisive and swift action to bring about a new education system for our province. I can assure you we have the will to act, but we require the authority to act."

The question to be posed to voters on referendum day, September 2, would read: "Do you support a single school system where all children, regardless of their religious affiliation, attend the same schools where opportunities for religious education and observances are provided?" If the majority voted yes, I noted in my speech, it would mean "nothing less than the removal of the churches from the governing of the schools. It

would mean the existing Term 17, which sets out denominational rights in the constitution, would be entirely replaced . . .
What will be the constitutional rights of the churches in such a
new school system? There will be *no* constitutional rights for the
churches in the new school system."

Unlike Clyde Wells, I intended to speak out in favour of the
referendum, and I committed the government to campaign on
behalf of our stand. The positions of the churches would be
delivered from the pulpit; our position would be delivered from
the legislature and from the premier's office. The Conservatives
under leader Loyola Sullivan were split, Sullivan opposing reform.
Jack Harris, the leader and sole NDP member, supported the
referendum question.

Roger Grimes and I, a Pentecostal and a Roman Catholic,
travelled the province seeking support for reform of the education system. We engaged in open debate with those on the other
side, and we corrected church representatives when they said
things that we thought were untrue. They claimed, for example,
that we were attempting to remove religion entirely from the
Newfoundland school system, when all we sought was to replace
the churches with school boards. The schools could continue to
provide religious studies in the curriculum, but the studies
would cover all religions—Catholicism, Protestantism, Judaism,
Islam and others.

We knew that the benefits of the reforms would take years to
make an impact. There would be upheaval and an extended
adjustment period, all leading to a better educational system. Our
efforts were rewarded on referendum night when the Chief
Electoral Officer announced that 73 percent of voters supported
the government. Newfoundland and Labrador, I reminded people
in a television address that evening, had joined Confederation
with a yes vote of just 52 percent; the Northwest Territories
had been divided to create the new region of Nunavut with a
54 percent majority; and Prince Edward Island chose to end its

island status by voting 59 percent in favour of a fixed link. So, 73 percent support was more than gratifying: it was convincing. Another reassuring point: of 48 constituencies in the province, majority votes in support of reform were cast in 47 of them. The constituency of Opposition Leader Loyola Sullivan was 90 percent Catholic, yet two-thirds voted in favour of reform. The entire southern shore of Newfoundland, predominantly Irish Catholic, supported reform by a ratio of about two to one.

I tempered my satisfaction by asking everyone to look at the wider picture. "Tonight is not about winning," I suggested in my television address.

> And it is not about losing. It should never be described in those terms. Tonight is about charting a new course, about setting a new direction for our education system and for Newfoundland and Labrador. This is not a time to analyze the result of the campaign, or the how or why of it. It is a time to accept a clear consensus when it has been expressed. It is a time to achieve what the people of the province have asked us to do for the benefit of the children of Newfoundland and Labrador.

Some resentment continued to be expressed by those opposing reform. This had, after all, been a campaign full of passion and determination, and the defeat of the church position changed things forever. Bonaventure Fagan, head of the Catholic Education Council, chose to attack me personally. "[The referendum] is an abdication of leadership on the part of the premier and his government," Fagan said. Melvin Regular, executive officer of the Pentecostal Education Committee, called the referendum "just opinion seeking" and claimed it had no legal standing, although he admitted "the provincial government will use it to frame a resolution."

Later, when emotions settled down, Dr. Regular agreed that it was time to move on in the best interests of the children's education. He acted with great dignity and wisdom, and I admire him for that. Catholic leaders refused to accept the reality that virtually every Catholic constituency had voted yes in support of reforming the system. They appealed the findings of the referendum all the way to the Supreme Court of Canada, asking to have the question and the referendum results thrown out. They lost at every step of the way.

It was a futile exercise in any case. To their credit, the opposition parties in the House of Assembly accepted the will of the people and the legislation passed unanimously.

THERE IS A TIME for politicians to trust the people. This was true in Montreal during the October 1995 separatist referendum when, given the opportunity, the people were relied upon to do the right thing when it mattered, and it was true in Newfoundland and Labrador on September 2, 1997. Although I had been confident we would win the referendum on educational reform, I knew that many things can affect a vote. The churches, after all, could be very efficient at getting out committed voters who would vote against reform. A high turnout by church supporters and a low turnout by those favouring reform could easily have defeated the question. So I had shown up on referendum night with two speeches in my pocket. I delivered the one acknowledging the passage and calling for reconciliation. I discarded the one that regretfully accepted the will of the people and announced my resignation.

In spite of that success and achievement, I remain opposed to referenda unless no other avenue can be pursued. Referenda deal in issues that tend to be black and white, and they often are a method of division instead of consensus. In this case, a previous referendum had identified at least a bare majority of people who approved the idea of reform, albeit in small measures. I saw no other way to resolve things except to either call an early election or return with a more clear and definitive question. In this case, the referendum was the most practical and, indeed, the only logical choice.

I'VE BEEN ASKED IF THE FINDINGS of the Mount Cashel inquiry influenced the referendum in any way. Certainly it reduced the status of the Catholic Church in Newfoundland and Labrador. Boys at Mount Cashel had been reporting abuse as far back as 1970, but their stories were dismissed or ignored entirely. Church authorities addressed the situation by implying that the boys were liars, and by shuffling the offending priests to far-off parishes where they were free to damage more lives.

The events at Mount Cashel in no way coloured my decision to press for the change in the education system, but as premier I took action to assist more than 40 men who were suing the Irish Christian Brothers, who ran the institution. As young boys, these men were physically and sexually abused by some of the Brothers, and all had suffered as a result. Some of the men had managed to make a life for themselves, while others were psychologically shattered. A few were dying of AIDS. All were asking the Brothers and the Catholic Church for recompense and recognition, but it was clear that some would not be alive by the time the legal jousting was settled.

Two fine lawyers, Jack Harris and Danny Williams, represented the Mount Cashel men. Jack was the leader of the NDP party in Newfoundland and Labrador at the time, and Danny Williams, from a solid Progressive Conservative family in St. John's, is now the Leader of the Opposition, and even their exceptional talents could not move the legal process along quickly.

Our legal advice stated that the plight of the Mount Cashel men was not the province's responsibility. Still, I saw the situation as outrageous. These men, who had already testified before a royal commission, would be required to come forward in a civil suit and recount the abuse and personal tragedies all over again. That seemed unconscionable to me. Could they not receive some settlement without repeating this painful procedure?

The cabinet agreed, and in December 1996 the province provided compensation of several million dollars to be divided among men who had become resigned to never seeing a penny had the suit dragged on for years. In return, the men assigned the right to sue the Christian Brothers to Newfoundland and Labrador, and none had to testify. Nearly six years later, the Christian Brothers settled with the province, which recovered the money advanced to the victims.

One more story from that period: While we were living in Ottawa, our son Adam attended a non-denominational public school in Ottawa and received religious instruction at our parish church. On the day of Adam's confirmation, Jodean and I were dismayed to discover that the children were to be addressed by none other than Archbishop Alphonsus Liguori Penney, the man who had left his post as Archbishop of Newfoundland after being severely criticized for his management of the situation at Mount Cashel. Fleeing Newfoundland and Labrador, the Archbishop had retreated to the labyrinth of the church to emerge now at our son's confirmation. To make things even more offensive, Jodean and I sat in stunned silence while he delivered a homily advising the children to respect their bodies as sacred temples.

It took some persuasion to convince Jodean to remain through the service and attend the reception afterward, which we planned to leave at the earliest convenience.

Before we could say our goodbyes, however, the local priest approached us, guiding the Archbishop by the arm. "You must know the Archbishop," the priest said to us, and Archbishop Penney smiled and offered his hand.

Jodean gripped the Archbishop's hand, looked directly into his eyes, and said: "Indeed I do. I know all about the Archbishop."

Her meaning was inescapable, and the Archbishop's response was immediate. He turned without saying a word and, with the confused priest in tow, fled the room.

THE MOST PROGRESSIVE
PROVINCE IN CANADA

WALLY ANDERSEN GREW UP IN MAKKOVIK, on the Labrador coast, and graduated from high school in North West River, near Goose Bay. He began working as a stock handler in the government-owned store in Davis Inlet and soon was transferred to Goose Bay as a buyer, eventually working his way up to manager of operations and purchasing.

Everything about Wally speaks of dedication, hard work and intelligence. More than that, Wally has strived all his adult life to assist Innu and Inuit youth to make the most of themselves (as he has done himself), and his efforts earned him acclaim as his community's citizen of the year in 1983.

Elected to the Newfoundland House of Assembly in 1996, Wally soon became one of the most popular members of caucus, a guy who worked tirelessly on behalf of the constituency of Torngat Mountains. He helped me and other members of the caucus understand the problems being faced by Inuit and Innu on the Labrador coast. As time passed, I grew aware of another side of Wally, one beyond the ambitious and hard-working government representative. It was the side that had to deal with the seemingly endless tragedies that befell young people in Inuit communities, and it was painful to see their effect on him.

Now and then, I would be informed that Wally was on his way to my office to share the burdens of his day. He would sit across from me, not asking for miracles or instant cures of long-standing social issues, but just needing to recount stories of teen suicides or infant deaths. Some days he would say, "Premier, this hurts. I'm hurting over this one." If an important caucus meeting or some other government event was upcoming, he would explain that he simply had to go home to his people, to be with his family, with the families of those who suffered the tragedy, with the elders, whoever. Over time, he engaged me and other members of the caucus in the reality of Native life on the north Labrador coast, and he helped set the stage for the province of Newfoundland and Labrador to embrace real Aboriginal reform.

My empathy for First Nations people had begun years earlier, thanks to Françoise Ducros, who later became director of communications to Jean Chrétien, is a passionate advocate for social justice where Aboriginal rights are concerned. Shortly after I had assumed the role of minister of fisheries and oceans, Francie, then an official with the Aboriginal affairs branch, sat me down and explained the ramifications of the *Sparrow* decision, the landmark Supreme Court ruling that defined Aboriginal rights over fishing and hunting. *Sparrow* established the guideline that Aboriginal people must be given priority to fish for food and for social and ceremonial purposes after conservation goals have been met.

I was having difficulty interpreting its impact on behalf of the ministry, and so Francie persuaded me to visit First Nations leaders in British Columbia, where events leading to the *Sparrow* decision had originated.

The leaders I met defied all the stereotypes that many Canadians harbour about the original inhabitants of this continent. They were charismatic, strong willed, intelligent and committed to the welfare of their people. They also welcomed me warmly, even when we disagreed on one point or another. I remember sitting with Ovide Mercredi, grand chief of the

Assembly of First Nations and Chief Joe Gosnell of the Nisga'a Nation and all of us watching a Nisga'a ceremonial drum dance until Ovide stood up and said, "Let's join in." And I did—a Newfoundland Irish Catholic copying the steps of a drum dance that was probably being performed when Captain Cook was sailing off Vancouver Island.

We travelled up to Carrier Sekani territory near Prince George, where Chief Ed John showed me the devastation created by river dams that had flooded the band's ancestral burial grounds, then invited me to a potlatch supper with community members including elders. As the guest of honour, I was invited to serve myself from the table first, and I scooped caribou and moose meat, beaver stew and other delicacies onto my plate. Returning to my table, I noticed a very old man, a band elder, smiling back at me. His canes were resting against his chair, and it was obvious that he would have difficulty walking to the table where the meal had been set out. So I did what any Newfoundlander would do in the situation—I offered him my food. He took it with a broad smile and a nod of thanks, and I walked to the end of the line.

That gesture, not uncommon in Newfoundland, elevated my status among the band members. I had shown respect for an elder, which is a hallowed tradition amongst Aboriginal peoples but too often lacking in the rest of society. First Nations people believe that an elder's experience should never be discounted or undervalued, a repeat of the lesson I had first absorbed back in 1978 when I encountered the dedicated captains in Newfoundland politics. The elders that day gave me a Carrier Sekani name that means Keeper of the Salmon.

Later I met Miles Richardson, a Haida leader on the Queen Charlotte Islands and a firebrand of a man who earned my admiration for his passion and insight. Rejecting formalities, Miles began our first conversation by glaring across the table at me and saying, "Listen here, Brian," before cataloguing all the failures of the federal government in dealing with Aboriginal issues. Miles talked and I listened. Later, Miles suggested I visit Haida Gwaii (the Queen Charlotte Islands) and see the ancient communities of longhouses and totem poles scattered among the towering trees. These long-abandoned communities were power-ful reminders of the Haida attachment to land. The Haida say, "We do not inherit the land from our ancestors, we borrow it from our children."

I returned to Ottawa with a new appreciation for the concerns of Canada's Aboriginal people and an admiration for the ability of their leaders. Years later, when Wally came into my office yet another time to tell me how much he was hurting over a youth suicide, I said, "If you're going home, Wally, I'm going with you." I travelled the northern Labrador coast with Wally and saw first-hand the state of the communities there. I saw no roads, no sewers, inadequate housing and makeshift schools. I returned to St. John's determined that something had to be done. I was ashamed, not of those I had met, but of myself and government leaders everywhere who had failed to address the basic human rights of a proud people.

Back in St. John's I discovered that many members of the provincial bureaucracy involved in Aboriginal issues were ready to move fast if given the green light. We quickly put in place plans for schools, housing, roads, water and sewer and recreation facilities. We fast-tracked negotiations on the Inuit land claim. Labrador Inuit Association president William Barbour and I agreed on a settlement area that provided 28,000 square miles of land and 17,000 square miles of adjacent ocean, extending 12 miles out from shore. An area covering 6,100 square miles, referred to as Labrador Inuit Lands, where the Inuit would retain most rights and benefits, was created within the settlement area. In addition, we negotiated with the Inuit to guarantee them a portion of provincial revenues from mineral developments and joint approval over mineral exploration on Inuit lands. Around the same time, Peter Penashue, the leader of the Innu nation, and I negotiated a memorandum of understanding to begin negotiations on the Innu land claims and self-government agreements.

With spring breakup the next year, the province constructed roads on the north Labrador coast for year-round use, built new housing, and made a major investment in Labrador schools, something that the DECs had never done. Under the DEC system, most schools in Labrador were archaic and unfit, barely measuring up to developing-country standards. They were never improved under the DECs, because the old system had served the communities with the strongest voice. Since the Labrador Inuit and Innu villages had virtually no voice, they received no funding. If the referendum-backed education reform program had done nothing else except raise the quality of Labrador schools to minimal acceptance levels, it would have been worthwhile. In reality, of course, it did much more.

All that expenditure took place while we, as a government, were seeking to maintain a balanced budget. How did we do it? By applying the savings from a reformed education system to where the need was greatest.

We built new roads on the south Labrador coast as well. The federal government had been providing a ferry service among communities on the Labrador coast and was committed under a constitutional agreement to maintain the service in perpetuity. We approached Ottawa with a proposal: instead of providing the inadequate seasonal ferry service year after year, Newfoundland would build a coastal highway serving the same communities. The province would release Ottawa from its constitutional obligation to operate the ferry service in return for the transfer of a one-time-only lump sum of money to Newfoundland to pay for the road construction.

The federal government agreed, and it was a good deal for everyone. We were able to construct a highway as far north as Cartwright (the cost of building a road beyond that point was prohibitive), a distance of about 250 miles from the coastal border with Quebec. The federal government, for its part, was released from an annual expense. During the construction period we had full employment on the Labrador coast, and when we finished, communities along the coast were finally connected by a good road. We even had money left over, which we used to improve the Trans-Labrador Highway from Goose Bay to the Quebec border.

You cannot underestimate the impact that good roads can make in the north. The improved highway to Goose Bay, for example, meant that residents of the area could enjoy fresh fruits and vegetables at reasonable prices, arriving year-round from Montreal on a regular basis. Until that highway was brought up to standard, perishable goods arrived either by ship, which meant they were never fresh, or by air, which meant they were terribly expensive. Cheaper and more plentiful fruits and vegetables meant healthier diets, which translated into a reduced burden on health care costs. Today, tourists can travel to Newfoundland, drive up the Great Northern Peninsula, take a ferry from St. Barbe across the Strait of Belle Isle to Blanc-Sablon in Quebec, and tour all the way up the coast to Cartwright—an unforgettable experience.

Whenever I recall the things we managed to do for Aboriginal rights in Newfoundland and Labrador, I think of Misel Joe, leader of the Conne River band of First Nations in Newfoundland. After a difficult first few meetings, where Chief Joe pressed for a number of things from me as premier and I had to convince him that I could not deliver everything he wanted, we developed a kinship that became cemented with his gift to me of a talking stick. Among Aboriginal peoples, a talking stick recognizes the creative aspirations of each individual. In a meeting or confer-ence, the person holding the talking stick must be listened to with respect and without interruption. He or she must, in turn, always speak the truth.

Misel Joe had personally crafted the talking stick he gave me, polishing and shaping it into a work of art before adding a traditional medicine bag near the top. When I saw how much work it represented, I refused to accept it. Misel Joe insisted that I take the talking stick and that I keep it in my office "so that, whenever I come here to talk to you, Premier, I'll know you are telling the truth!"

I asked how he could give away something so beautiful that he had obviously worked so hard to create.

"One day, you too will give it away," Misel Joe replied.

I assured him I would not.

"Yes, you will," he said. "You will know when, and you will give it to someone else."

A few years later, I left St. John's to attend a dedication of a statue honouring the Beothuk people, the original inhabitants of Newfoundland who were tragically and senselessly slaughtered. I took the talking stick with me because I planned to speak a few words at the event. At the dais I made my remarks, then told the story of how Misel Joe had created the talking stick especially for me and how much I valued it. In the middle of my talk, I looked across at Gerald Squires, the artist who had created the bronze statue of the Beothuk woman, Shawnadithit, that would mark the site. The power of Squires's work, and the knowledge of the Beothuk genocide, had moved everyone attending the ceremony. Suddenly I knew what to do, and I presented my talking stick to Squires. Like me, he at first refused to take it because it was so beautiful. Then, also like me, he accepted it and, I am sure, some day he will encounter the place, the person and the opportunity to pass it on to someone else, just as Misel Joe had predicted.

THE AGREEMENTS WITH THE INNU and Inuit were milestones marking important progress between government and Aboriginal groups. I'm proud of that achievement, but I am even more proud that the government was supported every step of the way by people throughout Newfoundland and Labrador. Many Canadians are surprised at the progressive attitudes of Newfoundlanders when it comes to social issues and equality of opportunity. In my experience, no region in the country is more open-minded on these matters than the people of Newfoundland and Labrador. I saw it demonstrated in the settlements with the Innu and Inuit, in the educational reforms we introduced to Newfoundland and in our decision to fund the Morgentaler clinics.

The impact of Dr. Henry Morgentaler on Canadian society is difficult to overestimate. A survivor of the Holocaust, he was one of the first physicians in Canada to perform vasectomies and provide IUDs for family planning. He was also one of the first to publicly request that the federal government repeal the law against abortion. His activities in this area resulted in a series of criminal charges against him in Quebec and Ontario. At each trial, he was acquitted by a jury, and instead of heeding the voices of the jury members, each acquittal spurred the governments, in what appeared to be fits of pique, to seek a retrial. No matter what your opinion on abortion may be, this process was not a search for justice but a policy of harassment and persecution, and it continued until the provincial governments realized they could not use the courts to batter someone whose activities and values were widely accepted by the community.

This policy of harassment was the product of petty minds, and petty minds do not give up easily. By the mid-1990s, medical facilities across Canada had for many years routinely provided the same abortion services that Dr. Morgentaler had been vilified for providing less than 20 years earlier, and the cost of these services was being covered by the public health system. Dr. Morgentaler was also providing abortion services in his own clinics throughout the country, and although the clinics could no longer be shut down, every provincial government refused to provide funding for them.

The female caucus members challenged me with a question. Did it make sense for Newfoundland to acknowledge and at least tacitly approve the existence and operation of the Morgentaler clinic in St. John's while barring it from public funds that clinics providing other services routinely received? Abortions were available at hospitals across the province. Why single out Dr. Morgentaler? The fact is, many women prefer the privacy of a Morgentaler clinic to a large, public institution.

We made a decision to provide full funding for the Morgentaler clinics, one made not without some controversy. A few caucus members feared it would hurt us politically, but we put the policy in place with barely a word of protest. In my view, the episode was an example of the community at large being far ahead of the political process.

A similar experience occurred when we provided amendments to the Human Rights Code for Newfoundland and Labrador, ensuring non-discrimination on the basis of sexual orientation. Again, there was much discussion within government that this change would upset people mightily and damage our position with voters. In fact, controversy over the legislation never occurred, and I found the public very supportive of the change.

There is a perception in this country that a basically rural populace necessarily has deeply conservative political attitudes. That simply isn't true. Newfoundlanders and Labradorians are tolerant, open and progressive in social policy, and proved it by supporting the government on those milestone initiatives.

TALL TALES FROM VOISEY'S BAY

O N A NATIONAL SCALE, nothing generated more controversy and outright hostility, in some quarters at least, than my stand on Voisey's Bay and Inco's claim to the enormous nickel deposits there. It led to one of the most lengthy and vitriolic discussions about Newfoundland and Labrador resources and politics to occur since the province had joined Confederation 50 years earlier.

Unfortunately, many of the details were unrevealed, unappreciated or simply ignored by many conservative commentators and politicians. At the height of the dispute, Diane Francis, writing in the *Financial Post*, claimed I was "pushing a personal agenda that proves he does not understand that nobody and no corporation owes Newfoundland or Canada a living."

Around the same time, then Ontario Premier Mike Harris said he was "shocked" by my handling of negotiations with Inco and that he favoured allowing Inco to process Newfoundland ore in its smelter in Sudbury, where the company had surplus capacity and where jobs would be created in Ontario. Mike Harris is a fine man, so even he might note the contradiction of being "shocked" that I would try to create jobs in Newfoundland, where I was elected, rather than promote the creation of jobs for Ontario. Seymour Schulich, a wealthy Toronto business leader, suggested that Prime Minister Jean Chrétien "should pull [my] chain and he will heel." Would Seymour Schulich support the idea of Canada's prime minister being able to pull a premier's chain under any other circumstances except for this one where he had a personal investment at stake? I doubt it.

Let's deal with the facts.

Voisey's Bay is a remote area about 200 miles north of Goose Bay. The Inuit called it Kauipuskats Shipish, which translates as Burning Spot Brook, but it was eventually renamed for Amos Voisey, a fur trader and his sons who operated a trading post there for many years, exchanging tobacco, flour and tea for furs.

In 1993, two prospectors, Chris Verbiski and Al Chislett, discovered significant deposits of nickel, copper and cobalt on the property, and they transferred the claim to a company called Diamond Fields Resources. The Inuit opposed exploration and development in the area for many years, citing the risk of pollution in the water and damage to sacred burial sites. When Labrador's Aboriginal peoples tried to evict prospectors and developers in early 1995, it led to a 12-day standoff between them and more than 50 RCMP officers. Eventually they were forced to relent, and Diamond Fields Resources resumed drilling for core samples. To Labrador's First Nations peoples, the development of Voisey's Bay became one more insult to their heritage, intensifying the impacts of low-level flight training, road expansion, industrial forestry and hydroelectric developments. Voisey's Bay was steeped in controversy from the beginning.

Overriding everything was the size of the ore body. More than 30 million tons of ore were identified, making Voisey's Bay one of the world's richest undeveloped nickel deposits. Arriving on the heels of the fisheries industry collapse, Voisey's Bay promised to be an economic godsend to Newfoundland and Labrador. Certainly Clyde Wells felt that way when, as premier in 1995, he took a hard and principled position with respect to the project's development and its benefits to the province. Those who believe that I launched a squeeze play against Inco over Voisey's Bay are mistaken. In reality, I was maintaining the same justifiable position that my predecessor had taken: Voisey's Bay should be developed in a manner that was fair to both the company and the people of Newfoundland and Labrador.

Remember that in the past Newfoundland and Labrador had suffered from a series of bad deals where resource development was concerned. The most notorious was Churchill Falls, in which Hydro Quebec reaped an enormous profit from power generated in Labrador and sold to them for less than three-tenths of a cent per kilowatt hour, a price fixed for 40 years with an option for Quebec to renew for an additional 25 years at an even lower rate. In effect, Quebec is guaranteed 5.2 million kilowatts of power until the year 2035 at a price less than one-tenth of the current market rate. Efforts by previous Newfoundland governments to renegotiate the deal and inject at least some fairness into the price were met by rejection and claims that "A deal is a deal!"

Churchill Falls is a scar on the psyche of Newfoundland and Labrador, and until we demonstrated that we could negotiate good deals, we would never be able to set aside the belief that we had been scuppered yet again. When it came to Voisey's Bay, Newfoundland was simply determined to ensure that, indeed, a deal *is* a deal.

The fiasco over bad deals had driven Clyde Wells from the Smallwood government back in the mid-1960s. He had put his political career on the line over it. He did the same thing with Voisey's Bay, except that now he was making decisions in the premier's chair and not being asked to go along with someone else's flawed plan.

Canada's nickel mining giants, Inco and Falconbridge, were still negotiating with Diamond Fields, who owned the Voisey's Bay rights, when I assumed the premier's office in St. John's. I was looking forward to bringing Voisey's Bay, Terra Nova and other developments on stream, but I was also determined to see that the deals were done fairly where the interests of Newfoundlanders were concerned.

Diamond Fields, led by controversial mining promoter Robert Friedland, initiated a long and bitter series of negotiations with the suitors for the Voisey's Bay rights, often using high-pressure tactics to squeeze the last penny for itself. This was considered tough but fair bargaining, even though it meant that Inco paid upwards of a billion dollars more than competitor Falconbridge had offered for the property. Yet, when the time came for Inco to sit down with the province to discuss its terms, our insistence that the mining company keep its original promises was considered unreasonable. Anyone who makes that claim is either unaware of all the details or is promoting the concept of an economic double standard where private corporations and provincial governments are concerned.

Too often in politics, you score points (or believe you do) just by making a deal. Politicians are frequently depicted shaking hands and smiling for the camera because a deal has been struck with a corporation or another level of government. Striking a deal, it is assumed, is always good news. But sometimes it is necessary to say no to an offer and walk away. Private corporations do it whenever they decide that the offer being tendered is not in the best interests of the shareholders. In politics, the shareholders are the voters and taxpayers who put you in power, and politicians owe them the best deal possible, just as a company president owes the same to the shareholders. The lack of a deal in politics should not be associated with failure; it may on occasion be more associated with principle.

Clyde Wells had stipulated a number of conditions to the nickel companies during preliminary discussions on Voisey's Bay, including the principle that the province would share in windfall profits should nickel prices increase dramatically. This was not a popular idea among the mining and investment communities, and so there was already an environment of tension and potential conflict when I arrived. An even bigger issue was Wells's insistence that Newfoundlanders must benefit from jobs created by the refining process. Instead of shipping raw ore elsewhere, it should remain in the province to be refined into nickel. Was that a tough or unfair stand? Only if you refuse to accept the fact that the ore belonged to Newfoundlanders and that they had every right to dictate the terms of its removal.

Inco agreed to this condition when it wrote Premier Wells in July 1995 to say, "Accordingly, Inco will use its best efforts to ensure that, to the greatest extent economically and technically feasible, the processing of all such ores will be done in the Province of Newfoundland. Inco also acknowledges your advice that the province may set conditions requiring that such processing be done in the province." Later, when Inco attempted to escape the processing requirement, the president claimed this "was not an unconditional commitment."

Both Falconbridge and Inco were preparing offers to purchase the Voisey's Bay rights from the mercurial Friedland and his Diamond Fields organization. At one point during the 1996 election campaign, Falconbridge president Frank Pickard called me to say he believed Falconbridge had won the bid to obtain the rights and that his company was totally committed to building a smelter and refinery in Newfoundland. Later, Inco delivered a knockout blow when it made a counter-offer of $4.3 billion, outbidding Falconbridge by a full billion dollars.

By going so far beyond the Falconbridge bid, Inco ensured that it would win the rights from Diamond Fields. Mike Sopko, CEO of Inco, soon called me to affirm that Inco would keep its commitment to develop ore-processing facilities in Newfoundland and Labrador.

That promise is the key to understanding the subsequent details of the story. Both companies committed themselves to building a refinery in Newfoundland during the bidding war. Was this offer part of a strategy to curry favour for their bids on the part of the Newfoundland government and its people? Undoubtedly. You don't secure a multi-billion-dollar bid without identifying all the interest groups involved and finding ways to get them on your side, and the refinery deal was welcomed by a province that needed the jobs and investment. At the same time, of course, a company does not offer to construct a smelter and refinery without assuring itself that the offer does not torpedo its chance to make a profit. Clearly, both Inco and Falconbridge believed that Voisey's Bay would make good economic sense if the ore were processed in Newfoundland and Labrador.

As soon as Inco obtained the rights to Voisey's Bay with its pre-emptive bid, the company dispatched consultants to research about a dozen potential sites for the smelter and refinery in Newfoundland and Labrador. It also signed a contract with a Japanese industrial giant to provide technology for the facility. By year's end, Inco had launched the required environmental review for the mine and mill facility, announced that Argentia was the chosen site for the smelter and refinery and contracted SNC-Lavalin Inc. as construction managers. Each of these announcements was made with much fanfare and handshaking all around. The idea of refining the ore in Newfoundland was not mine, nor was it an empty promise made only to secure a bargaining position; we believed it was a firm decision taken in the best interests of both Inco and the province.

Over the next year, things began to change in the Inco board-room. First came the realization that Inco may have overpaid for the rights to Voisey's Bay. Making matters worse, the price of nickel began to fall in 1997 and kept on falling. In February 1998, Inco announced the imposition of company-wide cost-cutting measures, a potential divesture of assets, a reduced dividend to shareholders and the re-evaluation of all major ongoing projects. Not surprisingly, one of the projects under review was Voisey's Bay and the firm's commitment to construct a refining facility in Newfoundland and Labrador.

These were the kinds of decisions any corporate management must take when faced with rising costs and reduced income, and their effects would be felt by various groups—employees, management, shareholders and investors. But when management decided that Newfoundlanders and Labradorians would also have to pay the price by releasing Inco from its commitment to build the refinery at Argentia so that the company could ship raw ore to its facility in Sudbury, an entirely new issue arose.

If one private corporation can overpay another private corporation for rights to a public resource, then later ask the public to absorb the impact of that error—in other words, pay the price of the corporation's own mistake—then we have changed the rules of free enterprise dramatically. Capitalism, by its very nature, entails risk. Those who take the risks earn the reward. Nothing I have ever read, however, says that the risk taker has a right to turn the clock back when the risk is discovered to have been ill taken. That was Inco's position in a nutshell. The company had taken a risk and lost, and now it wanted the people of Newfoundland and Labrador to cover its losses.

WHEN WE REFUSED TO RE-DRAFT THE AGREEMENT, Inco proposed building the prototype for a new hydro-metallurgical refining technology at Argentia. A portion of the Voisey's Bay ore would be shipped there to test the process. Meanwhile, substantial quantities of ore would be sent to Sudbury for refining under traditional methods, providing Inco with income during the demonstration period. We agreed to talk.

We entered a long and challenging series of negotiations with Inco, many of them shepherded by Roger Grimes, the minister of energy, and Bill Rowat, who had played such a pivotal role as my DM during the conflict with the EU over turbot. We agreed to work with Inco on the development of the new hydro-metallurgical technology. However, we wanted a guarantee that should the pilot plant fail to work, Inco would build a traditional processing plant in the province. In addition, Inco would have to return an equivalent amount of ore removed from the province during the demonstration phase back to Newfoundland for processing. I also asked the company to make a commitment that Newfoundland and Labrador–based suppliers of goods and services would be favoured, wherever possible. This latter point was not inflexible. If offshore or out-of-province suppliers offered a level of quality or price advantage that Newfoundlanders could not match, they would be awarded the work. I simply wanted to ensure that the people of the province were not systematically shut out of reaping the benefits of the project.

None of these requirements was beyond those I would expect any Canadian premier to place on the bargaining table. In spite of that, some commentators and editorialists in other areas of the country declared that I was attempting to squeeze unfair advantages from a private corporation and that I was unrealistic in my demands. Perhaps encouraged by these observations, Inco rejected the terms in the summer of 1998, and I informed Mike Sopko there would be no further negotiations as a result. Later that year, we passed amendments to the Mineral Act that gave government the power to withhold permits to companies if it felt the province was not receiving fair benefits. Talks resumed and continued intermittently through January 2000, when they were broken off for an unspecified period.

I have not a moment's regret over the position I took on Voisey's Bay. Not one moment. It ended a long history of Newfoundland politicians selling out and telling the province that half a loaf was better than none, after a whole loaf had been promised by both sides. Some editorial writers and business columnists missed that point. They wrote: "The opportunity of a lifetime has been lost. Tobin has caused the Voisey's Bay development to be stalled for a generation." Well, it was "lost" for barely two years. In June 2002, my successor, Roger Grimes, who worked alongside me as minister of mines and resources when we tried to hammer out a deal with Inco, announced that the project would go forward. The same terms that Inco had rejected earlier, including its commitment to replace any ore it took out of Newfoundland while the demonstration period was taking place, were agreed upon. In addition, Inco guaranteed a return to traditional processing technology if the hydro-metallurgical pilot plant failed. What was "impossible" barely two years earlier was doable now. I wish at least one of those political columnists and frantic financial gurus would acknowledge the fact that a two-year delay was worth 35 years of benefits for the province.

I am frequently surprised by the apparently perfect forecasting abilities of financial commentators in this country. Predicting economic developments even a few months in advance is less accurate than predicting the weather or the outcome of the NHL season. Yet these columnists and observers never hesitate to tell us where the market is going, where interest rates are headed and how likely you are to retain your job next year. All well and good; anyone in a free country should be able to express his or her opinion.

I become agitated, however, when self-appointed gurus attack a government branch that dares to question or challenge some aspect of business and free enterprise, as though elected officials have a less exalted view of reality than a newspaper columnist or TV commentator. I'm not saying they have a better view, although that's often possible. I'm simply suggesting that the view is usually on a par with others.

Let's not forget that many of the financial commentators who were vilifying me for my stand on Voisey's Bay in 1998 and 1999 were simultaneously praising people like John Roth, then president of Nortel. Roth, we were lectured by more than one conservative financial observer, was not only highly qualified to run Nortel, but could tell us how to run the country as well and do it more efficiently than anyone in Ottawa or the provincial capitals. Well, Roth is no longer running Nortel, and he certainly isn't running the country either. When I entered into negotiations with Inco over Voisey's Bay, Nortel stock was selling for about $100 (Canadian) per share and I was advised to forget about getting the smelter and refinery built in Newfoundland and Labrador. As I write this, Nortel is a penny stock. Inco stock, however, is almost twice the price it commanded when negotiations with Newfoundland and Labrador broke off.

WHEN THE INCO PURCHASE of the Voisey's Bay deposit was announced in 1996, lot of celebrations took place in Newfoundland. If I had permitted the company to break its promise about building a refinery in the province, the ore from Voisey's Bay would have been dug from the ground in Labrador, floated up the St. Lawrence to Montreal and loaded onto trains bound for Sudbury. The Ontario premier would have rightly claimed that another thousand or so jobs had been generated for Ontarians, and the people of Newfoundland and Labrador would have been convinced that they had been handed the short end of the stick again. And they would have been correct. That is why, backed by a unanimous vote in the Newfoundland and Labrador legislature, I had turned Inco down in January 2000.

The issue of Voisey's Bay was never one of a provincial government harassing a private company or playing hardball for strictly political purposes. The issue was whether the citizens of Newfoundland and Labrador would share in the added value of the ore once it was removed from the mine site.

I was personally involved in all aspects of the negotiations with Inco, and I got along quite well with Mike Sopko and Scott Hand, who is now president of Inco. There were tense and difficult moments in the meetings from time to time, but you expect that when the deal involves billions of dollars and the livelihoods of thousands of people. Both sides were under pressure. Inco was facing substantially reduced prices at that time for its product on the world market. I took the view we were not negotiating a deal based on the low prices in 1996, but rather a deal based on projected nickel prices over the next 35 to 40 years. I was representing a people who had been counting on jobs at the smelter and refinery to lift them out of unemployment. Inco was beholden to its shareholders; I was beholden to the people of Newfoundland and Labrador. Both of us wanted to go back to our people with the very best deal we could get.

Those who propose that governments act more like private corporations surely cannot criticize us for seeking the very best deal for everyone as well. As a government, we were determined to leave the ore in the ground until we were assured that the company would live up to its original commitment, and there is nothing wrong with that either.

IT WAS IN THE MIDST OF NEGOTIATIONS with Inco that I heard from Seymour Schulich. He had made a substantial investment based on Inco's assumed success with Voisey's Bay, even after I had told him that we expected Inco to keep its promise about an ore refinery. Seymour went ahead anyway, then visited me to urge that we get the deal completed. When I told him that nothing would happen unless and until Inco agreed to process the ore in Newfoundland, he became frustrated.

We had an otherwise cordial relationship, but Seymour kept warning me that if I kept saying no to Inco, I'd get hammered in the business press. At one point, he said, "Look what Diane Francis is saying about you in the *Financial Post*," and he read a severe personal criticism she had written about me over Voisey's Bay. In return, I gave Seymour an off-the-cuff observation of Ms. Francis.

A day or two later, I received a personal telephone call from Diane Francis. "I have been told," she said in a voice as cold as any January wind that ever roared through Labrador, "that you told Seymour Schulich I was a bitch. Is that right?"

"No, that is *not* right," I replied. "I did not say you were a bitch." I paused long enough for the words to sink in, then added: "I said you were a pompous bitch."

What followed is between me and Diane and is not the kind of stuff intended for a family audience. In what is surely a great irony, Diane Francis and I are both speakers for the same agency, and as I write this are appearing back to back, giving speeches across Canada. As usual, we still find much to disagree about.

VOISEY'S BAY WAS BOTH A WATERSHED for Newfoundland and a lesson for Canada. Newfoundland profited fairly from its own resource, and Inco obtained one of the most lucrative nickel ore bodies in the world. We should welcome the private sector and the investment it brings, and we should embrace free enterprise and celebrate the achievements of entrepreneurs. But we should never forget that the country's resources belong not to investors or private corporations, but to all the people of Canada.

HEALTH CARE IN CANADA—
PERSONALITIES AND PROPOSALS

M Y EXPERIENCE AS PREMIER provided me with a new perspective on government, of course. In federal-provincial relationships I was now on the other side of the fence in more ways than one, with a better understanding of the difficulties each level of government faces and some ideas on how they might be resolved.

One aspect of federal-provincial negotiations I especially enjoyed was the opportunity to work closely with people like Ralph Klein, Roy Romanow, Mike Harris and Lucien Bouchard.

Ralph Klein is difficult to get along with sometimes, and difficult not to like. He is a straight-talking personality who some people choose to define in right-wing terms exclusively, which I think is a mistake.

Ralph has come under attack from some quarters for his opposition to the Kyoto agreement, aimed at reducing greenhouse gases. Is he toeing the right-wing line when it comes to this particular environmental concern? I don't think so. Ralph wants to know how we are going to achieve the goals of Kyoto, which strikes me as a fundamental point to be established before signing an accord. He has a right and a duty to ask that question, as has every Canadian.

In discussions, Ralph usually begins by assuming a tough position and negotiating hard, but if a reasonable compromise is within reach, he is always prepared to move. I saw this strategy at work during discussions with the federal government on health care in September 2000. I had made a number of speeches prior to the conference, asking the federal government to restore health care spending levels. My position caused problems with people on both sides of the federal-provincial fence. My former federal colleagues were upset with me for pointing fingers at them, as though suggesting they were responsible for various troubles within the system; and my provincial friends were concerned that I might be trying to broker a deal on behalf of Ottawa.

Indeed, I had been part of the federal government that had slowed allocations to the provinces for health care in the mid-1990s as part of the federal government's efforts to deal with the deficit. My position in September 2000 was this: now that we have begun to put our financial house in order, it's time to reinvest in some services, health care prime among them.

I garnered support from other premiers by emphasizing the importance of standing together to reach an agreement acceptable to both sides. "As long as we are divided on this point [of increasing the federal government's allocation for health care]," I said at a previous session, "it will be like shooting fish in a barrel to them. If we do not learn to speak with one voice, if we are not coherent, if we are not capable of focusing our demands on a small number of key issues instead of a broad range of regional concerns, we'll lose. Why? Because the federal government, in the minds of most Canadians, would be quite right to say, 'These guys just have their hands out looking for a different list of priorities, and we can't afford to fund them all.'"

The provincial premiers had begun sharpening their focus during meetings in the period between 1995 and 2000, and it was paying off. Polls conducted at the beginning of that period indicated that Canadians saw the federal government in the role of guarantor of the health care system; any flaws in delivering health care were seen as the responsibility of the provinces. Over the next five years, however, opinions began to shift, and Canadians increasingly came to believe that the federal government was not paying its fair share.

For a number of years, Ottawa refused to do more in funding the system, centring its efforts on controlling the deficit. With an election coming up, however, the federal government agreed to support health care with an additional $20 billion in federal money. Prime Minister Chrétien arrived at the September 2000 meeting convinced that he had put a fair offer on the table. With this commitment, we managed to put a deal together that we knew Ottawa could accept and that the provinces could support. And all did—all but two, that is. Ontario Premier Mike Harris and Quebec Premier Lucien Bouchard said they could not support the agreement that the other provinces had approved. We needed a unanimous deal to send upstairs to the prime minister. Time was running out, and Harris and Bouchard appeared adamant: the deal was not satisfactory. Without concessions from Ottawa, they would not yield.

Ralph Klein had arrived at the conference with a similar attitude, even after the rest of us began to recognize the importance of accepting Ottawa's offer. Other provinces had also started out believing that their position was valid and represented the best solution. But as time passed, one province after another took the advice of Premier Romanow, who suggested we "pour a little water in our wine" and get on with it. Ontario and Quebec disagreed.

At one point, Premier Harris had lined up support against the deal from Quebec as well as from PEI, Nova Scotia and New Brunswick. This made him confident that he could either swing the conference to his point of view or, at the very least, walk out with the support of three or four other provinces.

The siding of the three Atlantic provinces with Harris and Bouchard was disconcerting to me. They had traditionally stood together with Newfoundland and Labrador on matters such as this because, despite our differing political affiliations—three

Conservative premiers and me, a Liberal—we recognized our common concerns. Once the other three Atlantic premiers had an opportunity to study Harris's plan in greater detail, however, they recognized the merits of Chrétien's offer and swung their support behind it again.

Premiers Harris and Bouchard remained firm in their opposition to the deal as it stood, and after a day and a half of effort, nothing appeared to have changed.

At dinner that evening, Ralph Klein spoke across the table to premiers Harris and Bouchard. "Fellows, enough is enough," Ralph said. "We have moved this file as far as we're going to move it. We need to stabilize the health care system; that's a priority. It's time to do a deal and Alberta for one is ready to sign off." Ralph saw the need for flexibility and supported the federal proposal in the wider interests of the country.

The following day was the last of the conference, and the prime minister was upstairs in the Lester B. Pearson Building waiting to hear if we had a deal. Roy Romanow and I agreed to make one final appeal to premiers Harris and Bouchard, who were insisting on more negotiations with Ottawa after the other premiers had agreed to the offer on the table.

Roy and I called Harris and Bouchard to the Newfoundland and Labrador delegation room, where we reminded them that everyone else was waiting on them. We pointed out that we had brought the federal government a considerable distance from its position at the beginning of the conference. There had been give and take on both sides. Eight of the 10 provinces were satisfied that they could go home with a deal acceptable to their constituents. "There is real money on the table," Roy and I said. "It's not as much as we wanted, perhaps, but it is a solid infusion of cash that will make a difference to the quality of our health care. Canadians want us to have a deal." Harris, in particular, appeared ready, as usual, to go it alone on an issue he felt strongly about.

Our words made an impact, but I could see it wasn't enough. Both premiers Harris and Bouchard indicated that they were still not satisfied and wanted further concessions from Ottawa.

There are times when your emotions rise to a level where they supersede logical argument, and this was one of those times for me. My father was gravely ill in St. John's. I knew that the vast majority of Canadians wanted—no, were *demanding*—a solution to the problems in our health care system that were directly linked to underfunding. As individuals, we can grumble about waiting too long in hospital emergency wards or paying user fees for services once covered by our provincial health plans. But when the health problem is literally one of life and imminent death—in this case my father's—things become clarified. They did for me. We were close, so close, to an agreement that I could not bear the thought of announcing we had failed.

I reminded premiers Harris and Bouchard that tens of thousands of people beyond that room were very ill. They wanted us to succeed. They wanted us to reach an agreement. And there were families all across the country who wanted their confidence in the health care system restored. How could we go back to them and say their elected leaders could not reach an agreement on the issue that was number one on the minds of all Canadians? How could we talk so long about a subject that Canadians had expressed such deep concern about and at the end of this conference just say, "No deal"? I could not believe that all our discussions, all our preparation, all the work that we had put into this conference had been wasted. "We've got to get this deal done today," I said, envisioning my father in his bed back in St. John's. Then I apologized, a little embarrassed, for the intensity of my comments. Mike and Lucien knew that my dad was gravely ill. They knew he was very much on my mind and that I wanted to go home to St. John's to be with him.

Harris and Bouchard left, assuring me they would talk things over once more. I didn't have high hopes, but both men called after a surprisingly short time to say they were returning. I asked Roy Romanow to join me, and he was there when Mike Harris and Lucien Bouchard arrived. "If we're going to support this deal," one of them said, tossing a printed sheet of paper in front of us, "we need to have this as part of it."

I scanned the paper. To this day I cannot recall exactly what they were asking for, because it seemed so trivial to me. It did not address the question of money; it was simply a change in the existing text, and meant nothing to the overall agreement.

I reached for the telephone, called Eddie Goldenberg in the PM's suite upstairs and told him to come down right away. Eddie had been waiting for word from us. If the prime minister learned that the talks had broken down because of the intransigence of Ontario and Quebec, he was prepared to take on Harris and Bouchard in the press, blaming them for the failure. When Eddie arrived, I handed him the paper.

Eddie scanned the text, then looked up in disbelief. "Is that it?" he said.

Mike Harris, Lucien Bouchard, Roy Romanow and I nodded our heads. That was it.

Eddie couldn't believe it. Things had almost collapsed over something that, compared with the big picture of providing adequate health care funding, was minuscule. He returned upstairs, the text was re-drafted and translated, press releases were prepared and within a short time we all gathered to announce that we had a deal. Canada's health care system was about to be revitalized under a unanimously supported agreement.

There were no villains and heroes in this drama, no white hats versus black hats. It's easy to assume that the premiers staked their claims and pointed their fingers, prepared to blame the other side for imminent failure. That just didn't happen. As conservative and hardbitten in their beliefs as Mike Harris and Ralph Klein might be, neither they nor any other premier were intransigent and accusatory. We were all equally dedicated to strengthening the health care system. True, we had fundamental differences about how to achieve this goal and about the role of the private sector. But we shared the same strong conviction that Canada needs a workable and effective health care system.

The September 2000 health care conference is a good example of the way in which provincial premiers can and must work together for a greater good. It challenged the perception that premiers speak only to and for their home province.

I PASSIONATELY BELIEVE in the Canadian health care system and abhor any suggestion that we Americanize it. Debates arise on this matter from time to time, between those who say the solution involves spending more money and those who preach that the problems can be solved by engaging the private sector. In my view, neither vastly higher expenditures nor a multi-tiered system is the answer as long as the health care system is captive to a plethora of interest groups that avoid assisting the broader situation. Provincial health care budgets are rising by 10 percent a year, a pace that cannot be maintained. As it stands now, the system is unsustainable and needs to be challenged and changed. But who has the will? Who has the solution?

Someone asks, "Should the nurses get more money?" and Canadians say, "Of course they should." A few weeks later we are asked, "Should the doctors get more money?" and we say, "Of course they should." Later the same people ask, "Should the people who clean hospital facilities get more money?" and we say, "Of course they should." Finally we are asked, "Should you pay much higher taxes to cover the health care crisis?" and we say, "Absolutely not!"

Then, what shall we do?

Canadians need to send a signal that they are ready for serious surgery on the system. We need to recognize where the private sector can do things better in some areas. I don't know why, in

Newfoundland for example, long lines of people appear at hospitals, waiting to get blood tests and X-rays. A hospital is where you should go when you are sick. For other procedures you should go to clinics or diagnostic labs, and if private sector clinics can do a better job and do it more efficiently, why not? Why drain the hospital's resources?

Why can't we differentiate between ICU nurses and those working in long-term care and pay them according to their qualifications and responsibilities? In Newfoundland and Labrador, the nurses' union was opposed to introducing pay levels commensurate with education and duties. The mantra that "a nurse is a nurse is a nurse" could not be challenged.

Why do we allow doctors a monopoly on the health care sector? Why can't nurse practitioners do more of the work we rely on doctors for, especially in rural areas where doctors don't want to practise anyway? There are dozens of ways to improve the health care system without assuming it will cost billions more. It takes the ability to see things in a new light, the commitment to find a solution, and the boldness to propose and implement the solution. It can be done. It must be done. I hope Roy Romanow's assessment of our health care system will address these questions and concerns.

Roy was an ideal choice as the person to prepare the report. Like Ralph Klein, Roy is more complex and flexible than some right-wing commentators might suggest, and he is driven less by political dogma than by down-to-earth pragmatism. In that sense, he is a reflection of Tommy Douglas who, like Roy, chose to look beyond his province's borders and address the benefits to Canada.

I recall a first ministers' conference in Quebec City in February 2000, one of the many interim events leading up to the health care agreement described above. We decided among ourselves that nothing would be released to the media until we had hammered out an agreement. No individual premier or group of premiers would comment on the proceedings until

Premier Bouchard, as host, made an announcement at the conclusion of the conference.

This silence, of course, raised all sorts of speculation among reporters and commentators. Many of them assumed, in this context, that no news was bad news. In their opinion, if things were going well, we would all be smiling and talking with the press. This wasn't happening, and so, in a leap of media logic, reporters deduced that we were battling among ourselves and that there might even be blood on the floor.

After a particularly long session one day, we took a washroom break and I told Roy Romanow that if he felt like having a little fun, he should follow me. He smiled and shrugged, and we both strode down a hall of the Château Frontenac and out a side door onto the Dufferin terrace. It was a lovely sunny day and the fresh air was invigorating after so many hours spent in the closed meeting room. The media had crowded the lobby and front entrance, assuming anyone leaving the meeting would pass through that area. Inevitably, one journalist spotted Roy and me strolling together, Roy still wondering what I meant about having some fun, until I suggested he look behind us.

When he did, he saw a mob of cameras, soundmen, reporters, journalists and radio commentators, all racing toward us, demanding to know what was going on and why no one was speaking to them. Roy and I did not share a reputation for saying "No comment" at times like that, but that's exactly how we responded that particular day. We kept walking, and when the reporters realized that we would not be saying anything about the proceedings inside, they began drifting back to the hotel.

That evening Roy and I had a chuckle when news reports claimed that the first ministers' conference had become so tense that premiers Tobin and Romanow were seen taking a break to strategize together and escape the strained mood inside the meeting room.

ROY AND I HAVE MAINTAINED OUR FRIENDSHIP since leaving political life. I'm pleased to say that I remain close with most other premiers I dealt with over the years, something that may surprise Canadians outside the political arena. Mike Harris and I often disagreed during premiers meetings; however, we frequently managed to sit together at the end of the day and enjoy each other's company over a glass of Scotch or, when possible, on the golf course. Working together under intense pressure you also get to know the staff and family members of other premiers. To one extent or another, you share in each other's triumphs and defeats, both public and private.

RETURN TO OTTAWA

T HE YEAR 2000 marked both a new millennium and a fundamental change in my personal life and political career. A provincial election the previous February had returned us to power with a two-to-one majority over the opposition parties, and while both the nurses' strike and the tug-of-war with Inco over Voisey's Bay continued, I sensed a more positive mood in the province than I had noted three years earlier. There was much to be done, and I was looking forward to it.

My father had not been feeling well for several weeks, and in June he was diagnosed with lung cancer. He had smoked all of his life—cigarettes, cigars and pipes—and had attempted, with little success, to stop. He had already suffered a heart attack and a stroke, both attributed to his smoking habit, and when he was told, with my mother, my brother Craig and me present, of a large tumour on his lung, he remained calm, focused and stoic. He assured us that he would fight it and win, perhaps bolstered by having survived the heart attack. He had also suffered from skin cancer when he was a very young man and prostate cancer a few years before the lung cancer appeared, and treatments for both were successful. So he was determined to take on the new challenge and win. "If I can get a few more years out of this," he said, "that will be great." But in his heart I think he knew he had run out of chances.

He came to St. John's for chemotherapy but discovered over the course of the summer that the disease had spread to his vital organs. I spent as much time as possible with him in the treatment centre until, in September, Jodean and I suggested he come to our house, where we would convert the living room into a semblance of a hospital room.

He knew there was little hope. More surgery and chemotherapy may have provided extra time, but the overall prognosis was not good, and we wanted him to be in comfortable surroundings, where friends and family could visit. Jodean and I agreed to do whatever it took to care for him and arrange for friends and family to visit.

Over the next few weeks, a constant stream of visitors came to visit my father as his strength ebbed. All of his children, my brothers and sisters, arrived, and their children as well. His own brothers and sisters visited, too. It was a commitment that all family members made and kept. At one time, I recall counting 26 people in the house, all there to speak with my father, which really meant saying goodbye. The visitors stayed with us or with my sisters Gloria and Janet, or in motels and guest houses around the city. My father was never left alone. Someone who knew and loved him was always there to talk or to listen or to help make him comfortable, 24 hours a day. If he woke at three in the morning, he would have someone to talk with, to fluff his pillow, to bring him a drink of water. Those who stayed with him through the night went to bed when others rose in the morning. Jodean's nursing education and experience, and the presence of visiting nurses from palliative care, helped manage things.

Looking back, I remember those weeks as an extended spiritual experience. Everyone had time for him, and he, of course, had time for them. He never complained, was never difficult and never lamented the disease that had invaded his body. He remained as sweet a man as he had been throughout his life. Even while we mourned what was happening to him, he was giving his blessing to us and to our children, smiling and offering encouragement. In his special way, he was making it easy for us. It was a wonderful lesson in dignity. If this makes my father sound like a modern-day saint, forgive me. He was a special man to me and to everyone in my family, and those who knew and loved him will understand why I am devoting so many words to him here.

He always had a special sense of humour, always found something to make his children laugh, and he never lost it in his final days. Near the end, my brother Ross, who had been sitting with him, came into the kitchen to join the rest of us. Ross was chuckling out loud. He had noticed my father's legs moving under the sheet as though he were pedalling a bicycle, and Ross asked why was he doing that. Was he uncomfortable? "No," my father said, "I'm exercising."

On October 5, 2000, Jodean came out of his room to tell the rest of us that Dad was slipping fast, and it was time. The family had remained nearby, and over the next few hours each of his children and most of his grandchildren entered the room alone to speak to him, to put their arms around him, to tell him they loved him. His nine children and most of his 35 grandchildren were with him that day. Each had this last private time with him, one on one. He listened carefully to us all, but he could no longer speak and so he could answer us only with gestures and expressions, but we knew he understood.

When everyone finished visiting with him, we gathered in the large room, standing where he could see us, all of his children and grandchildren there to say goodbye. My mother went to the bed and spoke to him. "Vince," she said, "have you had a good life?"

Unable to reply verbally, he enclosed her in one arm and pulled her toward him, and with his cheek against hers he nodded his head.

Someone began to sing the "Irish Lullaby," one uncertain voice at first. Then we all joined in, some shaky, others strong and sure. The entire family, brothers and sisters, nieces and nephews, granddaughters and grandsons, stood singing.

Over in Killarney many years ago,
My mother sang a song to me
In tones so sweet and low.
Just a simple little ditty,
In her good old Irish way,
And I'd give the world if she could sing
That song to me today.
Too-ra-loo-ra-loo-ral, Too-ra-loo-ra-li,
Too-ra-loo-ra-loo-ral, hush now, don't you cry!
Too-ra-loo-ra-loo-ral, Too-ra-loo-ra-li,
Too-ra-loo-ra-loo-ral, that's an Irish lullaby.

It was a family favourite. We had sung it together on many happier occasions, and nothing else seemed to fit the moment except to sing it then. And we did. We repeated the chorus, many of us sobbing, while my father died. We watched him take his last breath, and we kept singing.

Too-ra-loo-ra-loo-ral, Too-ra-loo-ra-li,
Too-ra-loo-ra-loo-ral, hush now, don't you cry!
Too-ra-loo-ra-loo-ral, Too-ra-loo-ra-li,
Too-ra-loo-ra-loo-ral, that's an Irish lullaby.

The next morning, I was scheduled to officially dedicate the provincial Fisheries and Agriculture building in St. John's, to be named after Senator Bill Petten. He had suffered a heart attack while attending a hockey game and died on March 6, 1999.

Bill had been a mentor to me, and Jodean and I considered him and his wife Bernice to be dear friends. They had greeted us upon our arrival in Ottawa in 1980, their daughter had been a babysitter for our children, and Jodean and I and our

children gathered at the Pettens' house every Christmas Eve
we spent in Ottawa.

We had been planning this dedication to Bill for many
months. Upon hearing of my father's death the evening before,
Heidi Bonnell assumed that I would ask John Efford, the fisheries and aquaculture minister, and Bernice Petten to take over
the duties. But I insisted on attending and speaking on Bill's
behalf. I owed him a great deal, and I felt no one else could
express what he had done on behalf of Newfoundland's fishery
better than I could.

I arrived at the building on Strawberry Marsh Road, the
realization of my father's death still resonating in my mind,
and I began to talk about all that Bill had accomplished in his
life and all that so many owed him. I spoke of his quiet
strength and his sense of fun, of his basic shyness and his strict
moral standards, of his great achievements in life and his joy at
hearing of the achievements of others. As I spoke I realized
that I was describing not just my late friend Bill Petten, but
also my late father, Vince Tobin. All the love that I felt for
those two men welled up inside of me, and I cut my speech
short and retreated to my office.

No one escapes the impact of the death of a parent, and I was
no exception. My father had been a strong, if often silent, presence throughout my life. Many times during my political career,
when I was facing a serious problem or questioning one thing or
another, I would call my father and discuss it with him. I
consulted with other people as well, of course, and absorbed their
comments and advice. But my father always provided a unique
outlook on things.

Much of the advice a politician receives is based upon what is
best for the party or the caucus. My father, like my mother,
always considered what was best for me as a person, something a
politician can lose sight of over time. Until you are in the public
spotlight 24 hours a day, surrounded by people who are either

looking to you for guidance or eager to provide you with it, you cannot appreciate the value of that kind of independent counsel. I went to my father with total freedom to discuss whatever was troubling me at the time, and they were often things that were impossible to discuss with professional colleagues—my fears, my aspirations, my doubts. It was a safe place to express these thoughts, a place that everyone needs but no one more, I suppose, than someone in public life. He listened with an open mind and responded with total honesty, free of any judgment about me either as a person or a politician. When he died, I lost not just a parent whom I had loved and respected all of my life. I also lost a special source of understanding.

Another effect of my father's passing was a reassessment of the time I was spending with my family—or more correctly the time I was not spending with them. I always loved family occasions celebrated with Jodean and our children, along with my brothers and sisters and in-laws. After my father's death, I valued family occasions even more and realized there is a finite number of opportunities to share those times. I wanted to make the most of those that were to come.

On top of everything else, I was being urged to return to Ottawa as a federal MP. I had been talking to the prime minister throughout that spring and summer. Jean Chrétien has a habit of calling various people as sounding boards for ideas. No longer a member of the federal caucus, I was someone he could speak with to test his views. There were several others around the country as well, and he would collect our various observations in evaluating an idea or making a decision. Sometimes the question dealt with public issues, sometimes with political concerns.

Remember, this was 2000, when Stockwell Day had just been chosen the new leader of the Reform Party and was receiving plenty of favourable press. He was dynamic, energetic and photogenic, all those things the media love in a leader. Some even called him the next Pierre Elliott Trudeau, the man to lead the Reform Party out of the wilderness and perhaps into power.

Many of the discussions I and others had with the prime minister concerned Stockwell Day and the effect he was having on the country. I suggested that the PM consider calling an election earlier, rather than later, before Day could make much of an impact in Parliament. I was confident the Liberals would win another majority government. I also felt it was important to take a stand against the Reform Party and its overly simplistic, black-and-white right-wing views of the country. We needed to make the case that Canada should continue to be a tolerant, open and multicultural nation and not become the kind of country that Stockwell Day and many of his supporters were proposing.

If the PM called an election, it would help the party to bring some new names to the federal scene. Jean Chrétien suggested the possibility of recruiting Frank McKenna, the former New Brunswick premier. Frank McKenna is one of the most capable and successful politicians this country has produced, and it would benefit everyone to have him sitting in Ottawa. Frank and I played a round of golf together that summer and I raised the idea with him, but he declined for personal reasons. He and his wife were enjoying private life together, and they chose to remain out of the spotlight.

We also discussed the idea of Roy Romanow crossing over from the NDP to join the Liberal Party, and I went to Ottawa to join Roy and the prime minister for lunch at 24 Sussex Drive. Roy shared our general concerns about Day and the potential impact of the Reform Party on Canada. He was concerned, however, about crossing from the Saskatchewan NDP to the federal Liberal Party in the relatively short time remaining, if the prime minister called an election that fall. The danger of a backlash against someone changing parties, especially just prior to an election, is a serious one. Roy also said that having spent a lifetime supporting the NDP, he could not abandon his friends there, and he eventually declined our invitation.

With two potential new faces out of the picture, Jean Chrétien began suggesting I consider returning to Ottawa. My initial response was negative. I told him that, rather than go to Ottawa, I was seriously considering leaving politics altogether. By that time, I had spent more than 20 years in public life. Since the age of 23 I had been immersed in decision making, campaigning, strategizing, managing and all the other facets of politics. My father's illness was a nagging reminder to make the most of my time with my wife and children. I felt it was time to do something besides politics; if there was more for me to do in the field, it was somewhere in the future. But many of the discussions I had with Jean Chrétien were related to issues that I felt quite strongly about, and at one point he said, "Brian, if you feel so strongly about that, why don't you put your convictions where your mouth is and get your running shoes back on?"

I had raised the question with my father, seated next to his bed one day. I explained my dilemma to him, as I often did, and he listened intently, as always. When I finished, he told me he understood the appeal of finding more time for my family by being outside the political arena. "Brian," he said, "you still have the political fire in your belly. You have to balance that against your personal desires." Then, as he always did, he said, "Follow your gut."

After my father's death, after the turmoil had settled down, I threw myself back into the fray, keeping myself busy, burning energy and time and reassuming reins that I had left in the hands of senior cabinet ministers during much of that summer. In that atmosphere, the idea of engaging myself in the discussions and decision making taking place in Ottawa became more appealing. I wanted to stand up and speak out against the encroachment of the Reform (recently renamed Alliance) Party in eastern Canada, especially in Ontario and Quebec. Looking back, I suppose I was responding to the loss of my father by immersing myself in the one thing that had occupied all my adult life to that point. Perhaps I didn't want change after all. Perhaps I wanted as many things as possible to continue as they had while my father was alive. Would I have made the same decision four or five months later? I don't know. Diving back into campaign planning, with all the adrenalin rush that it generates, was a method of seizing life once again, a way of fighting the sense of mortality that descends on everyone who loses a parent. When the prime minister offered me a cabinet post prior to the election writ being issued, I accepted.

Lloyd Axworthy had retired from public life and Jean Chrétien suggested I might replace him at Foreign Affairs. If I were going back to Parliament Hill, I wanted to play a role in Canada's economy. John Manley had been at Industry Canada for seven years and was ready for a change. He went to Foreign Affairs, and I happily took up responsibilities at Industry Canada.

Did I have ambitions beyond the cabinet? Of course. No one becomes a member of Parliament, let alone a cabinet minister, without ambition. I was as aware as anyone, of course, that the upcoming election would be Jean Chrétien's third and of the speculation that this would be his last term. Jockeying for the expected leadership race had already begun. Paul Martin was well ahead, with Allan Rock, Sheila Copps and John Manley as other leading candidates. Did I see myself as a potential candidate? Of course I did, although no commitment was asked for, nor was any given.

One of the most difficult hurdles in making this decision was the reaction of Newfoundlanders. Would they feel I was jumping ship to leave the province and return to Ottawa? Was I leaving a mandate unfulfilled? Yes, I was. But I have always thought that the public is more sophisticated than politicians appreciate. Most people, I believed, would recognize that I had managed to make substantial changes for the better during my time in office. Both the mood and the economy of the province were improved, and

I felt I had achieved much in the almost five years since I arrived from Ottawa.

On October 16, 2000, I held a press conference to announce that I had submitted my resignation as premier of Newfoundland and Labrador to Lieutenant-Governor Max House, and that I had further submitted my resignation both as leader of the Liberal Party of the province and as MHA for The Straits & White Bay North to the president of the Liberal Party of Newfoundland and Labrador and to the Speaker of the House of Assembly. I also announced that cabinet and caucus had unanimously recommended to the Lieutenant-Governor that Beaton Tulk be asked to assume the responsibilities of premier until the Liberal Party chose a new leader in convention, and that I would seek the nomination of the federal Liberal Party to represent Bonavista-Trinity-Conception in the federal election.

I thanked my family—Jodean, daughter Heather and sons Adam and Jack—for their support in helping me make my decision to re-enter public life on the national scene. Then I explained the motives behind my move. "Canada is more than a Monopoly board," I said, with clear reference to recent comments by Stockwell Day and Alliance Party supporters, "and the Canadian experience is more than a winner-take-all game of *Survivor*. The Alliance Party and all that it stands for . . . is the single most compelling reason that I have accepted the prime minister's request to consider a return to national politics."

I suggested that the coming election "should be about how we continue to build our country, not divide it. All governments in Canada have found ways to become more efficient. We have cut deficits. We have cut taxes. But we must never cut out the values of our collective community to share with each other . . . to protect our environment . . . to help the sick and the poor and the aged . . . and, most important, to see our children reach their full potential."

ONE MISCONCEPTION AROSE as a result of Jean Chrétien's decision to grant me a cabinet seat, and I would like to clear it up here.

In addition to other concerns involved in building a cabinet, prime ministers must pay attention to provincial representation. It would not do to have a province or region unrepresented at cabinet, nor to have a province or region receive more prominence at the table than its size may warrant. Does this mean good people can be left off a cabinet list because others from their province already have a seat at the table? Indeed it does, and that's one of those quirks that made Churchill describe democracy as the worst of political systems, with the exception of all the rest.

By tradition, Newfoundland qualifies for one cabinet position. In October 2000, when the prime minister invited me back to Ottawa, the province was represented at cabinet by George Baker, minister of veterans affairs. George is a first-class parliamentarian and a hard worker on behalf of his constituents. As much as I may have wanted to return to Ottawa, I would not sacrifice his cabinet position to do so, unless he consented.

When I approached George to say that the prime minister was offering me a cabinet post, he was surprisingly supportive. "I'm a maverick," George said. "Always have been, and I'm not very good at this cabinet stuff." I asked the prime minister if there was room for two ministers from Newfoundland and Labrador in the federal cabinet. The prime minister said, "There's only room for one." George, after more than 30 years of elected office, asked the prime minister for a Senate appointment. The prime minister agreed, and George serves there today with his usual high energy and effectiveness.

IN THE ELECTION OF NOVEMBER 2000, I spent perhaps half the campaign travelling across the country at the party's request. More than a few political columnists and observers were speculating that we could expect little more than a minority government in the face of the revived Reform/Alliance Party. If that happened, Jean Chrétien would either step down or be tossed aside to make way for a new Liberal leader. In fact, we won the largest majority of all three elections under Chrétien, and I was able to score a two-to-one majority over the PC candidate in my riding.

A YEAR ON PARLIAMENT HILL

M Y RETURN TO OTTAWA was very different from my arrival in 1980. Once more, Jodean and I decided not to interrupt the children's school year and I found myself again living in a spartan apartment waiting for my family to come and join me at the end of the school year. A significant number of my staff in St. John's—Heidi Bonnell, Paul McCarthy, Margo Brown and Tony Grace—also made the move to federal politics.

One of my first assignments upon filling the position of industry minister was to look into the events that became known as "Shawinigate." I recall turning to John Manley, my seat partner in the House, and congratulating him on his good timing. The allegations against the prime minister had been raised on his watch, and now it was my problem.

By christening the charges Shawinigate, echoing the Watergate scandal and the worst excesses of disgraced US President Richard Nixon, the press suggested that Prime Minister Chrétien was involved in a major crime. This was patent nonsense. To refresh your memory: Jean Chrétien owned a 25-percent interest in a golf course near his hometown of Shawinigan. Shortly before being sworn in as prime minister in 1993, he sold his share to a Toronto businessman, but the deal fell through and Chrétien didn't receive a penny until 1999. Three years earlier, in 1996, the prime minister had received a request that he support a

Business Development Bank of Canada (BDC) loan from the owners of the Auberge Grand-Mère, a hotel adjacent to the golf course. It was a routine inquiry, the kind that MPs receive on a regular basis. As the MP for his constituency, Jean Chrétien sought financial support on behalf of the hotel owners, telephoning the head of the BDC.

The Opposition charged that the prime minister's actions effectively raised the value of his quarter-share of the golf course—the share he had tried to sell three years earlier and for which he was still awaiting payment. The RCMP looked into the matter, at Joe Clark's insistence, and concluded there was no evidence to warrant a police investigation. Regardless, hysteria built until at one point Alliance Party MP Diane Ablonczy outrageously compared the prime minister's ethics and conduct with those of Yugoslavian warlord Slobodan Milosevic, surely one of the lower points in Canadian parliamentary debate history.

I looked at the file from every conceivable angle and discussed the details as appropriate with many officials involved. Since I am no longer a member of Jean Chrétien's cabinet, and Jean Chrétien, within little more than a year after I write this, will no longer be prime minister, my only motivation here is to tell things the way I see them. I do not believe that Jean Chrétien tried to reward himself in any manner through his request for a loan on behalf of the Auberge Grand-Mère.

I have never seen any evidence that he has one molecule of personal corruption in his body or in his psyche. I believed it from the first day I was sworn in as a cabinet minister, when the prime minister had Mitchell Sharp lecture us on the importance of ethical behaviour. I believed it as I watched the prime minister in countless cabinet meetings and strategy sessions. And I believed it after examining every relevant file provided to me as industry minister.

I became so passionate in defending the prime minister in the House that some commentators asked, "Isn't Tobin putting his own career at risk by defending the prime minister so vigorously?"

If you believe someone has done nothing wrong, you do not employ half measures in defending his or her integrity. Should ministers avoid taking any action that may cast the appearance of inappropriate influence? Yes, they should. Was the prime minister thinking, when he made that telephone call, that he was doing something to benefit himself personally? Absolutely not.

All MPs are advocates for their ridings. You are not sent to Ottawa to be Ottawa's voice in your constituency. You are sent to be your constituency's voice in Ottawa. Every MP receives requests for assistance in helping a local business or organization succeed. When that happens, your instinct is to pick up the telephone and see what you can do. The question that arises is one of appropriateness. What is appropriate action to take on behalf of your constituency? Increasingly, we are beginning to grapple with this point. Jean Chrétien's telephone call on this matter became controversial. I have no doubt that he wishes he had never made the call—just as I have no doubt that he harboured no expectations of personal gain from it.

Cabinet ministers routinely receive requests for financial assistance too, but the request usually originates with a provincial counterpart. Shortly after settling into the industry minister's chair, I received a request from the Quebec government to subsidize a proposed computer-chip manufacturing facility in Sainte-Anne-de-Bellevue on Montreal's West Island. The company, Taiwan-based Mosel Vitelic Inc., was looking for a billion-dollar grant to bankroll the plant, with funds provided equally by the federal government and the province of Quebec. I thought it was an astonishing amount of money, and I asked to see a review of the company, its products and its prospects for success.

Based on the economic analysis at hand, there was no justification for spending taxpayers' money on the project. The company was too small to play a dominant role in the market, its products offered no outstanding or unique qualities and world demand for computer chips was dropping. Quebec may have wanted a high-tech industry to brag about, but this one was simply not going to fly.

This decision had been made internally before I arrived at Industry Canada, but no one had communicated it directly to the Quebec government, so as to avoid handing the separatists an opportunity to say that Ottawa was thwarting the province's ambitions. For years, Ottawa and the Quebec government had played a game called "Who says no first?" in which the first one turning down a deal gets the blame. The more I looked into the file, the more I realized that this would not only be a bad investment for the federal government; it would also be disastrous for the Quebec government.

I called Premier Bouchard and explained that I wasn't interested in stalling a decision by saying the deal was being studied, which meant we hoped it would eventually die a natural death. "This is not a good deal for either of us," I said. It would almost certainly prove a debacle, I went on, costing hundreds of millions of taxpayer dollars. "You don't want this thing haunting you in the future," I added, "and I don't want it either. I'm telling you jack-blunt, Premier, that there is no way we can agree to our end of the deal."

Premier Bouchard understood our position and asked if I would communicate it directly to his industry minister, Bernard Landry. "Minister Landry," Bouchard explained, "has been deeply committed to this project for some time. Would you meet and discuss your decision directly with him?" The premier wanted to know that Landry and I were working with the same basic data on MVI and its prospects, avoiding any finger-pointing accusations later.

I agreed to meet Landry, who was flying in from the west the following day. We had a kitchen and small dining room at Industry Canada, and so Landry and I agreed to discuss the matter over dinner.

The next day, everything was laid on. The dining table was set, the meal had been prepared, and promptly at five o'clock Bernard Landry arrived at my office. We greeted each other, shook hands and before I had a chance to say, "Welcome to Industry Canada," Landry looked me in the eye and said, "If you are not prepared to give me half a billion dollars to support this project, then the meeting is over."

It was, I suppose, a straightforward attempt at intimidation and strong-arm negotiating tactics.

Instead of replying, I looked at my assistant Josée Bedard and said, "Please call Monsieur Landry a cab."

At that, Landry smiled, held up his hands and said, "Come on. This is not the way sophisticated people do business. We should talk about this."

Talk we did, although it did not lead to any agreement to fund the microchip manufacturer. On December 15, 2000, I held a news conference to announce our decision, explaining: "There is a limit to how much taxpayers should subsidize [an industry], even the development of new technology."

As difficult as relations between Ottawa and Quebec may be from time to time, both sides accept the fact that, at the end of the day, there is only one taxpayer base, one pot that we can draw cash from. With that in mind, we can reach across party differences and jurisdictional divides to do what is best for the country. And we do, more often than not.

DURING 2000, some members of caucus began looking ahead to a possible leadership review, and there was much speculation about whether Jean Chrétien would complete his term. Even before the prime minister began sending signals that he had led his last election campaign, a few cabinet members, notably Paul Martin, Allan Rock and Sheila Copps, already had their campaign organizations in place. With the belief that Jean Chrétien would not be seeking another term as prime minister, those members began preparing their leadership campaign. It takes only one individual to get the ball rolling, of course. If leadership hopeful A is discovered to be signing up supporters at various ridings, you can bet that hopefuls B, C, D and the rest of the alphabet will alert their campaign organizations and begin doing the same thing. Paul Martin and Allan Rock were already well along in their campaign planning when I returned to cabinet.

Paul Martin always possessed the skills, the ambition and the pedigree to fill any political position he chose. His father had been one of the country's leading statesmen, and so Paul was exposed to aspects of public life from a very early age. Establishing his ambition from the beginning without relying entirely on family connections, Paul always struck me as a guy willing to work hard and pay his dues.

When he arrived in Parliament in 1988, he focused his energies on the environment, foreign policy and the economy. His work on economic matters was so good that it earned him the Finance portfolio, where Paul built his current reputation. While it's true that good ministers influence the goals and values of their ministry, it is also true that a ministry can influence the cabinet minister over time, and I believe Paul Martin's long term as minister of finance has shaped his outlook. Finance, after all, deals with hard issues and bottom-line assessment, and I wonder if his nearly 10 years in that one capacity has perhaps narrowed his vision over time. Paul's departure from cabinet in July 2002, with an obvious level of antagonism on both sides, cleaved the Liberal Party, and to some degree the country, into two camps. Now that Paul is free of cabinet restrictions and able to forge his own path instead of following Jean Chrétien's lead, it will be interesting to see if he begins moving toward a progressive and activist agenda as opposed to his almost exclusively fiscal and monetary focus while in cabinet.

Much has been made of the working relationship between Jean Chrétien and Paul Martin. Were they bosom buddies?

No, they were not. Did they make things work? They certainly did, and that's the real test of both their relationship and their abilities. Remember that Jean Chrétien and Paul Martin fought a tough leadership battle in June 1990. Chrétien emerged the winner, and even though they were equally committed to the success of the Liberal Party and its policies, it's simply too much to ask that two men who competed against each other so vigorously could suddenly become the best of friends. In every political leadership race, the second-place finisher remains convinced that he or she is better qualified than the victor. It happened with Joe Clark and Brian Mulroney, with Preston Manning and Stockwell Day, with Jean Chrétien and John Turner, and later with Paul Martin and Jean Chrétien.

So the tension remained, even while both men worked together. It broke into the open at the March 2000 convention when some Martin supporters questioned Chrétien's intention to lead the party into a third election. The prime minister fended off the doubts rather easily but it left a scar or two, exacerbated by the unique relationship that exists between a prime minister and a finance minister.

The finance minister's most important job is to say no—no to expanded budgets that cabinet members want for their programs, no to MPs looking for government projects in their constituency, no to everyone calling for lower taxes when there is already not enough money to go around. These negative responses are provided to the individual ministers prior to the public announcement, usually in the context of a federal budget—or at least they should be. A finance minister needs the prime minister to soften the disappointment felt by others and to explain that the finance minister is doing his or her job. Of necessity, Jean Chrétien has had to stand behind Paul Martin and support often unpopular decisions handed down by the finance minister.

Eventually, the differences between Jean Chrétien and Paul Martin grew wide enough to split them apart. This came as no surprise to me and others who know them both well. It was inevitable. You can argue that one or the other could have deferred more than he did, I suppose. But these are two strong individuals, after all, and in some ways it is remarkable that they made it work so well for so long.

I am frequently asked, "Did Martin quit, or was he fired?" It's a moot point. When you have a process where a senior minister questions his role within the cabinet, the end is nigh. Paul Martin was on his way out. Whether the prime minister opened the door for him or Paul opened it himself is not the point. The finance minister was headed toward the door. The rest is semantics.

What matters now is the way each participant conducts himself, and in my opinion they have handled things well. Paul Martin, for example, responded graciously to the prime minister's announcement of his resignation timetable. Others within Martin's organization disagreed with it, but Paul said, "I accept the prime minister's time frame," and that was that.

With all the challenges facing Canada, both internally and externally, the supporters of each man must recognize that the obligation of the Liberal Party is to be a stable platform for dialogue, debate and decision. If the party begins turning inward to focus on questions of leadership almost exclusively, ignoring the demands and expectations of the wider community, we will pay a heavy price as Liberals.

THE PREVIOUS SUMMER, I had been approached about launching a leadership campaign. Steve Hudson, who built Newcourt Credit into a major international financial success, had years earlier assured me of his support if I did choose to seek the Liberal leadership. I contacted Steve in late 2000 and he assumed the task of organizing the fundraising structure. He became a source of advice on many topics and was especially careful about ensuring that there was no conflict of interest, apparent or real, in the assistance that he and others were providing me. Senator George Furey, my long-time friend and frequent campaign manager, served as chairman of the organization. Steve, together with Craig Dobbin, one of Newfoundland and Labrador's most successful entrepreneurs, put together a fundraising organization that they kept entirely separate from me as minister of industry. Steve, Craig and George Furey recruited Dave MacGuinness of the Canadian Association of Petroleum Producers as the day-to-day campaign manager, and they quickly opened offices in Toronto and Montreal. We soon had over a dozen full- and part-time employees attached to the Tobin campaign.

Given the size of my responsibilities as minister of industry and commerce, I frankly couldn't spare much time for the leadership campaign. Industry is a massive portfolio that includes, among others, the Atlantic Canada Opportunities Agency, Business Development Bank of Canada, Canadian Space Agency, Canadian Tourism Commission, Copyright Board Canada, Industry Canada, National Research Council Canada, and Statistics Canada. Four ministers reported to me and we all met, along with the deputy ministers, in a dining room each Wednesday. They were a good team of visionary public servants. I enjoyed working with them all. We had fun and we got some good things done.

One aspect of our activities at Industry Canada addressed the issue of readily accessible broadband service. The broadband agenda was already in place when I arrived at Industry Canada, and I brought a strong belief in the idea of extending the technology throughout the country. As premier of Newfoundland and Labrador, I had discussed the goal of providing broadband service throughout the province with John Manley while he was handling the Industry portfolio. John initiated the idea at Industry, and it formed part of the Liberal Party election platform in the 2000 election. So those who say that I cooked up the broadband idea out of thin air when I arrived at Industry are simply wrong: it was already part of the party's platform.

When I received a report from the National Broadband Task Force, a panel of industry and public sector experts who recommended that all Canadian communities be connected by broadband networks, I pointed out that we could not expect private industry to do it on its own. Millions of Canadians would not gain access to broadband service without some sort of government support.

"In this country that's founded on building bands of steel," I said in a speech accepting the report,

> surely it's appropriate at this point in time to build broadband and that we move quickly. The information revolution is picking up speed and new ways of innovation based on networks and information and communications technologies are transforming our society. The power of the Internet and the emergence of advanced applications represent a fundamental structural shift in our economy. Although the high-tech sector is experiencing some painful market corrections now, the people of Canada cannot and must not be distracted from this government's commitment to facilitate the acceptance and growth of electronic commerce.

By every measure, the broadband issue made sense to me. For a country that spends billions of dollars annually paying out unemployment insurance and billions more in welfare payments, year after year, why would we hesitate to make a one-time investment of a billion dollars to bring Canadians everywhere on-line? Consider it this way: we spend billions of dollars each year on Aboriginal communities, and we send them computers, even though most have no access to the Internet. Why wouldn't we spend some money to connect these communities to one another and, more important, to the rest of the world? The idea becomes especially attractive when you consider that this expenditure would result in greater efficiency and savings in delivering health care, education programs and economic opportunity. Telemedicine, for example, enables a health professional to exchange and obtain medical records, examination reports, diagnoses and specialized medical services directly from a computer keyboard—but only if broadband capability is available.

When we speak of a nation's infrastructure, we think of water systems, sewers, roads, bridges and power systems—and so they are. But in the globally linked contemporary society in which we live, broadband systems are as much a part of the infrastructure as the road you drive your car on and the pipelines that deliver water to your home. Some people may say that roads and sewers are necessary, and broadband service to provide Internet access is a frill. But that's not true for those who work at home, using the computer to deal with clients and customers. It's not true for businesses that require broadband access millions of times daily for transactions. And it is certainly not true for those who live in remote regions, far from health facilities, who could tap into improved health care via telemedicine.

We cabinet ministers were in the midst of shaping our programs and assessing prospects for the coming budget when the terrorists launched their horrific attacks on the World Trade Center on September 11, 2001. Like you, I and my family and staff spent the next few days in muted shock, trying to understand how the human mind could plan and execute such appalling destruction and the taking of innocent lives.

A few days later, I attended a meeting of a number of ministers in the prime minister's office to discuss a method of expressing our support for the people of the United States. I suggested we invite Canadians to gather en masse on Parliament Hill the following day, Sunday. Someone pointed out that the steps to the Parliament Buildings were under construction; I said we can build platforms over the steps if need be. Jean Chrétien asked, "What if it rains?"

"Prime Minister," I said, "if it rains, Canadians will bring their umbrellas. But they will be there."

To his credit, Jean Chrétien did not take the safe course and schedule an official event in a hall or cathedral, where we could overflow the venue with a few thousand people. "We're going to do this on Parliament Hill," he said. A number of ministers continued to express worries and wanted to hedge their bets. Others were concerned about security or were convinced that people would be reluctant to gather in a large crowd so soon after watching the World Trade Center disaster.

We were the only country to commemorate that terrible event and express our feelings with a public display. Other countries held services in cathedrals, or as part of official proceedings of one kind or another. Canadians gathered on our country's town square, as it were, and I think that speaks volumes about our commitment and concern for our neighbours in the United States. Jean Chrétien made the call and took the risk. If only a few people had shown up, the media would have said that Chrétien blew it. The truth is, 100,000 people gathered on less than one day's notice to express their support for the United States. Jean Chrétien did not put them there directly. But he had the courage to say, "Let's do it!" and he had the understanding to know that Canadians would arrive.

Post–September 11 Canada's priorities changed. We needed to make our country secure, to keep trade flowing across the Canada–US border, and to cooperate with other countries in combatting terrorism. However, I was concerned that we not throw away our long-term vision for the country. If we did that, I suggested, the terrorists in some way, would have won. Terrorists can never win a war; they can only cause us to fear, to fear each other and to fear the future.

I had been seeking $100 million to launch the broadband program in the coming year, much less than the $1 billion it would take to finish the job, and far less than the $3 or $4 billion that some reports said I wanted. When the federal budget was delivered in of December 2001, the $100 million was not allocated for the current year after all but was designated to be applied over several years, making the total effort impractical.

I had no knowledge of this cut in the expenditure before I and the rest of the country were informed when Paul Martin handed down the budget. I was genuinely surprised and disappointed at the decision. The prime minister had made it clear to me in the days leading up to the budget that the broadband item would be in the budget, no ifs, ands or buts. So this explains the shock I felt when details were delivered to the House that evening. When I enquired about the cuts, the prime minister told me that his instructions had not been followed. My response to that bit of news was to say, "Well, Prime Minister, if that is the case, you have an even larger problem than I have."

I knew that the full amount would not be made available for the broadband agenda, given the emphasis on security, and I took some comfort months later when Finance Minister John Manley and Industry Minister Allan Rock both announced their intention to carry forward the broadband agenda as I had originally proposed it.

But the broadband incident was something of a trigger for me. On its own, it was little more than the result of the strategizing and prioritizing you become familiar with at high levels of management, both in public and in private life. Years earlier, I might have rolled with the punches, altered my tactics and found a way to get the job done sooner or later. This time, however, it prompted a reassessment of all that I was doing, all that I had lost over the years as a politician and all that I had reconsidered with the death of my father. The broadband issue did not make me decide to leave politics. It did, I suppose, nudge me to examine things more closely and more critically than I had done before.

There was, of course, the question of the party leadership. I had a great team in place, and I was confident I could run a vigorous campaign. I looked forward to engaging in a public policy debate dealing with the future of the country. But I also became aware that Paul Martin had an insurmountable lead in organizing and funding his campaign.

In political life at the uppermost level, the personal commitment needed to fill a cabinet post or seek the leader's position must be absolute. I had been both a senior minister and a provincial premier, and I knew the amount of sacrifice and dedication needed to do the job successfully. You surrender both a private life and a private agenda. You compromise aspects of your family life that others take for granted.

What would be the benefit of working long and hard for the next several years, while maintaining my cabinet position, in pursuit of an unwinnable goal, beyond the opportunity to make a speech to the country live on prime-time TV? Would it be worth it to me? Would it be worth it to my family?

I excused myself from the ministry's Christmas party. My son Adam was arriving in Ottawa that afternoon, and my priorities had changed so much that I felt it was important to greet him personally at the airport and use the event to kick off the Christmas season with my family.

Over the holidays, I talked about my feelings with Jodean, Heather, Adam, Jack and my brothers and sisters. Early in the new year, I was scheduled to attend a series of meetings across the country, from St. John's to Vancouver, but after 24 years of active involvement in politics, I felt perhaps I had given enough. I had just turned 47 and was being touted, correctly or not, as the second-place candidate for the leadership running behind Paul Martin.

One question kept echoing through my mind: *run . . . for what?* I have never run to place.

I recognized this was an opportunity to have a private life, a family life, for the very first time. It was a chance to enjoy a life beyond politics. Jodean and I agreed to take time at Christmas to review things in detail. And we did. When you spend as many years in politics as I had, and others have made sacrifices to make it possible, there comes a time to pay for some of those sacrifices. You owe those who made them for you. I owed Jodean a great deal.

There was never any question of remaining in politics and simply slowing down. In politics, you either play flat out with total energy and passion, or you step aside and shift to a lower gear. Well, I don't know how to participate in low gear.

And what of the leadership? A leadership campaign can accumulate so much momentum and so much commitment from fundraisers, policy-makers, financial supporters, support staff and organizers that it takes on a life of its own and you, as the candidate, find yourself being carried along with the tide. There are no longer any buttons marked "Go" or "Stop." The thing is launched and impossible to shut down, and if you are unwilling to dedicate every ounce of your energy, every spare moment of your time to winning that prize, you don't just let yourself down. You let all those other people down, and you betray them.

I was not prepared to run for the leadership in the wake of all that I had gone through and in the certainty that Paul Martin was uncatchable. And I refused to betray all those who promised to work hard on my behalf by running a phony campaign.

In early January, I called the prime minister, who was in Florida at the time. I told him I understood he was planning to shuffle his cabinet upon his return to Canada and, if that were the case, it was important that he and I speak beforehand. I did not want him, I said, making a cabinet shuffle until he heard what I had to say. Having performed cabinet shuffles myself, I didn't want him going through all the choices he thought he had only to discover that a minister was leaving. I wanted to tell him upfront that I was leaving.

He returned from Florida on Sunday afternoon. I met with him that evening and told him my decision to step down.

Jean Chrétien was surprised at my news, and he spent the early part of that evening probing to see if I was indeed serious, or if I was angling for another job. I didn't want another job. Minister of industry was a great job. I didn't want a posting or a position elsewhere. I just wanted out.

The prime minister knows me well, and it didn't take him long to realize I was serious. His chief concern was "Why?" and he accepted my explanation that I wanted to spend more time with my family. I had spent much of my adult life in politics and I needed a new perspective. It was not an angry conversation. It was a discussion between two old friends rather than a meeting between a prime minister and a member of his cabinet. We did, I admit, talk about some aspects of the government and the way it was handling certain issues, and we did it with total candour. But the talk was conducted calmly and in strict privacy, and I must maintain that privacy now.

I reminded him that I was the longest consecutively elected member of his cabinet after himself and Herb Gray. For 24 years, one way or another, politics had dominated my life. I believed then, and I am more convinced than ever now, that everyone benefits from exploring new interests and achieving new goals from time to time. Working on this book has been one of those goals. It has proved healthy and refreshing, and has caused me to reflect on my thoughts and actions.

Toward the end of our meeting, the prime minister asked me to delay making my announcement for a day or two, giving him time to rethink his cabinet shuffle. I agreed, we shook hands and I left.

As I drove away from 24 Sussex Drive that evening, I noted a strange and not unpleasant sensation. I felt relaxed and free.

THE MEMBERS OF MY STAFF knew the fire had gone out of my belly with the announcement of the budget. When I called several of them the day after communicating my decision to the prime minister and said simply, "It's over," they reviewed all the worst-case scenarios that the media would explore: I was a quitter, I had an angry confrontation with the prime minister, I had personal family problems, I was planning a new strategy to seek the party leadership. They used them all. None was correct.

Steve Hudson arranged for Jodean, our son Jack, several staff members and me to fly to St. John's the following morning, with a stopover in Halifax to pick up our daughter, Heather, in her final year at Dalhousie University. When I called my mother to tell her my decision, she surprised me by saying, "Thank God—my prayers have been answered." Obviously, the slings and arrows of political life are tough on moms and dads as well as spouses and children.

The following morning, Heidi Bonnell arrived at our home in the ministry car, chauffeured by my driver, Guy Valin. When I invited Heidi in while Jodean and I finished our packing, Heidi reminded me that Guy was waiting outside in the car. "Send him back to the ministry," I told her. "I'll drive us to the airport, and I'll drive us home when we come back to Ottawa." The fact is, I was no longer the minister of industry and the minister's car was no longer mine to use. George Furey joined us on the flight, and once we were in the air I began writing out in longhand the speech I would deliver in St. John's.

When Heather joined us in Halifax, she was jubilant at the news. She asked me what I was going to do now, and I told her I wasn't sure. I asked what she was going to do when she graduated with a B.Comm. later that year. She grinned and replied, "I'm going to kick ass on Bay Street!" That's my girl.

Adam met us at the airport in St. John's. He knew of my decision, and I will never forget his words when we greeted each other. "You know, Dad," he said, "the rest of my life starts today, because I am no longer 'the son of . . .'"

Family and old friends were waiting for me at the Hotel Newfoundland, where Heidi had, with her usual magic, organized a press conference for later in the day. The plan was for me to call back to Ottawa and inform the ministry staff of my decision, then make it public at the press conference. Many people assumed I would be announcing a breakthrough on the negotiations with Inco over Voisey's Bay. Don Newman of CBC and Mike Duffy of CTV got wind of the press conference and called Heidi for details. She told them of my decision and asked if they would hold the story until after the press conference was completed. In return, each would receive an interview that evening.

Unfortunately, both Don and Mike rushed to the cameras and the staff in Ottawa learned of my decision not directly from me but over the television airwaves.

The news spread like wildfire. Paul Martin, Sergio Marchi and others reached me before the press conference to confirm what they had been hearing and to wish me luck. Finally, Jodean and I and our children stood before the cameras. "Let me be clear, before you ask, that this decision is not strategic, it is personal," I said after making my announcement. "During this holiday season, the scales tipped in favour of renewal and rejuvenation and a life beyond politics. When you hear about people going off for the weekend on a Ski-Doo, in politics you get to do that once a year, and maybe that's a photo op. I want more than photo ops with my family. My decision is about wanting to live a full life."

I anticipated the questions tossed at me by the press, most relating to the Liberal leadership race, my relationship with Jean Chrétien, the broadband issue and others. I answered them all as directly as I could, until one skeptical reporter commented: "Your kids are grown now, so why are you saying you're leaving politics to be with them when they are no longer babies?" Before I could reply, Jodean stepped up to the microphone.

"Excuse me," she said. "Your children are your children no matter what age they are. They will always need you and that is my responsibility as a parent."

There was nothing for me to add.

A NEW AND PRIVATE PERSPECTIVE

I N THE MONTHS SINCE, I have rediscovered many things. One of them is the special joy of unhurried time I spend with my family. I was excited to attend the university graduation of our daughter, Heather. I would have been there had I remained in politics, of course, but now I was able to take my time and accommodate her schedule instead of Heather accommodating mine. I grew more aware of the number of incidents in her life and in the lives of her brothers that I had missed while in public office. I will not fail to attend them in the future. The other pleasures of a private life that I am beginning to appreciate include opening the morning paper and not seeing a story about me, or a columnist's critique of something I have said, splashed across the pages.

Politics is a tough business. It's tough being in the limelight all the time, it's tough being the constant target of criticism from people who are convinced they can do the job better than you and it's tough asking your family to make sacrifices on your behalf. When I read about a politician in trouble now, I don't speculate about the spin that's needed or the backroom tactics that may or may not be involved. I think of his or her family and the things they will have to endure. I was no fan of Stockwell Day's, but I know his family paid a price during all the machinations performed to replace him with Stephen Harper, and I felt for Stockwell and for his wife and children. The unrelenting pressure on Joe Clark to resign has been uncomfortable to watch, because I know it distressed his family. The political wisdom of these men and others like them is not the issue here. It's the stress their families endure, and that's very real. When you take political risks, continually putting yourself in the spotlight, the attacks can become barbed and hurtful, not just to yourself, but also to those who love and care for you.

I took risks when risk was justifiable. Were all the decisions the safest to make, where my political career was concerned? No, they were not. Are some correct in calling me reckless, boisterous and rambunctious? I suppose. But you don't achieve change by standing alone on a hilltop, watching life pass by. You achieve it by becoming engaged in all the give and take, all the rough and tumble, of debate. You don't "roll the dice" and hope for the best, either. You do what you think is the right thing, and prepare yourself to accept both criticism and congratulations.

Will I return to politics in an active role? I have no plan to do so, but I have learned never to say never. Right now I'm finding it both fascinating and educational to sit back and watch the development and implementation of public policy as a private citizen, a taxpayer and a member of the business community. I look at the activities of many levels of government—the Council of the City of Ottawa where I live, the Legislative Assembly of Ontario, the Parliament of Canada, the House of Assembly in Newfoundland and Labrador—from the perspective of someone who will feel the impact of legislation without being involved in its creation.

I am free to express personal views on subjects without regard for maintaining the Liberal Party line or cabinet solidarity and free to consider wider issues than the current political agenda. Canadians do this all the time, of course. But to a person who was immersed in politics for so many years, it's a refreshing change to look at issues from an entirely personal perspective.

One subject I find myself pondering frequently is the state of Canada's multi-party system. I am as deep rooted a Liberal as you will find, but I am uncomfortable about the extended dominance of our party on a national basis, and the inability of any single party to appeal to multiple regions of the country. Canada needs a rejuvenated Conservative Party, one that can rise out of the ashes of the post-Mulroney years and provide a distinct alternative to voters.

I am also concerned about the decline of the NDP, which once acted as the country's social conscience. Many programs that Canadians value and support, from universal medical care and old-age pensions to workers' compensation and employment insurance, were spearheaded by the NDP. In recent years, the NDP appears to have discarded its pragmatic approach to issues, especially where fiscal matters are concerned.

Canadians look for government leaders who will guard the public purse. Grabbing at any and all sources of money by raising taxes and borrowing against tomorrow is ultimately disastrous. Until the NDP accepts this reality, I suspect the party will continue to lose adherents even from traditionally hard-core supporters such as autoworkers and steelworkers.

It is important for Canadians to have alternative political parties headed by experienced and trusted leaders. As much as I dislike the idea, I realize there will come a time when the Liberals will not win another majority. When that day arrives, I want to be sure that the federal government responsibilities are filled by experienced people who, though differing in view from me and other Liberals, are moderate, pragmatic and national in their vision.

Having no effective and viable Opposition works to the advantage of Liberals in the short term. In the longer term, Canada will suffer if strong representation is absent on the other side of the House. Competition makes us strong, and this works just as well in politics as it does in evolution. Nothing strengthens a party's effectiveness more than facing well-prepared Opposition. It keeps all of us on our toes, and it reassures the public that every side of an argument receives a fair hearing.

On a wider front, I remain uncomfortable about problems we face in spite of, and even because of, our free trade agreement with the United States.

I opposed free trade with the United States when Brian Mulroney proposed it during the 1984 federal election. Like John Turner, I worried that giving up the capacity to govern all aspects of a country's actions according to its own best interests constitutes an initial loss of sovereignty. Mulroney won the day, the deal was done and significant benefits accrued to Canada. I admire Mulroney for his boldness. However, the fact remains we diluted certain areas of our sovereignty by signing the free trade deal. "But so did the United States," I hear NAFTA authors point out. "Look how Europe's Common Market has evolved into a generally smooth-running economic engine. Doesn't that prove that everyone gains when trade barriers are removed?" Yes, and no.

The reality is that free trade works properly only when, to use the favourite analogy of the United States, the playing field is level. To continue the analogy, what happens if the field is level but larger on one side of midfield than on the other? That's the difference between Europe and North America. The French and Germans may be at loggerheads over one aspect or another on trade, but they are generally equal in size when it comes to markets and population, counterbalanced by the presence of other members of the organization who can cast their vote one way or another.

We lack that balancing arrangement with the United States. Even that problem could be dealt with, however, if NAFTA rules were applied universally and consistently. They are not, and while this may not surprise experts on international trade agreements, it's critical for Canada to deal with them as an issue and not as a series of crises that happen from time to time in various corners of that clichéd playing field.

It comes down to this: *you cannot be a free trader of conven-ience.* You cannot manage free trade and still support its original goals. I fully acknowledge that a country as massive and diverse as the United States inevitably encounters situations where an industry or region will feel wounded by its trade policy. We endure this in Canada from time to time, in matters ranging from Alberta oil and gas to Atlantic fisheries. That's when a government committed to honouring its agreements must spend political capital within its jurisdiction. Political capital to a government is like gold to a miser: you can hide it away, or you can put it to work when it's needed. When it comes to free trade issues, the US federal government needs to invest a little of its political capital within its own borders to support its endorse-ment of free trade principles.

Washington, of course, answers to its own people, not to Canadians. We cannot sway 300 million Americans to our point of view overnight. But we can, and we must, start speaking frankly, directly and clearly to the US government about issues before they spring up and surprise us. If the United States, the world's free trade champion, cannot make the concept work with its closest neighbour and friend, with whom it shares more language, cultural, economic and security values than with any other country, how can it expect to make the idea work anywhere else? The point is not a new one, but I suspect it has not been made boldly enough.

Virtually every resource, industry and region in Canada is affected by the United States in its attempt to manage free trade. Softwood lumber, durum wheat, PEI and New Brunswick pota-toes, TV and film production, steel and fisheries on both coasts operate from year to year under a Damocles-style sword that threatens to drop at the first outcry of a US senator, congressman or interest group, regardless of the merits of the argument. During the most recent softwood lumber protest, one US senator from a lumber-producing state called Canada's policy on lumber pricing "Soviet style," which did little to deal with the issue but succeeded in inflaming emotions on both sides of the border. These actions should not be viewed, in my opinion, as individual occurrences but as a pattern of US protectionism regardless of NAFTA's guidelines.

Trudeau's elephant-and-mouse analogy still holds true today when it comes to US-Canada relationships. Overly aggressive proposals in dealing with trade issues could prove self-destructive. We cannot, for example, link our energy sales to the United States with our softwood lumber concerns. But neither can we continue to assume that virtual paralysis is our only recourse. In spite of NAFTA, protectionist walls continue to be erected around many US markets. Our door is always open for entry, but going the other way, into the United States, lately requires Canada to sometimes climb a fence.

Canada's relationship with the United States is and will always be our number one priority. We need to know we can count on each other. From trade, to security, to combatting global terrorism, Canada has a vested interest in ensuring there are no misunderstandings between us. The United States is our best friend, and we should reflect that in our dealings with them. Likewise, Canada is the United States' best friend, and they ought to reflect that reality in their dealings with us.

On a wider scale, Canada should be able to demonstrate better than any other nation on earth that it is possible to be open, progressive and tolerant and still be efficient, competitive and capable of wealth creation. For years, a debate has revolved around the foolish notion that a country is either a bastion of free enterprise and lower taxes or a socially progressive nation. We should never be forced to choose between the two. In fact, Canada is both. It's true we don't need more government everywhere, but there are strong arguments for active government policies in at least three corners of our lives.

First, we are living in an age of globalization, which raises the spectre of multinational corporations taking it upon themselves to act like governments or, where self-interests demand it, supersede public policy. As globalization fosters more powerful international corporations driven by their pursuit of maximum profits and minimal social responsibility, who will provide the necessary balance if not a strong central government?

Second, globalization can be a creator of new wealth and opportunity, but as September 11 taught us, the effects of remote conflicts can arrive on our doorstep with sudden and appalling impact. We now realize that the problems of the Middle East are our problems as well, not just those of Jews and Arabs. How does a passive government position deal with these questions? It cannot.

Third, we have seen the economic fallout of scandals and mismanagement on the part of top-level executives at Enron, WorldCom and other corporations. Who will protect employees, investors and pensioners of corporations engaged in similar conduct? The courts cannot, until governments recognize the widespread fallout of this kind of corporate immorality and pass appropriate laws to root it out.

These examples should remind us that we need a world in balance, one that is less ideologically hidebound. Those of us trying to create the best possible world for ourselves, our children and our society must become more than witnesses to an ideological struggle between capital and labour. We must continue building bridges between the two. Much of the world is looking for a model for people of different languages, religions and cultures living together in peace and tolerance. Fulfilling that role, within a strong and free economy, would be a gift from Canada to the world. It would be a gift to ourselves as well.

All these challenges are for the current and next generation of political leaders to grapple with. They will shape the debates of tomorrow and in so doing reveal the future of Canada— all in good time.

INDEX

Ablonczy, Diane, 241
Aboriginal issues. *See* First Nations people
abortion, 33–34, 204–205
Air Canada, 145–146, 148
Alaska, 92
Alexander, Ben, 30, 32, 33
Alliance Party, 233–234, 235, 237, 239
Alpha and Omega II, 90
Anderson, Wally, 197–198, 200
André, Harvie, 58
Angus Reid, 141
Anstey, Gary, 143
Auberge Grand-Mère, 241
Axworthy, Lloyd, 145, 236
Aylward, Joan Marie, 162, 164–165, 166
Aylward, Kevin, 186

Baker, George, 238
Baltic States, 108
Barbour, William, 200
Barry, Leo, 156
Bartleman, Jim, 3, 5–6, 117, 118, 124, 129
beauty of Canada, 14
Beck, John, 95, 100, 104, 110, 121, 126

Behind the Embassy Door (Blanchard), 149–150
Benjamin, Les "Boxcar," 38–39
Beothuk people, 203
Bettney, Julie, 161–162
Bird, Cyrus, 16
birthplace, 7–8
Blanchard, James, 90–91, 93, 149–150
blizzard campaigning, 71
Bloc Québécois, 59, 66, 77–78
Bonino, Emma, 100–101, 102, 104, 109–110, 121, 126, 129, 130, 131, 132–133
Bonnell, Heidi, 107, 163, 232, 240, 256
Bouchard, Lucien, 59, 65–66, 69, 83, 127, 140, 144, 150–151, 152–153, 218, 220–223, 226, 243
Boudria, Don, 56, 58, 59
Bourassa, Robert, 74, 75
Bourgon, Jocelyn, 87, 123
Briffett, Julie, 34
British fishermen, 139
Brittan, Sir Leon, 112, 129
broadband program, 248–250, 251–252
Broadbent, Ed, 52, 54–55
broadcasting, 23–24
brothers, 11

Brown, Margo, 164, 240
Bruton, John, 175–180
Bryden, Joan, 132
Byrne, Gerry, 102

cabinet appointment, 78, 236, 238
Cabot, John, 174–175
Caesar, 14
Campbell, Kim, 63, 77
Canada AM, 147–148
Canadian Airlines, 146, 148
Canadian Charter of Rights and
    Freedoms, 29, 44–47, 74–75
Canning, Patty, 27
Cape Roger, 4, 6, 124–125
Carter, Walter, 156
Catholic Education Council, 184, 192
Charest, Jean, 150–151
Cherry, Don, 120
childhood, 11, 12
children, 32
Chislett, Al, 207
Chrétien, Jean, 2, 39, 40, 42, 45, 46,
    50, 51, 57, 63, 67–74, 78–79, 107,
    112–114, 116, 120, 123–124,
    131, 146–147, 150–151, 153,
    173, 220, 233–235, 236, 238,
    239, 240–242, 244, 245–247,
    250–251, 254–255
Churchill Falls, 208
Clarity Bill, 69
Clark, Joe, 29, 30, 55, 64, 241, 259
Clinton, Bill, 91
Coastal Fisheries Protection Act
    (Bill C-29), 83, 88–89, 89, 108,
    112, 116
cod stock depletion, 82, 137
Collenette, David, 98, 115–116
committee work, 60–61
community welfare, 21
Confederation, 41
Conne River band, 202
Constitution, 29, 44–47

Copps, Sheila, 56–57, 59, 236, 244
Corner Brook (Nfld.), 29–35, 72
corporate scandals, 264
Cossitt, Tom, 38
Counterpoint, 23
courtship, 22–23
Coyne, Deborah, 75, 157
Crosbie, John, 24, 29, 78, 80, 81–82,
    84–85, 93, 155
Cummins, John, 121, 127

Davey, Keith, 52
Day, Stockwell, 233–234, 237, 258
DC-3 aircraft ride, 12–13
deal-making, 209
"deals," 65
debating club, 16–17
Denominational Education Commit-
    tees, 183
Diamond Fields Resources, 207,
    208–209
Dicks, Paul, 168, 186
Diefenbaker, John, 30
distinct society clause, 74–75
Dobbin, Craig, 248
doctors, 225
Douglas, Tommy, 225
Drew, George, 41, 62
Ducros, Françoise, 85, 143, 198
Duffy, Mike, 257
Dustan, John, 42–43

educational reform
    background, 182–185
    campaign, 191
    generational change, 187
    need for reform, 188–189
    referendum in 1995, 184
    referendum in 1997, 189–193
    royal commission, 184
    sectarian identity, 184–185
    separation of church and state, 187
Efford, John, 121, 232

Elizabeth II, Queen of England, 175–181
emotional commitment, 118
Encylopedia of Newfoundland and Labrador, 173
essay writing, 16–17
Estai, 1, 3–4, 124–129
ethics, 79
European Union, 83, 88–89, 100–101, 103–104, 106, 108, 110–111
see also Turbot War

Fagan, Bonaventure, 192
Falconbridge. *See* Voisey's Bay
family, 9–11
family life, 233, 257
Faour, Fonse "The Fonz," 30, 31, 32, 33
father. *See* Tobin, Vince
federal election (1993), 77–78
federal election (2000), 238–239
federal politics
  cabinet appointment, 78, 236, 238
  Corner Brook (Nfld.), 29–35
  election of 1993, 77–78
  election of 2000, 238–239
  entry into, 25–35
  first election, 29–35
  growing support, 48
  leadership campaign, 247–248, 252–254
  maiden speech in House, 40–41
  MP, role of, 242
  resignation from cabinet position, 254–256
  return to, 233–237
firefighters, 10
First Nations people
  Beothuk people, 203
  elders, respect for, 199
  leaders of, 198–199
  negotiations, 200–201

road construction, 201
Sparrow decision, 198
support for, 204
talking stick, 202–203
Voisey's Bay. *See* Voisey's Bay
Fisheries and Oceans Canada, 82
fisheries minister
  agenda, 80
  Atlantic fishery troubles, 80–81
  British fishermen, 139
  cabinet appointment, 78
  cod stock depletion, 82, 137
  flags of convenience, 83–84, 86–87, 89
  impending overfishing, 137–138
  management style, 86
  moratorium, 82
  NAFO. *See* North Atlantic Fishing Organization (NAFO)
  overfishing, 80, 81–82
  quotas, 82
  salmon fishermen, 92
  scallops, 89–92, 93
  sedentary species, 90, 91, 92, 93
  straddling stocks, 83
  transit fee, 92
  turbot. *See* turbot quota
  unilateral action, 84–85
Fisheries Resource Conservation, 94
Fitzpatrick, Ross, 145
flags of convenience, 83–84, 86–87, 89
Foote, Judy, 161
Foreign Affairs, 116, 131, 134–135
France, 80–81, 89, 121
Francis, Diane, 206, 216–217
Frank, Barney, 91
Fraser, Graham, 65
free trade, 66, 108, 110, 261–262
Friedland, Robert, 209
friendships in politics, 65–66
Furey, Chuck, 52, 156, 186

Furey, George, 248, 256
future sovereignty referenda, 69

Gallant, Felix, 7
Gatineau, 136
Glavine, Gerry, 163–164
globalization, 263–264
Goldenberg, Eddie, 72, 73, 117, 223
Gonzales, Felipe, 133
Goose Bay, 11–14
Gosnell, Joe, 199
Gotlieb, Allan, 84
Goudie, Mona, 16
Gourd, Robert, 43
Government House, 78
Grace, Tony, 164, 240
Grand Banks, 1–6, 83
    see also fisheries minister; Turbot
    War
Gray, Herb, 56, 59, 97, 255
"Great Debate of the Decade," 24
Greenland halibut. *See* turbot quota
Grimes, Roger, 182, 188, 191, 212,
    213

Haida Gwaii (Queen Charlotte
    Islands), 199–200
Hand, Scott, 215
Happy Valley–Goose Bay, 11–14
Harmon Air Force Base, 8, 11
Harper, Elijah, 76
Harper, Stephen, 161, 258
Harper, Tim, 55
Harris, Hollis, 145–146, 227
Harris, Jack, 191, 194
Harris, Mike, 206, 218, 220–223
health care issues
    conference 2000, 224
    reform, 224–225
    support from premiers, 219–223
Heighton, Peter, 16
Hibernia petroleum development
    project, 169–170

hockey, 10–11
Hodder, Mary, 162
Hosek, Chaviva, 91
House, Max, 237
House of Commons, 68
Hudson, Steve, 247–248, 256
Hulan, Bud, 120
Humber–Port au Port–St. Barbe
    (Nfld.), 30, 35
Hydro Quebec, 208

Inco. *See* Voisey's Bay
individualism, 21
Industry Canada, 236, 243–244,
    248–250
Innu, 13, 197, 201
    see also First Nations people
Innu Healing Foundation, 80
Innu Nation, 80
Inuit, 13, 197, 201
    see also First Nations people
Ireland, 175–180
Irish Christian Brothers, 194
Iron Ore Company of Canada, 28, 55
island living, 16
Italy, 175, 177

Jamieson, Don, 14–15, 27, 29–30,
    31, 35, 48
Japan, 99
Joe, Misel, 202–203
John, Ed, 199
John Cabot, 24–25
Jones, Yvonne, 162
José Antonio Nores, 112
journalism, 23–25

Keeper of the Salmon, 199
Kelly, Sandra, 162
Kennedy, Ted, 91
kissing the cod, 72
Klein, Ralph, 147, 218–219, 220,
    221, 223

Korea, 102
Kristina Logos, 86–87

Labrador. *See* Newfoundland and Labrador
Lacey, Ted, 24–25
Ladies' Hospital Auxiliary, 9, 10
Lalonde, Marc, 39, 40, 41, 42, 64–65, 67
Landry, Bernard, 153, 243–244
Lapierre, Jean, 56, 58–59
Lapointe, Paul, 130–131
Law of the Sea, 131
leadership campaign, 247–248
LeBlanc, Romeo, 49
Leonard J. Cowley, 4, 119, 125
Lévesque, René, 29, 41–42, 43, 152
Liberal Party
    leadership convention (1990), 72–73
    in minority position, 54–55
    regaining power, 77
    sympathies with, 26

MacDonald, Ron, 104–106
MacEachen, Allan J., 36–37
MacLaren, Roy, 108
magazines, 16
Major, John, 114–115, 127, 133
Maldoff, Eric, 73
Malépart, Jean-Claude, 56, 58, 59
Manley, John, 236, 248, 252
Mansbridge, Peter, 151
Marchand, Jean, 42
Marchi, Sergio, 257
marriage, 22–23
Martin, Paul, 69–70, 236, 244, 245–247, 252, 253, 254, 257
Martins, Licino, 126
Mathews, Lloyd, 188
Matthew, recreation of voyage, 174–181
Mazankowski, Don, 60–61

McCarthy, Jack, 33, 34, 240
McCurdy, Earl, 101
McInnis, Dave, 248
McKenna, Frank, 144–145, 147, 234
Meech Lake Accord, 66, 73–76, 155, 157
Memorial University, 23, 173
Mercredi, Ovide, 198–199
Mills, Eva, 34, 163
Mineral Act, 213
Miquelon fishermen, 80–81
Montreal rally, 143, 144–150
Moores, Frank, 28, 173–174
Morgentaler, Henry, 204–205
Mosel Vitelic Inc., 242–244
mother. *See* Tobin, Florence
Mount Cashel orphanage, 187, 194–195
Mulroney, Brian, 28, 44, 50, 51–52, 54–55, 63–64, 65–66, 74, 78, 93, 261
multi-party system, 259–260
Murphy, Bill, 101

NAFTA, 261–263
National Broadband Task Force, 249
National High School Debating Championship, 17
net incident, 129, 130–133
Never a Dull Moment (Carter), 156
New Democratic Party, 54–55, 260
Newfoundland and Labrador, 8–9, 13, 15, 32, 34, 41, 118, 137
Newfoundland and Labrador Manufacturers Association, 170
Newfoundland and Labrador politics
    Aboriginal issues. *See* First Nations people
    abortion, 204–205
    confidence, restoration of, 169–171
    decision to run, 158–159
    educational reform. *See* educational reform

election, 161
first year in office, 167
fiscal matters, 167–168
Hibernia petroleum development
    roject, 169–170
loneliness, 159
nurses, 165–167
offshore oil and gas policy, 170
pension payments, 159–160
provincial deficit, 162
public service workforce reduc-
    tions, 162–163, 167–168
resignation, 237
sector growth, 170–171
staff, 163–165
Terra Nova negotiations, 170
tourism, 174–175
wage freeze, 165
Wells's resignation, 155–158
women candidates, 161–162
Newfoundland School Society,
    182–183
Newman, Don, 257
nickel mining. *See* Voisey's Bay
Nickerson's, 48–49
Nielsen, Erik, 58
Noradina, 119
Nortel, 214–215
North Atlantic Fishing Organization
    (NAFO), 83, 88, 94, 96, 99, 100
Norway, 89
NTV, 24
Nunziata, John, 56, 57–58, 59
nurses, 165–167, 225

objection procedure, 103
offshore oil and gas policy, 170
Olivier, Jacques, 43
opinions, 259–264
Opposition party, 77, 260
Ouellet, André, 112, 117, 123
overfishing, 80, 81–82

Pardos, José Luis, 88–89
Parizeau, Jacques, 140, 144, 151–152,
    153–154
Parti Québécois, 37
    see also referendum of 1995
Patricia Nores, 112
Pearson, Lester, 41
Peckford, Brian, 39
Pedra Rubia, 112
Pelletier, Gérard, 65
Penashue, Peter, 80, 201
Penney, Alphonsus Liguori (Arch-
    bishop), 195–196
pension payments, 159–160
Pentecostal Assemblies. *See* educational
    reform
Pentecostal Education Committee,
    184, 192
periodicals, 16
Pescarmar Uno, 129–130
Petten, Bernice, 231, 232
Petten, Bill, 83, 231–232
Philip, Prince of England, 175, 178
Pickard, Frank, 210
Pickersgill, Jack, 61–62, 173
political debts, 65
politics
    during Conservative era, 54–55
    "deals," 65–66
    federal. *See* federal politics
    friendships in, 65–66
    provincial. *See* Newfoundland and
        Labrador politics
    sexism in, 56–57
    tough business of, 258–259
    and wealth, 159–160
Portugal, 95–96, 106, 121, 126
prime minister's powers, 61
Progressive Conservatives, 29
Provincial Airlines, 124
provincial politics. *See* Newfoundland
    and Labrador politics
public service, 65

public service workforce reductions, 162–163, 167–168

public trust, restoration of, 79

Quebec
  Clarity Bill, 69
  distinct society clause, 74–75
  Lévesque, René, 41–42, 43
  Mosel Vitelic Inc., 242–244
  Rat Pack and, 58–59
  referendum (1980), 42–44, 46
  referendum (1995). *See* referendum of 1995
  separatists in, 140–141
Question Period, 61–62, 120

Rabinovitch, Victor, 85
Radwanski, George, 73
Rand, Ayn, 21
Rat Pack, 55–62
Rawson, Bruce, 84, 86, 87
Reagan, Ronald, 55
"Red Rump," 54
referendum of 1995
  Canadian message, 144
  CBC "Decision Desk," 151
  Chrétien's activity, 150–151
  Montreal rally, 143, 144–150
  narrowness of no victory, 154
  overview of situation, 146
  polls, 141–143
  popular support, 148–150
referendum process, 46–47, 187, 193–194
Reform Party. *See* Alliance Party
Regular, Melvin, 192–193
religion. *See* educational reform
resettlement, 137
Richardson, Miles, 199–200
Rideau Canal (Ottawa), 15
Riggs, Bernie, 125
Riggs, Newman, 124, 125
road construction, 201–202

road hockey, 72
Robert Leckie High School, 16
Rock, Allan, 97–98, 236, 244, 245, 252
Roman Catholic Church. *See* educational reform
Romanow, Roy, 218, 221, 223, 225, 226–227, 234–235
Rompkey, Bill, 40
Roth, John, 214–215
Rowat, Bill, 3, 5, 87–88, 102, 120, 124, 129, 133, 134–136, 143, 212
Rowe, Bill, 25–26, 27, 28
Rowe, Malcolm, 164
Roy, Jacques, 112
rules of engagement, 108–109, 116
Ryan, Claude, 42

salmon fishermen, 92
salmon stocks, 92
Santor, Jacques, 124
Scalfaro, Oscar Luigi, 175, 177
scallops, 89–92, 93
Schulich, Seymour, 206–207, 216
Scottish Whitefish Producers Association, 127
screech, 72
sectarian identity, 184–185
sector growth, 170–171
sedentary species, 90, 91, 92, 93
September 11, 250–251, 264
Severin, Timothy, 25
sexism in politics, 56–57
Sharp, Mitchell, 78–79, 241
Shawinigate, 240–244
Short, Max, 2–3, 5–6, 101–102, 125
siblings, 11
Sir Wilfred Grenfell, 4, 125, 129–130
sisters, 11
Smallwood, Joey, 24, 41, 155, 172–174
Smith, Gerald, 188
Smith, Ginger, 22

Smith, Gordon, 3, 5, 112, 117, 123, 124, 129, 134–135
Smith, Jodean. *See* Tobin, Jodean
Smith, Joseph, 22
Society for the Propagation of the Gospel in Foreign Parts, 182
solitude, 15
Sopko, Mike, 210, 213, 215
sovereignty association, 140
Spain, 1–6, 86, 88–89, 94, 95–96, 106, 110, 111–112, 122–123, 126–127, 129–130, 133
Sparrow decision, 198
Special Joint Committee of the House of Commons and Senate on the Constitution, 45
speeches, 73
Squires, Gerald, 203
St. Brendan, 25
St. Pierre fishermen, 80–81
Stephen B., 87
Stephenville (Nfld.), 7–8, 22
Stevens, Sinclair, 59, 65
Stirling, Geoff, 24
straddling stocks, 83
Strowbridge, Leo, 124
student council, 18
student protest, 17–18
Sullivan, Loyola, 191, 192
Sun Microsystems, 170
Sussman, David, 73

t-shirts, 120
Team Tobin, 11
teenaged years, 15–21
teleprompter, 73
Terra Nova negotiations, 170
Thistle, Anna, 162
Tobin, Adam, 195, 237, 253, 256
Tobin, Florence, 9–10, 230
Tobin, Heather, 32, 160, 237, 253, 256, 258
Tobin, Jack, 237, 253, 256

Tobin, Jodean, 15, 22–23, 31–32, 34, 139, 149, 159, 184, 195–196, 229, 230, 237, 240, 253, 256, 257
Tobin, Terry, 52
Tobin, Vince, 9–12, 228–231, 232–233, 235
Tonks, Alan, 57–58
tourism, 174–175
transportation services user fees, 61
travel, 14
trickle-down economics, 55
Trudeau, Pierre Elliott, 26–27, 29, 37–38, 39–40, 41, 42–44, 47, 50, 63, 64–65, 67–68
truth, 49
Tulk, Beaton, 121, 163, 188, 237
turbot quota
  Beck's comments, 104–106
  Chrétien's letter, 112–114
  declining stocks, 93–94
  diplomatic channels, 116–118
  emotional commitment, 118
  European Union, 100–101, 103–104, 106, 108, 110–111
  ministers' support, 98
  potential for armed encounter, 108–109
  response to possible objection, 107–108
  rules of engagement, 108–109, 116
  Spain, 94, 95–96, 110, 111–112
  united front, 97–98
  victory with NAFO, 102
  war. *See* Turbot War
Turbot War
  armed confrontation prospects, 136
  Canadian reactions, 127–128
  crumbling EU support, 133
  Estai, 1, 3–4, 124–129
  EU reactions, 125–126, 127
  false bulkhead, 128
  fence-sitters, 125–126

Foreign Affairs, 134–135
negotiations, 126, 129, 133–138
net incident, 129, 130–133
news coverage, 130–133
operational plan, 136
Operations Centre, 120
political partisanship, 121
principles behind actions, 121–122
provocative action, 135–136
public relations program, 119–120
Question Period, 120
Spain's "goodwill gesture," 122–123
Spanish hostilities, 129–130
t-shirts, 120
two sets of logbooks, 128
Turner, John, 50–54, 60, 63, 65, 67, 68, 69, 70, 71, 261
two solitudes, 8–9, 46

United Kingdom, 89, 114–115, 127, 139–140
United Nations Conference on Straddling and Highly Migratory Fish Stocks, 130
United States, 20–21, 83, 89–93, 262–263
United Way, 120
US-Canada relationships, 263

Valin, Guy, 256
Verbiski, Chris, 207
Verge, Lynn, 161
VIA Rail, 146, 147
Vietnam War, 18–20
Vigia, 129–130

Voisey's Bay
agreement, 213–214
background, 207
conditions, 209–210, 212–213
controversy, 206–207
Diamond Fields Resources, 207, 208–209
falling nickel prices, 211
hydro technology development, 212
Inco's commitment, 210–212
negotiations, 209–210, 212–213
personal involvement in negotiations, 215–216

wage freeze, 165
Walters, Sam, 170
warp-cutters, 108
Warrior, 89–90
Wells, Clyde, 74–76, 127, 132, 147, 155–158, 175, 184, 207, 208, 209–210
White, Bob, 166
Williams, Danny, 194
Windsor, Earl, 27
Windsor, Jack, 27
Winsor, Hugh, 61
Woodward, Mel, 156
work-to-rule strategy, 17
World Trade Center attacks, 250–251, 264
Wright, David, 122–123

Zedcomm, 170–171